Personal Letters From Kenneth

A Legacy

of Letters

2 0 0 0 - 2 0 0 5

KENNETH
COPELAND
PUBLICATIONS

A Legacy of Letters, Volume 3
Personal Letters From Kenneth Copeland to His Partners

ISBN 978-1-60463-097-8   10-4000

15 14 13 12 11 10   6 5 4 3 2 1

© 2010 Eagle Mountain International Church Inc. aka Kenneth Copeland Ministries

Kenneth Copeland Publications
Fort Worth, TX 76192-0001

For more information about Kenneth Copeland Ministries, call 800-600-7395 or visit www.kcm.org.

Table of Contents

2000

2001

2002

2003

2004

2005

Foreword

When I first came back to Jesus in December 1977, Kenneth Copeland was the man God used to drastically impact my life, and that of my family, as we began our great adventure with God. If I were to try to describe him, I would say he is a mighty man of faith, a heroic giver in every sense of the word, relentlessly true to his calling to teach faith to the world. He visited me in prison, and has stood beside me when many walked away. He is my friend, and taught me with his life what a real friend does.

As I sit here reading this manuscript, I cannot help but reflect on a time when the pain, injustice, loss and hopelessness I felt in my soul had all but taken my life. Even those I loved deeply could not seem to get through the hurt. I felt numb from the inside out; and among other things, I had lost my song.

Now, you must understand, I have been a believer for many years, and in my life the Word of God has been my final authority. I knew the only way I could ever make it through this horrific time was to fill my eyes, my mouth and my heart with what God had to say.

During that time, I had taken Kenneth's first book of letters, *Dear Partner,* with me to prison. I can honestly say that those letters saved my life. I read them every day. They are letters from a man, yes, but they are filled to overflowing with the Word of God, woven into real life by one of the most anointed teachers in the world.

I will never forget my brother Kenneth telling me how Oral Roberts one day had thrown his Bible to him asking, "What is this?" Kenneth looked hesitatingly. "These are letters! This is a book full of letters," Oral said.

Now, as I read the consistent letters of a man who has stayed the course, I think of the countless tens of thousands of lives just like mine who will be encouraged, strengthened, and given hope by the words on these pages. Take the time to open your Bible and read the verses along with Kenneth, and allow the Holy Spirit to guide you. I know He will.

Thank you, Kenneth, for all you have invested in my life and ministry.

Your friend and brother,

Phil Driscoll

Dear Partner

I will never forget the day Oral Roberts ministered to me how much of the New Testament is a book of letters...letters from the Apostle Paul to the people with whom he had partnered. They were letters from the heart of God, through the heart of this preacher, to the hearts of the people.

That day, the Lord set in my heart the desire to communicate with my Partners through a monthly letter. So I began writing these letters—and haven't missed a month since!

Every month, the Lord gives clear direction as to what He would have me say to you. And He doesn't do it in some formulaic way. I may be sitting on the back porch in the hours before dawn. I might be in a meeting hearing the Word preached. I might be stuck on a ski lift in Colorado, not even thinking about the letter. And, yes, most often I am sitting in my big easy chair, deliberately praying over the letter. Whenever and wherever the letter's message comes to me, I am ready to receive it. I know how important His words are for you.

Often the heart of these messages is the beginning of a major word the Lord needs the Church to hear. And my Partners are the first to get in on it. That thrills me!

This book is a collection of all my Partner Letters between 2000 and 2005. In them our Father made us to understand His kingdom and His way of doing things in the face of many important world events.

Starting with the questions that surrounded Y2K, God made sure we understood that the world is not our source, but Jesus is! He zeroed in on the importance of standing together as Partners no matter what the circumstances, and that His heart is to take care of His own people.

When the terrorist attack of September 11, 2001, struck the U.S., He declared an all-out war on fear, and the letters from 2002 were His words of courage and strength. In 2003 we learned how to be established in His love for us, because love is the key to everything God does.

As we planted ourselves firmly in the foundation of love, He began to pour on His blessings. He filled us with the knowledge of His provision, the Father's heart to fulfill His plan and purpose for our lives, and the potential of fully awakened faith. For me, and I believe for you, too, life has never been the same since He gave us these truths.

So, as you read my Partner Letters from these years, don't focus on the events that happened but on the eternal truths God has given us. World events will come and go, but His Word remains true and sure...it will stand forever!

I love you, Partner. One of my greatest joys in life is receiving God's Word for you and writing these letters. Enjoy them!

Jesus Is Lord!

Ken

Happy, Blessed, Overflowing, Abundantly Prosperous,
Victorious, To-Be-Envied-by-the-World New Year!

Dear Partner

This January 1st gives an all-new meaning to the phrase "new year." So many things will change with the coming of this new year. A new millennium, a new century, and a new number on the calendar and in our computers—along with whatever that brings. <u>The big news, however, will come in the world of the spirit.</u> The manifestations of God's power have already drastically increased over the last several months, and I believe the release of power from on high as the Y2K comes in is going to be awesome, to say the very least.

There is an anointing that was manifest in the life of Jesus that we've not yet seen in our time. That's the anointing to make the maimed whole. Let's look at Matthew 15:30-31.

> 30   And great multitudes came unto him, having with them those that were lame, blind, dumb, maimed, and many others, and cast them down at Jesus' feet; and he healed them:
>
> 31   Insomuch that the multitude wondered, when they saw the dumb to speak, <u>the maimed</u> to be <u>whole</u>, the lame to walk, and the blind to see: and they glorified the God of Israel.

The Greek word translated *maimed* in that verse means "distorted," or "crooked," or both. Now look at Luke 14:13: "But when thou makest a feast, call the poor, <u>the maimed,</u> the lame, the blind."

The word translated *maimed* in this verse means "deprived of a limb"—either the loss of a limb or being born with limbs missing. I have heard of things such as the replacement of limbs, but I have never seen them firsthand. This is just one more area of signs and wonders that must take place before Jesus comes. That, then, brings up John 14:10-12:

10   Believest thou not that I am in the Father, and
the Father in me? the words that I speak unto
you I speak not of myself: but the Father that
dwelleth in me, he doeth the works.

11   Believe me that I am in the Father, and the
Father in me: or else believe me for the very
works' sake.

12   Verily, verily, I say unto you, He that believeth
on me, the works that I do shall he do also;
and greater works than these shall he do;
because I go unto my Father.

Verse 10 points out that the works were by the anointing. Verse 12 is the great promise that the anointing would not only come because He went to the Father, but also that a time would come when the anointing would increase in power until greater things would begin to take place than what He did while He was on earth.

I believe the beginning of that time has already come. I know the anointings on this ministry are increasing at a more rapid pace than ever before. Instead of over a period of years, it is now over a period of days. Gloria and I have seen it recently increase drastically from one meeting to the next—especially in the preaching and teaching of the Word.

If you, or someone close to you, falls into this category of "maimed," don't give up. Get into every meeting you can where healing is being ministered. Stay in the Word. Watch the *Believer's Voice of Victory* broadcast every time it comes on. We are pressing in with all our faith to these levels of anointing and blessing.

Jesus said, "Because I go to my father." Well, He went to His Father, and He's far more powerful there than He was while He was here on the earth. He said just after His resurrection: "All power is given unto me in heaven and in earth" (Matthew 28:18). All power! All power! You and I are directly connected to all power. Ephesians 3:20: "Now unto him that is able to do exceeding abundantly above all that we ask or think, according to the power that worketh in us."

Above all we can ask or think. Something has to happen to our ability to ask and think in areas where we have never before walked or had <u>any</u> experience.

Let's look just above verse 20 to verse 16: "That he would grant you, according to the riches of his glory, to be strengthened with might by his Spirit in the inner man." That's where we are now—believing for the strengthening of our spirit by the Holy Spirit <u>to bring us into a higher level of insight, concepts, and Word-produced ideas so that we can ask and think bigger than ever before.</u>

There are no limits in God. There are no limits in our reborn spirits. The problems we have are mostly in our thinking—especially in things that look to us like they are way out there.

But look where we've come from. Things we daily walk in now, considering them almost commonplace, only a few years ago seemed so far out a lot of people thought we were crazy to believe. (Some still think so!) The beautiful part of it now is how fast things are growing. What looked far-out yesterday looks easy and perfectly natural to believe for and receive today. That's because of the Power that worketh within us. All of this is working alongside the great outpouring of revelation from heaven concerning our finances. It's time for all this to come together.

That's the reason Gloria and I need the strength of your prayers and the prayers of all our Partners. We are hearing the Spirit of God calling us out there with Him. We are stretching ourselves on the inside <u>and</u> on the outside. Just to get ourselves ready for a million Partners has been a major step of faith and growth. <u>But we're there!</u>

God blessed us with a <u>totally</u> new computer system that took over three years to bring online. But it will handle well over a million Partners and help us do a far better job of ministering to you than ever before. We've built a brand new Partner service facility of over 100,000 square feet so that we can serve you the way Gloria and I have always wanted to.

The self-generated electric plant <u>is finished!</u> What a joy it is to not have to depend on any outside aid or support for our electricity or natural gas, or water or sewer treatment plant services. <u>We have our</u>

<u>own.</u> Thanks to our God, His Word, faith and, of course, our Partners.

See what I mean about walking in areas of faith that only a few years ago seemed far, far out and impossible? It wasn't, but it seemed to be. The maimed being made whole is not far out. It just seems to be. What seems impossible about your situation today is only a few hours spent in meditating the promises of God away. The Word of our covenant has within itself the power to bring itself to pass.

Take Psalm 112 and read it and meditate on it until it becomes a <u>reality</u> in your inner man that it is a picture of you. It is the profile of a prosperous believer. Imprint it on your heart and mind. It's a picture (image) of Jesus. It's a picture of Abraham, and it's a picture (profile) of <u>you.</u> Romans 8:29 says we are to be conformed to the image of Jesus. The power to bring to pass is in the Word itself.

As you sow your financial seed this month, hold it in your hand and read Psalm 112 out loud. Then tell your seed, "Seed, I'm supposed to prosper. I'm a covenant person. Devil, I'm supposed to prosper and be in good health. I'm supposed to be made whole in Jesus' Name."

Jesus said in Luke 13:16: "And ought not this woman, being a daughter of Abraham, whom Satan hath bound, lo, these eighteen years, be loosed from this bond on the sabbath day"? Ought not this Partner of Kenneth and Gloria Copeland be whole, seeing they're the seed of Abraham? Joint heir with Jesus? Yes! A million times, Yes! Do it right now!

Gloria and I love you and pray for you every day!

Jesus is Lord.

Love,

Let's Get in the Field

Dear Partner

Just before the first of this year, I was talking to a close friend in the ministry about the year 2000. He said, "Brother Copeland, I believe our time has come." Those words have been ringing in my spirit since that day.

I believe that this is our day. This is the time that our heavenly Father has been looking forward to since the Fall of Adam. We think we've been through a lot getting here, but just think about what He's been putting up with. Especially the past 2,000 years.

He paid the total and ultimate price for the salvation of the whole world. Because He loved the world, He sent His only Son, Jesus, to die as the sacrifice for our sins and to totally defeat death and hell.

Instead of being praised for it, He's been ridiculed, hated, accused, cursed and rejected. Why?

At first glance it doesn't make any sense. Why would the majority of people hate and curse the One who loved them so much? The answer is <u>pressure.</u>

In the first chapter of Job, when satan was trying to get God to break His covenant with Job, the enemy revealed his purpose. He said, "He [Job] will curse You to Your face." Satan's desire is to get men to curse God to His face. <u>Satan knows that for him or his devils to curse God has no effect on God and certainly brings no heartache to Him. However, when a human does it, it brings pain to the heart of God.</u> And that's what satan desires to do, especially if he can get God's own children to turn against Him—even if only for a moment.

Satan's ways of doing this are simple, but effective, if not stopped in the life of a believer. Even in times of great outpouring like we are in right now, we have to vigilantly stand guard over our minds and bodies, over our money and goods, etc., to keep him from stealing right out from under our noses.

He'll do anything he can to discredit God and His Word. He'll do all he can to make it look like what is being preached isn't working. Especially for you. Then the next temptation is to cry out of desperation and care or pain, "Why did You let this happen?"

I know it doesn't seem like it at the time, but that is a form of cursing God. Whatever happened was not His fault. He has never broken covenant with you or me or anyone else—EVER!

So what is going on in that situation? PRESSURE!

Let's look at the definition of the word *press:*

> To act on with steady force or weight;
> To push steadily against;
> To squeeze;
> To force—as to press into service;
> To lay stress on;
> To be insistent about;
> To emphasize;
> To distress or embarrass;
> To urge or drive on;
> To force one's way.

Now who does that sound like? Right! The devil.

Jesus, in Mark 4:14-19, explains the five ways satan brings pressure on hearers of the Word. They are affliction, persecution, cares of this world, deceitfulness of riches (believing you can trust money), and the lusts (or pressures) of other things. Now, that's all satan has to work with. Everything he tries to do comes under the heading of those five things one way or another.

However, there is a small, two-word key to satan's operation in verse 19: "entering in"!

None of these five things will work if they are not allowed to enter in. If they don't enter in, they can't work. Satan cannot force them into your inner being. If they can't enter in, they can't choke the Word. If the

Word is not choked, it will produce power and victory.

The people in Mark 4:20 who brought forth fruit 30, 60 and a hundredfold all had the same pressure put on them that the others did. But they didn't allow it to work. Satan does not have the power or authority over a believer to make or force his pressure to work. When he is resisted, he must flee! Every time!

Jesus said in Luke 16:16-17, "The law and the prophets were until John. Since that time the kingdom of God has been preached, and everyone is pressing into it. And it is easier for heaven and earth to pass away than for one tittle of the law to fail" *(New King James Version).*

When we press in to what is preached under the anointing, the Word will not fail. Our failures, whatever they are, are never failures of the Word of God. His Name never fails. His blood never fails. The failure is on our part. Yielding to pressures and not standing on the Word in faith is where the failures come.

The Apostle Paul said in Philippians 3:13-14, "Forgetting those things which are behind, and reaching forth unto those things which are before [things that have not yet come to pass], I press toward [forward to] the mark for the prize of the high calling of God in Christ Jesus."

Look at that. I press—act on with steady force. I push, squeeze, force, lay stress on, am insistent about, emphasize, urge, drive on and force my way forward and upward. Upward toward the highest place in God and in His Anointing. This is a constant, persistent, steady pressing with faith through to those things that have been preached and that you know in your heart belong to you. Your healing, deliverance and peace in life. Your financial prosperity and all that goes with it.

It may look like everybody is prospering but you. It may look like everyone is healed but you. Push, press those thoughts out of your mind! Roll the cares of life over on your God. Read this out loud NOW! First Peter 5:5-10:

> 5   Likewise, ye younger, submit yourselves unto the elder. Yea, all of you be subject one

to another, and be clothed with humility: for God resisteth the proud, and giveth grace to the humble.

6 Humble yourselves therefore under the mighty hand of God, that he may exalt you in due time:

7 Casting all your care upon him; for he careth for you.

8 Be sober, be vigilant; because your adversary the devil, as a roaring lion, walketh about, seeking whom he may devour:

9 Whom <u>resist</u> stedfast in the faith, knowing that the same afflictions are accomplished in your brethren that are in the world.

10 But the God of all grace, who hath called us unto his eternal glory by Christ Jesus, after that ye have suffered a while, make you perfect, stablish, strengthen, settle you.

That word *suffered* in verse 10 means "pressed." After I have pressed and stood in faith awhile, even the toughest situation will have to give in. Our pressure is always greater than satan's pressure. All of his stuff is from the world. Our weapons are not carnal but powerful through God to the pulling down of strongholds.

Recently, Gloria and I have been through some of the worst pressures we've ever had to overcome. This has been especially true in the past three months. We've built more and stretched more and have preached in more places than ever before in this ministry. Satan has tried his best to make it look like our finances were not going to hold up—that we've outrun our supply. Well, we have stepped out—way out, beyond our present income—but we have not and will never, ever outrun our supply! His Name is Jesus, and He's more than enough!

The key to the whole thing is to keep your mind on Him and His promises. Don't look back even for the slightest moment. Open your mouth and shout at the problems and the pressure to think about them. Even when every part of your mind and feelings are resisting praise and faith, talk. DO IT ANYWAY! I mean it. Now! Do it!

Don't even think about accusing God for not doing more for you. Take charge! Go forward! Look up! Press. Press. Press onward and upward. Your victory is drawing nigh!

I've preached myself happy writing this letter to you. <u>You're one in a million!</u> Together we're going to get this job done in spite of all the devils of hell.

As you sow your financial seed this month, use it as a weapon against the forces of darkness. When it arrives here, that's what we're going to use it for.

This is our time. We're the harvesting generation. Let's get in the field with everything we have.

Gloria and I love you and pray for you every day.

Love,

You're One in a Million

Dear Partner

I know beyond any doubt <u>Gloria and I have the greatest Partners of any ministry in the world!</u>

During the year 1999, we stretched ourselves, our faith and our money as far as it would go. <u>Sometimes we stretched further than we thought we could.</u> It reminded me of Gen. George Patton during World War II. He headed his tanks and troops toward Germany and didn't look back. He outran his supply lines and still wouldn't stop. The only reason he finally came to a halt was because his tanks and trucks ran out of gas.

That's the way we were last year, and this year is no different. We were told to build, so we built. We were told to go, so we went. We were told to get on new television stations, so we did. We spent all the money we had. We pushed the devil and his work back until we ran over him. We traveled, preached, prayed, sang and did anything else the Lord Jesus wanted done.

We ended 1999 with the greatest year of ministry in our 33-year history. I know that happened, first of all, <u>because of our Partners' faithfulness</u>—their faithfulness to pray.

In Philippians 1:19 the Apostle Paul told his partners, "For I know that this shall turn to my salvation <u>through your prayer,</u> and the supply of the Spirit of Jesus Christ." He depended on the prayers of his partners to connect to the power and anointing of supply through the Holy Spirit. He not only expected them to pray, but he also said, "I know I'll be saved from all this through your prayers." <u>When his partners were praying, he knew the Holy Spirit would move.</u>

Now look at Verse 20: "According to my earnest expectation and my hope, that <u>in nothing</u> I shall be ashamed, but that with all boldness, as always, so now also Christ shall be magnified in my body, whether it be by life, or by death." He <u>earnestly,</u> or intently, expected to be victorious in every situation because he knew the high caliber and faithfulness of his partners. He said, "I don't expect to be ashamed or defeated in anything." Now you can see why he was so bold. He said "with all boldness, AS ALWAYS"! I fully understand where he was coming from. He knew his partners were there.

I know my Partners are praying and standing with us all the time. That's one of the reasons we're so bold to go do anything and everything the Lord has for us to do.

Now, let's look at verses 23-25:

> 23 For I am in a strait betwixt two, having a desire to depart, and to be with Christ; which is far better;
> 24 Nevertheless to abide in the flesh is more needful for you.
> 25 And having this confidence, I know that I shall abide and continue with you all for your furtherance and joy of faith.

His very reason for staying on this earth, rather than to die and head for heaven and be with Jesus was to continue to receive revelation from heaven and further their joy and faith.

<u>That is the center of my life</u>—to live and continue with you, serving God with all my heart and ministering to you to continue to build up your joy and faith. I pray for you <u>every</u> day. My Partners are at the very center of my prayer life. KCM has a highly trained staff of prayers—people who pray all the time, who pray for the prosperity and victory of Jesus in <u>your</u> life every day. We are totally committed to the improvement of your faith and your style of life in this earth.

Just in the past few days, our new super computer system went online. We spent three years and over $6 million putting it in place, just for our Partners. We did it so we can serve you—and a million more—with speed, accuracy and a lot of other ways we were not able to in the past. Not only that, but we also built you your own 100,000-plus square foot building—the "Partner Service Center"—to help take care of your needs. I'm telling you all this because I want you to know, and the Lord

Jesus wants you to know, that we love you because He loves you, and we care for you very much.

We are an "anointing family." The anointing on Gloria and me and on this ministry is on you. Depend on it more. Remind yourself every day that because you are connected to this ministry through prayer and through your financial support, you are connected to its anointing.

I want to show you something from Ephesians 4:16: "From whom the whole body fitly joined together and compacted by that which every joint supplieth, according to the effectual working in the measure of every part, maketh increase of the body unto the edifying of itself in love." Jesus has joined us together. However, we are compacted, or held together, by that which every "joining" supplies.

That is a divine connection. Each one of those connections creates an anointing that none of the parts could have had on its own. The personal members of Jesus' staff—Peter, James, John and others—had His Anointing on them. Then, as the Body of Christ, the Anointed One, grew, so did the effectiveness of His Anointing in the Body. These connections are precious in His sight because in them His burden-removing, yoke-destroying power is able to compound and spread all over this world.

Think about over a million of us joined together, praying for one another, preaching literally all over this entire earth by television and the many other ways we're reaching out with His Word. If Gloria and I are out there, you're out there with us. We're doing the going; you're doing the praying and buying the airplane gas that gets us there. We're like Patton in that we are going all out full speed ahead, and not looking back. The difference is we'll never outrun our supply lines—not as long as we have the most faithful Partners in the world like you!

You're One in a Million, Partner.

Gloria and I love you and pray for you in faith every day.

Love,

"I can do the work only because of your financial support and prayers. Thank you for being a vital part of this harvest. KCM and its Partners have a great reward." —Reinhard Bonnke

Keep Believing! What? That Jesus Is Anointed!

Dear Partner

What a time we live in! Every voice—TV, newspapers, radios, magazines, anything that can speak—is shouting at the top of its lungs: "It's time for Jesus to come!!" On one hand the world is filled with sin and judgment, and on the other the Glory of God is being poured out like a flood.

A few days ago I talked with Reinhard Bonnke, who gave me a report on a six-day meeting he had just finished in Nigeria. In those six days 1,758,158 answered the altar calls for salvation. More than 25,000 counselors prayed with over 800,000 people one-on-one, and they still couldn't get to everyone! Miracles and healings flowed like a river.

He was giving me this report because <u>KCM paid the budget on this meeting.</u> That means you and I as Partners receive the rewards of God in that harvest just as though we did the preaching. Take a moment and let that sink into your spirit. That's only one meeting. These same kinds of staggering results are happening all over the world.

We received a letter yesterday from a satellite broadcasting company we just went on several months ago that has <u>ADDED</u> over a million households to receive our broadcast—<u>in China.</u> That satellite is already broadcasting over most of Asia and the Far East, as well as Russia.

We are getting letters from places we have never heard of. In fact, the flood of mail has hit at the same time we have been switching to our new super computer system. It has our mail department working double shifts to catch up! And this is only the beginning! What a time to be alive. I mean really alive—alive on the Word and on the power of God. Our God is on the move, and you and I are right in the middle of it all!

In this letter I want to share some things with you about opening up your life—or becoming totally subject—to the authority of Jesus' Anointing.

Remember, Isaiah 10:27 says that the anointing is the burden-removing, yoke-destroying power of God. Then Isaiah 11:1-3 says it is the spirit of wisdom, counsel, might and quick understanding. So let's say it like this, "becoming totally subject to the burden-removing, yoke-destroying spirit of wisdom, counsel, might and quick-understanding anointing power of Jesus."

That covers it all. Everything in life comes under the anointing one way or another. The more we learn to walk in it and be controlled by it, the more we become like Jesus.

Let's look at Mark 5:21-43:

21   And when Jesus was passed over again by ship unto the other side, much people gathered unto him: and he was nigh unto the sea.

22   And, behold, there cometh one of the rulers of the synagogue, Jairus by name; and when he saw him, he fell at his feet.

23   And besought him greatly, saying, My little daughter lieth at the point of death: I pray thee, come and lay thy hands on her, that she may be healed; and she shall live.

24   And Jesus went with him; and much people followed him, and thronged him.

25   And a certain woman, which had an issue of blood twelve years,

26   And had suffered many things of many physicians, and had spent all that she had, and was nothing bettered, but rather grew worse,

27   When she had heard of Jesus, came in the press behind, and touched his garment.

28   For she said, If I may touch but his clothes, I shall be whole.

29   And straightway the fountain of her blood was dried up; and she felt in her body that she was healed of that plague.

30   And Jesus, immediately knowing in himself that virtue had gone out of him, turned him about in

the press, and said, Who touched my clothes?

31 And his disciples said unto him, Thou seest the multitude thronging thee, and sayest thou, Who touched me?

32 And he looked round about to see her that had done this thing.

33 But the woman fearing and trembling, knowing what was done in her, came and fell down before him, and told him all the truth.

34 And he said unto her, Daughter, thy faith hath made thee whole; go in peace, and be whole of thy plague.

35 While he yet spake, there came from the ruler of the synagogue's house certain which said, Thy daughter is dead: why troublest thou the Master any further?

36 As soon as Jesus heard the word that was spoken, he saith unto the ruler of the synagogue, Be not afraid, only believe.

37 And he suffered no man to follow him, save Peter, and James, and John the brother of James.

38 And he cometh to the house of the ruler of the synagogue, and seeth the tumult, and them that wept and wailed greatly.

39 And when he was come in, he saith unto them, Why make ye this ado, and weep? the damsel is not dead, but sleepeth.

40 And they laughed him to scorn. But when he had put them all out, he taketh the father and the mother of the damsel, and them that were with him and entereth in where the damsel was lying.

41 And he took the damsel by the hand, and said unto her, Talitha cumi; which is, being interpreted, Damsel, I say unto thee, arise.

42 And straightway the damsel arose, and walked; for she was of the age of twelve years. And they were astonished with a great astonishment.

43 And he charged them straitly that no man

should know it; and commanded that something should be given her to eat.

Jairus openly and publicly threw off his religious position, and image. He was willing to change anything because he believed Jesus was anointed. Remember that everywhere He went, Jesus preached the same message He preached in Luke 4:18, "The Spirit of the Lord is upon me for He has anointed me...." In Acts 10:36-38, Peter taught that Jesus preached that same message throughout all Judea.

Now when Jairus fell at Jesus' feet, he had <u>only one thing to say:</u> "Come lay your hands on my daughter and she shall live!" That was a bold statement of faith in Jesus and His Anointing. It's important to notice that he did not go into "his story." He didn't say a word about the problem. He didn't try to talk Jesus into going home with him or anything else. He just talked his faith: "...she shall live!"

Let's take a look at some things that could have stopped the power of the anointing—even though Jesus was there:

1. Being a ruler of the synagogue, he could have condemned the woman because of her being in public with an issue of blood.
2. He could have criticized Jesus for stopping and taking time to listen to her testimony. Had he done that he would have missed Jesus' teaching on faith.
3. He could have accepted the death report and yielded to fear. That would have negated what he had just seen—the woman had received her healing. What he had just heard—her powerful testimony and Jesus teaching her about faith—all would have been wiped out.
4. He could have become puffed up with pride when Jesus left that whole crowd to go home with him.

In all of these opportunities to fail, <u>Jairus didn't say another word.</u> He stayed with his faith. He had said "she shall live!" That statement brought him into and under the authority of Jesus and His Anointing.

Now look again at verse 40. Jesus took over Jairus' household. That sounds great, and it is, but look at it again. This is a funeral—a death in the family—and Jesus ran the whole bunch out. The uncles, aunts and cousins, the synagogue high-ups, the whole FAMILY and FRIENDS! What an opportunity to become offended at Jesus for being so "insensitive" in their time of grief.

But Jairus didn't. He obeyed what Jesus had said for him to do when the servant came and told him it was all over. His daughter was already dead.

In verse 36, Jesus said, "Stop the fear and keep believing!" Keep believing what? Keep believing what you said by faith—"she shall live." Why did you say that in the first place? Because, Jairus, you believed Jesus was anointed with the burden-removing, yoke-destroying power of God. Keep believing that and keep saying she shall live.

Jesus Christ, the Anointed One and His Anointing—the same yesterday, today and forever. What is He anointed to do today? The same thing He did in Jairus' case. He watched over Jairus' confession of faith and by His Anointing saw to it that it came to pass. Hebrews 3:1 declares that He is appointed and anointed by God our Father as High Priest over our words of faith.

Go to the New Testament. Find the promises that cover your situations. Put them in your eyes. Put them in your mouth. Keep them there. Even when you don't feel like it—hold on to them. In the face of the bad reports—don't say anything else. In the face of family and friends—don't say anything else. In the face of death—don't say anything else. Don't fall for any of the devil's tricks. Don't yield to fear. Stay with faith, and keep believing Jesus is anointed.

Take your seed offering for this month, lay your hand on it, pray over it, and then shout your faith like Jairus did. Even if you don't have any seed to plant at the moment, do it anyway. Send something, even if it is only a note of faith, so all of us here at KCM can take hold together with you like Jesus did with Jairus. Jesus told Peter, James and John to go into Jairus' house with Him. We're your "Peter, James and John."

We're going together with Jesus and you to total victory. We are Partners! The anointing is flowing all over me while I'm writing this. This is it! Total breakthrough!

Gloria and I love you very much and pray for you every day. Stand with us and pray for us.

Love,

God Has a Plan!

Dear Partner

Regardless of what the situation is, and no matter what the devil has done, God has a marvelous plan for your victory.

Let's take a look at Ephesians 1:3-5:

> 3   Blessed be the God and Father of our Lord Jesus Christ, who hath blessed us with all spiritual blessings in heavenly places in Christ:
>
> 4   According as he hath chosen us in him before the foundation of the world, that we should be holy and without blame before him in love:
>
> 5   Having predestinated us unto the adoption of children by Jesus Christ to himself, according to the good pleasure of his will.

Verse 3 states that God <u>HAS</u>—not "is going to someday" but "has already"—blessed us with <u>all</u> spiritual blessings in heavenly places in the Anointed One and in His Anointing.

It is not a matter of God deciding whether or not to bless you. He's already made that decision. In fact He did that before the world was ever created. He saw you and chose you before the creation of the world—<u>before Adam was created and before sin came into the world.</u>

God blessed us and made promises to us long before the Fall of Man and the problems we face today came into existence. First Peter 1:19-20 and Revelation 13:8 both declare that Jesus, the Lamb of God, was slain <u>before</u> the foundation of the world. The picture God has of each of us is that perfect and beautiful image before all the sin and destruction ever came.

Look at Titus 1:2: "In hope of eternal life, which God, that cannot lie, promised before the world began."

God actually promised and blessed you and me in Christ Jesus <u>before</u> anything we know about was ever created. Then He formed the plan of redemption to keep us from losing all He planned for us.

<u>There is a place of abundance in God for every believer</u>—a wealthy place of divine health and prosperity, a glorious place of power and victory in Him. Jesus went to the cross and was raised from the dead in order for us to live in that place of victory. Psalm 66:12: "Thou hast caused men to ride over our heads; we went through fire and through water: but thou broughtest us out into a wealthy place."

That "wealthy place" is where the Spirit of God is always endeavoring to lead us. Ephesians 2:10 says, "For we are his workmanship, created in Christ Jesus unto good works, which God hath <u>before</u> ordained that we should walk in them." "Before ordained" is referring to <u>before</u> the foundation of the world.

All of God's paths, works, ways, roads and plans lead to that overcoming, wealthy place in Him. Not just in heaven.

Heaven is where we're heading all right, but He planned for us to have days of heaven on earth (Deuteronomy 11:18-21). Of course we have to fight the good fight of faith to receive it, but it's ours. It belongs to us. Jesus bought and paid for our victory—spirit, soul and body. It's ours just as much as it was <u>before</u> the foundation of the world.

There's more to walking in victory and abundance than getting our bills paid and having our bodies healed. Our bodies belong to Jesus. We are the Body of Christ, the Anointed—not just figuratively but literally. Our bodies are the temple of the Holy Ghost.

Our bodies are necessary to Jesus in this earth. The same is true of our finances. If we don't have it, He doesn't have it.

We need a well, healthy body; a keen, anointed mind; and money enough to do what Jesus needs done in this earth. Remember the madman of Gadara out of whom Jesus cast the legion? In Mark 5:15-19 we read:

15   And they come to Jesus, and see him that was possessed with the devil, and had the legion, sitting, and clothed, and in his right mind: and they were afraid.

16   And they that saw it told them how it befell to him that was possessed with the devil, and also concerning the swine.

17   And they began to pray him to depart out of their coasts.

18   And when he was come into the ship, he that had been possessed with the devil prayed him that he might be with him.

19   Howbeit Jesus suffered him not, but saith unto him, Go home to thy friends, and tell them how great things the Lord hath done for thee, and hath had compassion on thee.

Jesus healed him <u>and clothed him,</u> but it was for a purpose and calling.

Look at Luke 19:30: "Saying, Go ye into the village over against you; in the which at your entering ye shall find a colt tied, whereon yet never man sat: loose him, and bring him hither." Jesus told His disciples to get a colt for Him to ride. In verse 31, He said, "If any man ask you why do you loose him, you say because the Lord hath need of him."

Jesus needs you and me to prosper and be in health even as our souls prosper. There's far too much to do in this earth for sick, broken-down, always-hurting people to get it done without them being spiritually, physically, and financially able.

It's time for <u>all</u> of us to rise up in faith, and fill our hearts and mouths with the Word of His promises and power until it overflows out of our mouths with a mighty force. The seed of that overflow is in you right now. It was planted in you when you made Jesus Lord of your life—the seed of every great thing God saw in you before the foundation of the world.

Finally, look at 1 Corinthians 2:9: "But as it is written, Eye hath not seen, nor ear heard, neither have entered into the heart of man, the things which God hath prepared for them that love him."

God's plan for your wealthy place is far beyond anything you or I could ask or think. But, thank God, there's more to us than just you and me.

Look at verse 10 and verse 12:

> 10   But God hath revealed them unto us by his Spirit: for the Spirit searcheth all things, yea, the deep things of God.
>
> 12   Now we have received, not the spirit of the world, but the spirit which is of God; that we might know the things that are freely given to us of God.

Glory to God! It's all ours NOW. Every blessing in heavenly places. Take hold of it. See just how big you can believe and ask.

Gloria and I are your Partners, and we are believing bigger and releasing our faith for our Partners more than ever before. We have to. We are being called on by the Lord Jesus to do more than we've ever done. But that's the whole point: *Together* we—Jesus, you and Gloria and me and all this ministry—can and will get it done.

Gloria and I love you very much and pray for you every day.

Love,

Ken

Send me your picture! We're building picture displays for the new Partner Service Center and other administrative buildings. Even if we already have one, send me a new one. Nothing fancy. Just the "real you" snapshot.

Dear Partner

I want you to know how much this ministry loves you. Never a day goes by that Gloria and I don't pray for you and earnestly believe God that you "prosper and be in health even as your soul prospers" (3 John 2). We have prayer staff who are assigned to pray for all of our Partners and specifically for your needs that you tell us about.

When we pray for you, we don't just mumble a few words like "God bless our Partners, Amen." I'm going to take you through my personal prayer that I pray every day, so you can know and agree with me in faith.

The <u>first</u> thing I pray each day, in order to be obedient to the written word, is 1 Timothy 2:1-2:

> 1   I exhort therefore, that, first of all, supplications, prayers, intercessions, and giving of thanks, be made for all men;
>
> 2   For kings, and for all that are in authority; that we may lead a quiet and peaceable life in all godliness and honesty.

The key issue in this prayer is that we, the Church, may lead peaceable, or quiet, lives. This is the place to pray for our leaders and over such matters as the elections. <u>I am praying for a record-breaking Christian turnout to vote this November,</u> standing on the word "peaceable." I ask and believe I receive directions on whom I vote for and any involvement the Lord wants from me.

The next order of my prayer is to obey what Jesus said in Matthew 5:44: "But I say unto you, Love your enemies, bless them that curse you, do good to them that hate you, <u>and pray for them which despitefully use you, and persecute you.</u>" This is a good place to do a personal check for such things as unforgiveness and offense. There's no use going any further until all of these types of issues are dealt with.

The next step is to pray "Father, I pray for my Partners, my staff and my family. I pray that we prosper and be in health even as our souls prosper. Father, You know each one of us by name. We are Your children. Holy Spirit, I'm asking You to call each individual Partner's name, according to the Lamb's Book of Life, before the throne of grace as I pray. I hold each one up to You now with my faith. <u>You are the Most High God!</u>"

Father, in Jesus' Name I pray the 23rd Psalm:

1   The Lord is my shepherd; I shall not want.
2   He maketh me to lie down in green pastures: he leadeth me beside the still waters.
3   He restoreth my soul: he leadeth me in the paths of righteousness for his name's sake.
4   Yea, though I walk through the valley of the shadow of death, I will fear no evil: for thou art with me; thy rod and thy staff they comfort me.
5   Thou preparest a table before me in the presence of mine enemies: thou anointest my head with oil; my cup runneth over.
6   Surely goodness and mercy shall follow me all the days of my life: and I will dwell in the house of the Lord for ever.

I pray that _____ never has a want unfulfilled. They will follow the Great Shepherd, Jesus, to their green pastures of rest and peace. They will live alongside still waters of abundance and prosperity.

Father, I pray for every Partner who is going through the valley of the shadow of death. We stand together fearlessly and boldly on Your Word. We come to the table of provision by the blood of Jesus.

Father, I pray the 91st Psalm. I pray that _____ dwells in the secret place of the Most High. Together with _____, I say of the Lord:

2   He is my refuge and my fortress: my God; in him will I trust.

3   Surely he shall deliver thee from the snare of the fowler, and from the noisome pestilence.

4   He shall cover thee with his feathers, and under his wings shalt thou trust: his truth shall be thy shield and buckler.

5   Thou shalt not be afraid for the terror by night; nor for the arrow that flieth by day;

6   Nor for the pestilence that walketh in darkness; nor for the destruction that wasteth at noonday.

7   A thousand shall fall at thy side, and ten thousand at thy right hand; but it shall not come nigh thee.

8   Only with thine eyes shalt thou behold and see the reward of the wicked.

9   Because thou hast made the Lord, which is my refuge, even the most High, thy habitation;

10 There shall no evil befall thee, neither shall any plague come nigh thy dwelling.

11 For he shall give his angels charge over thee, to keep thee in all thy ways.

12 They shall bear thee up in their hands, lest thou dash thy foot against a stone.

13 Thou shalt tread upon the lion and adder: the young lion and the dragon shalt thou trample under feet.

14 Because he hath set his love upon me, therefore will I deliver him: I will set him on high, because he hath known my name.

15 He shall call upon me, and I will answer him: I will be with him in trouble; I will deliver him, and honour him.

16 With long life will I satisfy him, and show him my salvation.

I pray now the 103rd Psalm. I believe _____ receives every benefit promised:

1   Bless the Lord, O my soul: and all that is within me, bless his holy name.

2   Bless the Lord, O my soul, and forget not all his benefits:

3   Who forgiveth all thine iniquities; who healeth all thy diseases;

4   Who redeemeth thy life from destruction; who crowneth thee with lovingkindness and tender mercies;

5   Who satisfieth thy mouth with good things; so that thy youth is renewed like the eagle's.

6   The Lord executeth righteousness and judgment for all that are oppressed.

7   He made known his ways unto Moses, his acts unto the children of Israel.

8   The Lord is merciful and gracious, slow to anger, and plenteous in mercy.

9   He will not always chide: neither will he keep his anger for ever.

10   He hath not dealt with us after our sins; nor rewarded us according to our iniquities.

11   For as the heaven is high above the earth, so great is his mercy toward them that fear him.

12   As far as the east is from the west, so far hath he removed our transgressions from us.

13   Like as a father pitieth his children, so the Lord pitieth them that fear him.

14   For he knoweth our frame; he remembereth that we are dust.

15   As for man, his days are as grass: as a flower of the field, so he flourisheth.

16   For the wind passeth over it, and it is gone; and the place thereof shall know it no more.

17   But the mercy of the Lord is from everlasting to everlasting upon them that fear him, and his righteousness unto children's children;

18   To such as keep his covenant, and to those that remember his commandments to do them.

19   The Lord hath prepared his throne in the heavens; and his kingdom ruleth over all.

20   Bless the Lord, ye his angels, that excel

in strength, that do his commandments, hearkening unto the voice of his word.

21 Bless ye the Lord, all ye his hosts; ye ministers of his, that do his pleasure.

22 Bless the Lord, all his works in all places of his dominion: bless the Lord, O my soul.

(Spend some time here filling your mouth with good things according to verse 5.)

Father because of what Jesus did for us in Isaiah 53, _____ and I sing and shout Isaiah 54:

1 Sing, O barren, thou that didst not bear; break forth into singing, and cry aloud, thou that didst not travail with child: for more are the children of the desolate than the children of the married wife, saith the Lord.

2 Enlarge the place of thy tent, and let them stretch forth the curtains of thine habitations: spare not, lengthen thy cords, and strengthen thy stakes;

3 For thou shalt break forth on the right hand and on the left; and thy seed shall inherit the Gentiles and make the desolate cities to be inhabited.

4 Fear not; for thou shalt not be ashamed: neither be thou confounded; for thou shalt not be put to shame: for thou shalt forget the shame of thy youth, and shalt not remember the reproach of thy widowhood any more.

5 For thy Maker is thine husband; the Lord of hosts is his name; and thy Redeemer the Holy One of Israel; The God of the whole earth shall he be called.

6 For the Lord hath called thee as a woman forsaken and grieved in spirit, and a wife of youth, when thou wast refused, saith thy God.

7 For a small moment have I forsaken thee; but with great mercies will I gather thee.

8 In a little wrath I hid my face from thee for a

9   moment; but with everlasting kindness will I have mercy on thee, saith the Lord thy Redeemer. For this is as the waters of Noah unto me: for as I have sworn that the waters of Noah should no more go over the earth; so have I sworn that I would not be wroth with thee, nor rebuke thee.

10 For the mountains shall depart, and the hills be removed; but my kindness shall not depart from thee, neither shall the covenant of my peace be removed, saith the Lord that hath mercy on thee.

11 O thou afflicted, tossed with tempest, and not comforted, behold, I will lay thy stones with fair colours, and lay thy foundations with sapphires.

12 And I will make thy windows of agates, and thy gates of carbuncles, and all thy borders of pleasant stones.

13 And all thy children shall be taught of the Lord; and great shall be the peace of thy children.

14 In righteousness shalt thou be established: thou shalt be far from oppression; for thou shalt not fear: and from terror; for it shall not come near thee.

15 Behold, they shall surely gather together, but not by me: whosoever shall gather together against thee shall fall for thy sake.

16 Behold, I have created the smith that bloweth the coals in the fire, and that bringeth forth an instrument for his work; and I have created the waster to destroy.

17 No weapon that is formed against thee shall prosper; and every tongue that shall rise against thee in judgment thou shalt condemn. This is the heritage of the servants of the Lord, and their righteousness is of me, saith the Lord.

Now, Lord, I pray these powerful, Holy Ghost prayers in the New Testament.

Ephesians 1:16-23:

16 [I] cease not to give thanks for _____,
    making mention of [them] in my prayers;
17 That the God of our Lord Jesus Christ, the
    Father of glory, may give unto [them] the spirit of
    wisdom and revelation in the knowledge of him:
18 The eyes of [their] understanding being en-
    lightened; that [they] may know what is the
    hope of his calling, and what the riches of the
    glory of his inheritance in the saints,
19 And what is the exceeding greatness of his
    power to us-ward who believe, according to
    the working of his mighty power,
20 Which he wrought in Christ, when he raised
    him from the dead, and set him at his own
    right hand in the heavenly places,
21 Far above all principality, and power, and
    might, and dominion, and every name that is
    named, not only in this world, but also in that
    which is to come:
22 And hath put all things under his feet, and gave
    him to be the head over all things to the church,
23 Which is his body, the fulness of him that
    filleth all in all.

Also, Father, I pray Ephesians 3:14-20:

14 For this cause I bow my knees unto the Father
    of our Lord Jesus Christ,
15 Of whom the whole family in heaven and
    earth is named,
16 That he would grant _____, according
    to the riches of his glory, to be strengthened
    with might by his Spirit in the inner man;
17 That Christ may dwell in [their] hearts by
    faith; that [they], being rooted and grounded
    in love,
18 May be able to comprehend with all saints what

is the breadth, and length, and depth, and height;

19 And to know the love of Christ, which passeth knowledge, that [they] might be filled with all the fulness of God.

20 Now unto him that is able to do exceeding abundantly above all that we ask or think, according to the power that worketh in us.

I pray Colossians 1:9-11:

9 For this cause we also, since the day we heard it, do not cease to pray for _____, and to desire that [they] might be filled with the knowledge of his will in all wisdom and spiritual understanding;

10 That [they] might walk worthy of the Lord unto all pleasing, being fruitful in every good work, and increasing in the knowledge of God;

11 Strengthened with all might, according to his glorious power, unto all patience and longsuffering with joyfulness.

Also, Father, I pray 1 Thessalonians 5:23 that "The very God of peace sanctify _____ wholly; and I pray God [their] whole spirit and soul and body be preserved blameless unto the coming of our Lord Jesus Christ."

Now, Lord, I plead the blood of Jesus over my Partners, my staff, and my family for protection against every evil spirit, every evil person, every evil thing, and every evil plan of the devil. I bind you, satan, according to the Word of God.

It is written: "In my name cast out the devil" (Mark 16:15-20). It is also written: "Whatever you bind on earth is bound in heaven." I bind you! "Whatever you loose on earth is loosed in heaven." I break your grip, satan, and loose you from my Partner _____ and all that is theirs.

It is written: "Give no place to the devil" (Ephesians 4:27). So I take from you any place you think you have in _____'s life. Take your hand off, NOW! You have no place! It is written: "Ye are of God, little children, and have overcome them: because greater is he that is in you, than he that is in the world" (1 John 4:4).

We overcome you and all your work by the blood of the Lamb and the word of our testimony. Our testimony is 1 John 5:1: "Whosoever believeth that Jesus is the Christ is born of God: and every one that loveth him that begat loveth him also that is begotten of him." We believe that!

First John 5:4: "For whatsoever is born of God overcometh the world: and this is the victory that overcometh the world, even our faith." We are world overcomers together. Now!

First John 5:18: "We know that whosoever is born of God sinneth not; but he that is begotten of God keepeth himself, and that wicked one toucheth him not." We are born of God, satan, therefore the seed of sin is not in us. The seed of righteousness is in us. You touch us not! We plead the blood of Jesus!

Now, Father, I pray for _____ according to the full wisdom, will, and knowledge of God. I pray in the spirit for _____ according to 1 Corinthians 2:7: "But we speak the wisdom of God in a mystery, even the hidden wisdom, which God ordained before the world unto our glory."

I pray also that I interpret—a word, a conviction, an inward witness or direction—Your full vision and direction for this ministry. I believe I receive the mysteries while they are yet mysteries. Colossians 2:2-3:

2   That their hearts might be comforted, being knit together in love, and unto all riches of the full assurance of understanding, to the acknowledgement of the mystery of God, and of the Father, and of Christ;

3   In whom are hid all the treasures of wisdom and knowledge.

All of these treasures are ours through the blood covenant, resurrection, and glorification of Jesus our Lord and Savior. We release them, now, by faith.

My Partner, _____, and I stand together in this calling to take the word of faith to all the world. We'll preach it without compromise from the top of the world to the bottom and all around the middle. Father, reveal to each one of us our part of this. What must I do? What must I pray? What must I sow? _____ and I together in faith can do anything You want us to do. We can do all things through the anointing which strengthens us.

I pray this for you every day, seven days a week. That's my assignment from heaven. Out of that prayer comes all the revelation I receive to preach. You are with me everywhere I go and in everything I do. Ministering to you is Gloria's and my priority in life.

Take the time to pray this every day. We are Partners in all of this. Add your name in the blanks along with Gloria's and mine. Write them there. These words will be a springboard in the spirit that will lead you into areas of prayer you've never experienced before. Deuteronomy 11:21 will be the result: "That your days may be multiplied, and the days of your children, in the land which the Lord sware unto your fathers to give them, as the days of heaven upon the earth."

Gloria and I depend on your prayers of agreement and faith. We need you.

Send me your picture as soon as possible. Nothing fancy. Just a snapshot will do. Even if we already have one, send a new one. I cannot wait to see what a million pictures on the wall will look like!

You are truly special to Gloria and me, and to all of us at KCM and Eagle Mountain International Church. You're One in a Million.

Love,

Ken

The Wisdom of God—His Divine
Ability to Use Knowledge

Dear Partner

There has never, ever been a time when God has made Himself
known and available as He is making Himself known now. This is the
time to draw close and take full advantage of all He is doing.

He is pouring out of Himself in ways never before seen. He is
teaching, explaining, revealing and giving insight into His way of doing
things. He has always been willing to do these things. But now there's
just something special about the way He's opening His wisdom and
knowledge and its treasures to anyone who will dare seek Him for it.

That's what this ministry has always been about—digging,
searching and praying for everything we can get to remove burdens
and destroy yokes, then sharing it all with you, our Partner.

Let's begin by looking at Proverbs 4:5-13:

5	<u>Get wisdom, get understanding:</u> forget it not; neither decline from the words of my mouth.
6	Forsake her not, and she shall preserve thee: love her, and she shall keep thee.
7	<u>Wisdom is the principal thing;</u> therefore get wisdom: and with all thy getting get understanding.
8	Exalt her, and she shall promote thee: she shall bring thee to honour, when thou dost embrace her.
9	She shall give to thine head an ornament of grace: a crown of glory shall she deliver to thee.
10	Hear, O my son, and receive my sayings; and the years of thy life shall be many.
11	I have taught thee in the way of wisdom; I have led thee in right paths.
12	When thou goest, thy steps shall not be straitened; and when thou runnest, thou shalt not stumble.

13   Take fast hold of instruction; let her not go:
keep her; for she is thy life.

Notice the command, "Get wisdom. Get understanding." Now you know God well enough to know that He would never command us to do something that we couldn't do. Nor would He command us to get something that was unavailable to us.

It is true that His wisdom and understanding has to be received according to the rules and laws of faith, because <u>He has hidden His wisdom from our enemy, satan, and all who follow his ways.</u> Lucifer was the anointed cherub and had at least some wisdom. But Ezekiel 28:17 says his wisdom became corrupted, and he's been barred from being able to get his hands on any of the wisdom of God since. It has been hidden from him.

Let's read 1 Corinthians 2:7-8:

7   But we speak the wisdom of God in a mystery,
<u>even the hidden wisdom,</u> which God ordained
before the world unto our glory:

8   Which none of the princes of this world knew:
for had they known it, they would not have
crucified the Lord of glory.

That Word says God not only hid His wisdom from satan, but also that before the foundation of the world He ordained it, or set it aside, for <u>our</u> glory. Don't you know that tears satan up? Now look at Ephesians 3:8-10:

8   ...that I should preach among the Gentiles the
unsearchable riches of Christ;

9   And to make all men see what is the fellowship
of the mystery, which <u>from the beginning of
the world hath been hid in God,</u> who created
all things by Jesus Christ:

10   To the intent that now unto the principalities
and powers in heavenly places might be known
by the church the manifold wisdom of God.

The wisdom of God, set aside for us, is available for all men to see.

Where did God hide His wisdom? It had to be in a place where angels could not get it. Devils could not access it. But all men, by faith, could receive it, understand it and walk in it. In fact, He hid it in plain sight. Proverbs 1:20-23:

> 20 Wisdom crieth without; she uttereth her voice in the streets:
> 21 She crieth in the chief place of concourse, in the openings of the gates: in the city she uttereth her words, saying,
> 22 How long, ye simple ones, will ye love simplicity? and the scorners delight in their scorning, and fools hate knowledge?
> 23 Turn you at my reproof: behold, I will pour out my spirit unto you, I will make known my words unto you.

God fixed it so that the devil doesn't have a clue about God's wisdom, but all the time it's available to anyone—even people on the street. Look at Proverbs 2:7:

> 7 He layeth up sound wisdom for the righteous: he is a buckler to them that walk uprightly.

If that isn't strong enough, read 8:1-9:

> 1 Doth not wisdom cry? and understanding put forth her voice?
> 2 She standeth in the top of high places, by the way in the places of the paths.
> 3 She crieth at the gates, at the entry of the city, at the coming in at the doors.
> 4 Unto you, O men, I call; and my voice is to the sons of man.
> 5 O ye simple, understand wisdom: and, ye fools, be ye of an understanding heart.
> 6 Hear; for I will speak of excellent things; and

> the opening of my lips shall be right things.
>
> 7 For my mouth shall speak truth; and wickedness
> is an abomination to my lips.
>
> 8 All the words of my mouth are in righteousness;
> there is nothing froward or perverse in them.
>
> 9 They are all plain to him that understandeth,
> and right to them that find knowledge.

Now let's check out some New Testament scriptures, and it will become very clear what God planned where His wisdom is concerned. In Luke 11:49 Jesus referred to the written Word as the wisdom of God. Then in 1 Corinthians 1:30 the Word says Jesus was of God made unto us wisdom:

> 30 But of him are ye in Christ Jesus, who of God
> is made unto us wisdom, and righteousness,
> and sanctification, and redemption.

In fact, 1 Corinthians 1:24 says Jesus' Anointing is not only the power of God but is also the wisdom of God. In fact, Jesus is the wisdom of God and He has been given to us. When you received Jesus as your Lord and Savior, you received the wisdom of God! Colossians 2:2-3. Look at it. No, shout over it!

> 2 That their hearts might be comforted, being
> knit together in love, and unto all riches of
> the full assurance of understanding, to the
> acknowledgement of the mystery of God, and
> of the Father, and of Christ;
>
> 3 In whom are hid all the treasures of wisdom
> and knowledge.

If these treasures are hidden in Him, they're in you! If He's in you, then everything that's in Him has to be in you. In fact, 1 Corinthians 2:12 and John 16:14-15 say that's the reason the Lord Jesus sent the Holy Spirit to dwell in you—to reveal all that God had invested in you.

Colossians 1:9 says all wisdom and understanding is available until we become filled with it.

How do we get it from being a mystery hidden in us to becoming understanding? First of all, a constant reading and meditating on the Proverbs bring faith. According to Proverbs 1:2, that's the reason they were written:

>2 To know wisdom and instruction; to perceive the words of understanding.

James 1:5-7 just says outright that we either get it by faith or not at all. Faith cometh by hearing and hearing by the Word of God. Once faith has asked, then knowledge of the way God thinks about certain things keeps us from thinking the way the world thinks and being drawn into their so-called wisdom. The world's way of doing things is one of the major problems among God's people now. Dump it! God's way (wisdom) works.

However, there's a lot more to it than that. That's just where you start. We need specific answers for specific situations—NOW! That's where praying in the spirit comes in—BIG TIME!

Remember those scriptures we read about the hidden wisdom in a mystery—1 Corinthians 2:7; Ephesians 3:9, etc.? Now look at 1 Corinthians 14:2:

>2 For he that speaketh in an unknown tongue speaketh not unto men, but unto God: for no man understandeth him; howbeit in the spirit he speaketh <u>mysteries.</u>

No wonder satan has fought praying in tongues so. He cannot get in on what's coming out of you going to God and what's coming out of God going to you.

That verse says men don't understand what you're speaking, but it does not say understanding is not available <u>to you. It's coming out of you. It belongs to you!</u>

Verses 13-15 give the process for receiving understanding. First, pray that you interpret. Then pray in the spirit and pray with your understanding. Then sing awhile in the spirit and also with your understanding. Let it flow. Don't struggle with it.

Remember James 5—<u>without faith, this process doesn't work.</u> The knowing, understanding, insights and concepts will begin to emerge. You'll wake up in the morning with a knowing of what to do, what to say, or maybe what to pray in a certain situation. Proverbs 18:4 and 20:5 promise that the process works, but it takes time spent doing it.

Think about it! The wisdom of God—His divine ability to use knowledge—is only about 18 inches below your head! Get busy and begin drawing it out. Health, riches, honor and happiness filled with joy is ready to change your life forever.

<u>You and I have a job to do that's beyond just our own wits and human knowledge.</u> We've already stretched ourselves out far beyond that. Without the mighty wisdom of God we've had it! But, thank God we're not without it.

Spend time praying with Gloria and me and all of us here at KCM and EMIC. Your prayers provide our supply through the Holy Ghost. Our prayers provide your supply as we pray for one another—we together strengthen one another to receive. Together in <u>Christ</u> Jesus we can do <u>all</u> things.

Sow your seeds this month expecting a flood of divine wisdom. In fact, sow toward that. It's there just waiting to be released.

We love you and pray for you every day!

Love,

Ken

Be Still and KNOW!

There is no doubt about it—I <u>know</u> for a fact that I have the best, strongest and most faithful Partners in the world. No ministry anywhere has partners equal to mine. I am so grateful to God for you. You are partakers of my grace.

Have you ever come to the place where it seems as though you've come to a dead end of everything all at once? You know the wisdom of God is in you, but you haven't received any more instructions. At the same time, the money has run out. At the same time, several other things seem to just hit the wall. What do we do now? Fast? Pray more? Confess more scriptures? What?

Those are all good things to do but there are three things that are especially powerful at a time like this. What we don't want to do is to start trying to <u>make</u> something happen and get over into doing something in the power of the flesh. That only compounds the problems and adds to the pressure and frustration.

The three things I mentioned we should do are these:

1.   Meditate the Word of God. (Joshua 1:8)
2.   Praise God for His goodness, mercy
      and wisdom. (Psalm 8 and Psalm 37)
3.   "Be still, and <u>know</u> that I am God."
      (Psalm 46:10)

Let's look at Joshua 1:8.

8   This book of the law shall not depart out of
      thy mouth; but thou shalt meditate therein
      day and night, that thou mayest observe to
      do according to all that is written therein: for
      then thou shalt make thy way prosperous, and
      then thou shalt have good success.

Meditation in the Word of God gives your heavenly Father opportunity to reveal the meat of His Word to you. It will build your capacity for faith. Meditation is not reading large amounts of scripture, but taking a verse or two and meditating on them. Ask yourself, "How does this verse change my situation? What if the Lord Jesus was standing right here in front of me, called me by name and said this verse to me?"

If you were meditating Philippians 4:19, it would begin building and enlarging your capacity for faith for finances. If you were meditating 1 Peter 2:24, it would increase your inner man's capacity to receive healing for your body, and so on. It is also a great source of rest.

Now praise. Read Psalm 8.

1   O Lord our Lord, how excellent is thy name in all the earth! who hast set thy glory above the heavens.

2   Out of the mouth of babes and sucklings hast thou ordained strength because of thine enemies, that thou mightest still the enemy and the avenger.

3   When I consider thy heavens, the work of thy fingers, the moon and the stars, which thou hast ordained;

4   What is man, that thou art mindful of him? and the son of man, that thou visitest him?

5   For thou hast made him a little lower than the angels, and hast crowned him with glory and honour.

6   Thou madest him to have dominion over the works of thy hands; thou hast put all things under his feet:

7   All sheep and oxen, yea, and the beasts of the field;

8   The fowl of the air, and the fish of the sea, and whatsoever passeth through the paths of the seas.

9   O Lord our Lord, how excellent is thy name in all the earth!

Praise stops the work of the devil! It stops confusion. It takes over your mind and helps flush out all the stuff that is causing the pressure and unrest. Those are the thoughts that feed doubt and unbelief.

Now the third, and most of the time the hardest thing to do: "Be still, and know that I am God." We should all practice this often—not just when everything has hit the wall.

Be still!

It's a whole lot easier to make your body be still than it is to quiet your mind and emotions. That's the reason meditation and praise are so important.

One really important fact to remember here is that no one can fight thoughts with thoughts. God created you and gave authority to your tongue. Meditation and praise is powerful when released with the words of your mouth. Your mind has to stop and see what your mouth has to say. Once your mind is quiet, begin to say, "I know You are God. I know that You know what You are doing. I know that I am in Your hands. I know that You love me. I know You gave me Jesus."

Since it was God who said, "Be still," He is responsible for your "knowing." Here are a few definitions of "to know":

A. To perceive with certainty
B. To understand clearly
C. To preclude all doubt
D. To have intimate relation with
E. To have full assurance...

THAT HE IS GOD!

There is a knowing that comes in the spirit that brings total peace to your mind and emotions. It passes all human understanding. This is our advantage over the world and all the forces of darkness. To know by revelation that He is God—the Most High God—our God— changes everything.

As you pray over your financial seed this month, aim it toward the "knowings" of the Bible. <u>Know</u> that you are entire, wanting nothing. <u>Know</u> who you are in Christ Jesus. <u>Know</u> the love of God. Study the <u>knowings</u> of the New Testament and then be still and <u>know!</u> It won't be long until you'll be up and running full blast in faith again shouting, "Out of my way, devil, I <u>know</u> He is God!"

Gloria and I love you very much and we pray for you every day.

Love,

Ken

You Can Be One Who
Knows Instead of Wonders!

Dear Partner

In last month's letter, we talked about being still and <u>knowing</u>. Psalm 46:10 says:

> 10   Be still, and know that I am God: I will be
>   exalted among the heathen, I will be exalted
>   in the earth.

Notice it did not say, "Hope that I am God," nor did it say, "Be still and maybe I'll be God." No! He <u>is</u> God! He is God and He wants us to <u>know</u> it.

The first dictionary definition of *know* is "perceive with certainty." It means "to come to a clear understanding."

There is something that God has put deep on the inside of every human being that is very hard to describe with words. It is that part of your born-again spirit that can <u>KNOW</u>. There is a deep place that can become so convinced about something or someone that even the threat of death cannot change it. It's more than just making up your mind. It's deeper than that. In fact, it can totally change or renew your mind.

Ephesians 3:19 says that we can know beyond our knowledge. Philippians 4:7 says:

> 7   And the peace of God, which <u>passeth all</u>
>   <u>understanding,</u> shall keep your hearts and
>   minds through Christ Jesus.

How do we get to that peace? It can't come out of the mind alone because it passes, or goes beyond, all understanding. It comes up from your spirit's innermost being—from your "knower."

You can be taught something until you have understanding. You can practice until you have a working knowledge of something. But you will never <u>KNOW</u> it until you take quality time to be still and know.

If there is one major handicap among believers it is never taking the time to be still—especially in our generation. We are all too busy, or at least think we are. Almost everyone is working day and night, going to school or taking children to school—or both, working at church, and on and on.

However, we seem to have time to spend from one to four hours a day, or more, watching TV. That's self-imposed busyness. Only a portion of this time spent being quiet before God in order to open up our knowing to Him would change things drastically. And, I might add, it wouldn't take long to do it.

Let's take a look at some "knowings" from the Word.

This is a great one. Ephesians 6:5-8:

> 5 Servants, be obedient to them that are your masters according to the flesh, with fear and trembling, in singleness of your heart, as unto Christ;
>
> 6 Not with eyeservice, as menpleasers; but as the servants of Christ, doing the will of God from the heart;
>
> 7 With good will doing service, as to the Lord, and not to men:
>
> 8 <u>Knowing</u> that whatsoever good thing any man doeth, the same shall he receive of the Lord, whether he be bond or free.

Think about how much pressure would be lifted during a day's work if you <u>knew</u> that. I'm not talking about just having been taught that or having even a working knowledge of it after having been to a Believers' Convention or two, or having listened to some tapes. All of that is good foundation, but there's something deeper that's available.

There's <u>knowing</u> that will come right on the job when it's needed most—when the devil and his crowd are really trying to break your spirit—if you've spent the time beforehand meditating, praising and being still before God. You've opened up your knower. You've allowed the Holy Spirit to take you beyond your own understanding. In fact, you'll be amazed at yourself—at how peaceful and above it all you are when you should be coming apart at the seams.

Look what an edge that will give you in your work. You'll still be in control and doing a good job when everyone else is folding up. Not only that, but during your still times is when you begin to <u>know</u> things about your job that only God knows. Inventions, ideas, solutions and promotions all come from God showing you how to do good things for others and receiving from the Lord.

Also, take hold of the last part of that verse "whether he be bond or free." Think what freedom can reign in your life when the devil can no longer get you under pressure over your past, your race, your education, your have-nots—whatever they are. <u>You have the knowing ability on the inside of your spirit</u> to completely move all that entirely out of your consciousness. GONE! Not just covered up only to rise up and knock you down when the pressures of life come rolling in.

In closing, I want to open up another area of knowing. Be still and know giving and receiving. "Lord Jesus, where should I invest Your money and prosperity?" It's one thing to seek God for the harvest we need, but it's quite another to seek Him and <u>know</u> where and what to give. When we sow in the right places, harvesting is not nearly the problem as when we miss it and sow out of His will. There's a great confidence that comes after we've sown <u>knowing</u> where and how much and when. Obedience is greater than sacrifice, the Word says.

When we know what to do beyond our own understanding, and we obey, there's a level of faith that comes that is so great that harvesting that seed cannot be denied. When we do it <u>knowing,</u> we cannot be talked out of our blessing.

Take the time not only to pray over your seed this month, but also to be still before God and know. Know that your money is going into the harvest field of souls.

Know that Gloria and I are somewhere at this very moment preaching a noncompromised message from God's Word because you obeyed God and bought the fuel for us to get there. Know that you paid for the airplane, the trucks, the sound systems, the material and the clothes on our backs! And know that you get the same reward for sending us as we do for preaching.

These are truths—not just words. Take the time to know them.

Know also how very much Gloria and I love and appreciate you. You are One in a Million!

We love and pray for you every day.

Love,

You share equally in the rewards, both in heaven and on earth, for everyone saved, healed and set free from drugs and suicide at the Healing of the Nations Motorcycle Rally, in Kayenta, Ariz.

Wake Up, Boy! That Corn
Won't Put Itself in the Barn!

Dear Partner

All the prayers I've prayed for more than 30 years for the North American Indian people are coming to pass. At the time I'm writing this letter I am in Kayenta, Arizona, in the heart of the Navajo Nation.

A young native pastor, Ellson Bennett, started the Healing of the Nations Motorcycle Rally here last year. This year's rally has been absolutely outstanding. We've seen people saved, healed and set free in every service.

The meetings are outside, of course, in a rodeo-grounds arena. Last night, right in the middle of my message, a windstorm blew in, and sand and dirt began blowing everywhere. I kept on preaching and nobody left. Pastor Bennett gave an invitation and people came. They stood at the altar in the wind and dirt, covering their eyes with their hands as Pastor led them in prayer. It was a glorious, windy time of great breakthrough.

The same outpouring of the Holy Spirit is happening all over the Navajo Nation. The president and chief of the Navajo Nation, Kelsey Begaye, is a mighty man of God—a Spirit-filled, faith-filled man of the Word.

It's happening among the other Host Nations people from the northeastern tribes to the southernmost tribes of North America to the northwestern tribes of Canada. I am so thrilled and honored to be part of it all.

I'm even more thrilled when I think about you and all our Partners who pray and give and stand with this ministry. You're the ones who get us even to the most remote places all over the world to preach this uncompromised message of faith.

You paid for most of this rally in Kayenta. I didn't. You did! You get credit and reward for every salvation, every healing, every deliverance, every young Indian teenager set free from drugs and suicide. There have been many of all of these, and there will be many, many more. You get the same heavenly and earthly reward for sending Gloria and me as we receive for preaching this uncompromised message.

The outpouring of the power of God for the great harvest of souls is underway. It's increasing in intensity every day. That means that the great financial harvest and wealth transfer talked about in the Word for the last days has also begun. <u>The financial harvest and end-time wealth transfer is for the purpose of financing the harvesting of souls.</u> They run together at the same time, one complementing the other— one supporting the other.

However, without constant faith we can't receive the fullness of either the soul harvest or the financial harvest. It's so easy to sow our money and then sit back and wait for the harvest to come in. It won't. That will never happen with a natural crop, nor will it happen with a spiritual crop. Let's look at Mark 4:3-8:

3   Hearken; Behold, there went out a sower to sow:
4   And it came to pass, as he sowed, some fell by the way side, and the fowls of the air came and devoured it up.
5   And some fell on stony ground, where it had not much earth; and immediately it sprang up, because it had no depth of earth:
6   But when the sun was up, it was scorched; and because it had no root, it withered away.
7   And some fell among thorns, and the thorns grew up, and choked it, and it yielded no fruit.
8   And other fell on good ground, and did yield fruit that sprang up and increased; and brought forth, some thirty, and some sixty, and some an hundred.

<u>The moment the sower went out to sow he had problems.</u> He had to choose productive ground. He couldn't just go out the door and throw a bunch of seed. The same is true of spiritual seed. The only way to know good ground to sow in is through prayer and listening to God.

It takes time to pray, and it takes time to hear.

Next the sower had problems with satan. To get a harvest of any kind we must be obedient to Ephesians 6:10-18:

10   Finally, my brethren, be strong in the Lord, and in the power of his might.

11   Put on the whole armour of God, that ye may be able to stand against the wiles of the devil.

12   For we wrestle not against flesh and blood, but against principalities, against powers, against the rulers of the darkness of this world, against spiritual wickedness in high places.

13   Wherefore take unto you the whole armour of God, that ye may be able to withstand in the evil day, and having done all, to stand.

14   Stand therefore, having your loins girt about with truth, and having on the breastplate of righteousness;

15   And your feet shod with the preparation of the gospel of peace;

16   Above all, taking the shield of faith, wherewith ye shall be able to quench all the fiery darts of the wicked.

17   And take the helmet of salvation, and the sword of the Spirit, which is the word of God:

18   Praying always with all prayer and supplication in the Spirit, and watching thereunto with all perseverance and supplication for all saints.

Our victory is assured, but only if we suit up and take our stand of faith against the enemy.

It doesn't, however, stop there either. Mark 4:8 is not the end of Jesus' teaching: "And other fell on good ground, and did yield fruit that sprang up and increased; and brought forth, some thirty, and some sixty, and some an hundred."

Look at 4:29: "But when the fruit is brought forth, immediately he putteth in the sickle, because the harvest is come." The crop came up. The seed did its part. The ground did its part. Now someone has to gather it in.

Every farmer knows that all the hard work spent caring for and watering the ground, then the long hours planting, are to no avail if he doesn't get that crop into the barn. It will rot in the field if he gets lazy. The real work and long hours just begin when it's time to put in the sickle.

This is all especially true when it comes to spiritual harvesting. We must do all the same things as in a natural harvest. The ground of our hearts must be prepared through the Word and prayer including repentance, etc.

Then, as I said earlier, time must be spent praying and listening to God about the places He wants us to sow into, such as our church, ministries, people and places of His choice—not just the ones who make the loudest noise.

When we do these things, our harvest is there. Spiritual things don't take as long as natural things to return their harvest. However, spiritual things have to be transferred into natural money, or goods, or into whatever we were believing to receive when we sowed in faith and obedience. This is where the sickle has to be put to work.

What is the sickle?

Calling things that be not as though they were! Your tongue is your instrument of harvest. There's no getting around it. Without a constant, exerted effort of filling our mouths with our faith from the Word and speaking it, the harvest will hang there just out of reach in the unseen world. It's there, but it has to be brought in.

I realize this is the hardest job of all. It seems as though you're just talking to the wind, or the devil will say, *What possible good could all that confession stuff and naming and claiming do anyway?* He has to try something to stop you because he knows what "good" it will do. It will cost him everything he has.

What is actually happening? Hebrews 3:1 and Mark 11:23-24 tell the story.

Hebrews 3:1:

> 1   Wherefore, holy brethren, partakers of the heavenly calling, consider the Apostle and High Priest of our profession, Christ Jesus.

Mark 11:23-24:

> 23   For verily I say unto you, That whosoever shall say unto this mountain, Be thou removed, and be thou cast into the sea; and shall not doubt in his heart, but shall believe that those things which he saith shall come to pass; he shall have whatsoever he saith.
> 24   Therefore I say unto you, What things soever ye desire, when ye pray, believe that ye receive them, and ye shall have them.

<u>Jesus is the One backing our words of faith.</u> It's when we fill our mouths with His promises and in faith, pray, speak, shout and praise them back to Him that the transfer from the world of the spirit to the natural, material world begins.

Always see Him, your High Priest, right in front of you when you speak the Word of your harvest. <u>Never just speak into thin air.</u>

<u>Never!</u>

He's there. He's in you. He's around you. He promised He would never leave you nor forsake you. He's ready to do His part. The main problem has been that without us doing our part of speaking in faith continually, He has little or nothing to work with. If we do our part, the possible, He will <u>always</u> do His part, the impossible.

Harvest time is here! Stand up and call it in. Sharpen your sickle with the Word and bring it in. We've a huge job to do and a short time to do it. The souls are hungry and ready. Together we can fill the house of the Lord.

Pleeeease—if you haven't already sent me your picture, do it now. We're getting everything together to move into the great new Partner Service Center, and it's important that I have a picture of every Partner. Just a snapshot will do. We will be praying over a real face instead of just a name. Hurry. You're One in a Million!

Check out the new Web site! It's dynamite—Internet radio, the *Believer's Voice of Victory* TV broadcast and a ton of other stuff to keep your faith right up on top!

Also, check into and pray about becoming a part of CFAITH.com. It's the greatest thing ever for people like you and me.

Thank you from the bottom of our hearts for continuing to stand with us in prayer and faith and also with your financial sowing into this ministry. We're going for every TV station in North America that will accept our broadcast and then every station in the rest of the world. God will have His witness! Together we can and will do it.

Gloria and I love you very much and we pray for you every day— along with hundreds of people here at KCM.

We Love You,

Ken

Never Give Up On Your Dream!

Dear Partner

When Gloria and I married in April of 1962, she had a dream to someday have a nice house for her family. It was only a spark, but it was there nonetheless. Then, six months after we married, we both accepted Jesus as our Lord and Savior. That began to change everything.

The changes came slowly at first because we knew so little of the Word of God. But that small dream was in her, and she held on to it even when things looked so impossible around us.

Our children were born. Our life's direction was changed. We went from a career in aviation that was out of the will of God, to answering God's call to serve Him in the ministry. I finally said yes to that call in the latter part of 1963, not having the slightest idea what to do next. We bounced around from place to place, always broke and deeply in debt.

We lived in some really strange places during those years until I finally agreed with God to enroll in Oral Roberts University. Then in December of 1966, we moved to Tulsa and into another strange, beat-up, dirty, little house. It was awful! However, after the shock of first sight we moved in, and with a little paint and a lot of soap and water, things began to look better.

About this same time a book by Oral Roberts came into our hands. In that book Brother Roberts said to write your dreams down and don't let anyone talk you out of them. Gloria did that. Right after the things concerning ministry and family, she listed her house.

That's when the little spark took root in her soul—<u>that place where dreams are</u> <u>born, nourished</u> and <u>grown</u> <u>until they are turned over to faith to be brought to pass.</u>

At the time I am writing this letter, Gloria and I have lived in the final manifestation of her dream <u>for one week!</u> It is wonderful! It is as much a place prepared by our heavenly Father as the Garden of Eden was for Adam and his wife.

There were many times over the past 38 years when it looked as though there was no way for that dream to come to pass. But Gloria paid no attention to those times. She just kept on collecting magazines, pictures, articles, videos and anything else she came across to help shape the final product.

The most important thing, however, has been the many Scripture promises she collected. She has house scriptures, land scriptures, tree scriptures, furniture scriptures, water scriptures (for the well) and all kinds of treasure scriptures. She has peace scriptures, blessing scriptures, love scriptures and ministry scriptures for anyone who enters her home.

She has God's Word for <u>everything</u> that has had anything to do with that house. Even scriptures that covered finding the right contractor. Our experience with our builder and his subcontractors and workers has been wonderful. Not some nightmare, like so many stories I have heard. Gloria even got to where she was a pretty good architect and a better-than-good interior decorator. As a result, she has had a large hand in designing the buildings the ministry has built over the years. That was because of the anointing that has developed in that area of her life. It's there because she refused to let go of her dream.

Let's look at 1 Corinthians 13:13: "And now abideth faith, hope, charity, these three; but the greatest of these is charity." These three are abiding—or living—forces: faith, hope and love.

Hope, the one in the middle, is the living force where our dreams and desires are developed. <u>Hope is the blueprint</u> drawn by the living promises of God that the force of faith brings to pass. Faith is the substance of things <u>hoped</u> for. Without faith there is no substance. Without hope there is no pattern for substance.

Look at Hebrews 6:17-20:

17   Wherein God, willing more abundantly to show
unto the heirs of promise the immutability of

his counsel, confirmed it by an oath:

18 That by two immutable things, in which it was impossible for God to lie, we might have a strong consolation, who have fled for refuge to lay hold upon the hope set before us:

19 Which hope we have as an anchor of the soul, both sure and stedfast, and which entereth into that within the veil;

20 Whither the forerunner is for us entered, even Jesus, made an high priest for ever after the order of Melchisedec.

Notice in those verses that hope is set before us and (1) must be laid hold upon, (2) is the anchor of the soul both sure and steadfast, and (3) it enters into that within the veil, or into God's very presence.

The hope we are talking about is not what the world calls hope. What the world calls hope is the same as to wish. "Will you be healed?" "Well, I sure do hope so." There is no place to put any faith substance in that. It has no scripture, therefore it has no foundation. There's no way anyone could lay hold on that kind of hope.

Real Bible hope, however, is totally different. It is set before us in the Word of God. In Acts 26:6, we read in the words of the Apostle Paul: "And now I stand and am judged for the hope of the promise made of God unto our fathers." And 2 Peter 1:4 says, "Whereby are given unto us exceeding great and precious promises: that by these ye might be partakers of the divine nature, having escaped the corruption that is in the world through lust."

The Bible word *hope* literally means "earnest expectation." So faith is the substance of things earnestly expected.

"Will you be healed?"

"Oh, yes!"

"How can you be so sure? How do you expect to be healed when everyone else with that has died?"

"Because I have God's Word on it. It is written, 'By his stripes I am healed.'"

Can you see the Word foundation? See how easy it is to apply faith when the Word is the basis for expectation?

Let's talk about the blueprint of faith—the hope that is set before us.

One of the most important things Gloria did was to write down her dreams. Every one of them has come to pass. There is something strong that happens on the inside when you write down your dreams—especially along with the promises of God—then talk as if you were already standing in the midst of them NOW. That's calling things that be not as though they WERE. Not someday—NOW.

"Lord, it's so good to be living in my dream home. It's so good to be debt free. It's so wonderful to be totally healed and free of pain. I remember when I was so deep in debt and so sick. I remember those old bills all piled up. I remember what a thrill it was to pay them all. Just look all around me now. Your wonderful Word has come to pass. Oh, praise Your wonderful Name!"

Take the time to do this every day. Read your promises and your dream list, then see yourself with it. Not someday but NOW. That's living hope and living faith at work. It doesn't matter what your natural eyes are seeing or what your natural brain is reporting. Those images are without power. Our dreams anchored solidly to the Word of God will eventually drive those so-called facts first out of your mind, then out of your body, and finally completely out of your life.

"Brother Copeland, this sounds like that stuff the world does like mind over matter or imaging and such."

No. All that stuff sounds like this. Those are satan's counterfeits to the real thing. God told Joshua: "See, I have given you Jericho." He told Abraham, "I have made thee the father of many nations"—not "I am going to" but "I have."

As you continue to hope and use your faith, your inner image will develop into the perfect will of God for you. Proverbs 16:3 from *The*

Amplified Bible says: "Roll your works upon the Lord [commit and trust them wholly to Him; He will cause your thoughts to become agreeable to His will, and] so shall your plans be established and succeed."

Over a period of time your inner thoughts—not the ones on top of your head, but the thoughts and intents of the heart—will conform to God's will for your life and calling. Then you'll be like Joshua in Joshua 1:8:

> 8   This book of the law shall not depart out of thy mouth; but thou shalt meditate therein day and night, that thou mayest observe to do according to all that is written therein: for then thou shalt make thy way prosperous, and then thou shalt have good success.

Hope becomes revelation from heaven, and patience will have her perfect work. You <u>will</u> be entire, wanting nothing.

Gloria and I have taken a stand on God's Word for you and your dreams. This is the scripture God gave us, and we are standing on it <u>for</u> and <u>with</u> you. Isaiah 54:2-4 *(New King James Version):*

> 2   Enlarge the place of your tent, And let them stretch out the curtains of your dwellings; Do not spare; Lengthen your cords, And strengthen your stakes.
>
> 3   For you shall expand to the right and to the left, And your descendants will inherit the nations, And make the desolate cities inhabited.
>
> 4   Do not fear, for you will not be ashamed; Neither be disgraced, for you will not be put to shame; For you will forget the shame of your youth, And will not remember the reproach of your widowhood anymore.

My dream is to take the uncompromised word of faith to the nations. Pray over your seed this month and listen for the Spirit of God to instruct you concerning sowing into your dream—how much, where, when. Then obey. See yourself harvesting your dreams together with us—an overflowing, overpowering harvest.

You are part of my dream. Gloria and I love you very much, and we pray for you every day.

Love,

Ken

If You Don't Take the Bait,
You Won't Fall Into the Trap.

Dear Partner

There's never been a time like this. Every generation before us has been on the world's clock—the world's timetable. But you and I are not on Adam's clock and <u>never</u> ever will be again. Nothing in this world order is the same. It's no longer a time of waiting, then waiting some more—of long, dragged-out times of either everything being "the same ol' same ol'" over and over again, or just plain nothing happening at all.

We have all moved over onto God's time clock. There's no more time left. He has declared certain things will happen at certain times, and they must not miss their appointed times by one second. Only one moment late would make God a liar and subject to satan. That must not and will not happen. You may be assured, however, that satan and all hell are doing everything they can to stop God's Word from coming to pass. That means he's out to steal, kill and destroy every way he can.

For those of us who walk in the Word, it is the very best of times. It is the fullness of times. We are standing at the crossroads of the ages. This is the greatest of all times to be alive on the earth. We have front-row seats. We are the blessed of the blessed. Every prophet of every generation before us pointed to this time as the time to be alive.

However big God has to show Himself alive and strong in order to make His appointments, that's just how grand He'll be. Whatever the devil does, however wild he gets, it's not wild enough. Jesus said in John 10:10, "The thief cometh not, but for to steal, and to kill, and to destroy: I am come that they might have life, and that they might have it <u>more</u> abundantly." Abundance always overcomes stealing. It always overcomes death, and it always overcomes destruction.

Let's look at that verse again. Jesus did not say I have come that you may have life abundantly. He said <u>more</u> abundantly. "More" in this verse changes everything. Regardless of what satan plans, there's <u>more</u> abundance. <u>Satan has limits. God does not!</u> <u>More</u> means <u>more!</u>

There are some things we <u>must</u> be very careful to watch for in order to keep the forces of darkness out of our lives and ministry. This is no time to be lazy and loose about the things of the spirit. This is the time to be vigilant and stay strong before the Lord. The devil is running out of time and he knows it. He is seeking those whom he may devour.

This is no time to be wandering around outside the sheepfold in the dark. This is the time to stay as close to the Shepherd as we can get. He is leading us into the greenest pastures we've ever seen. We are coming along beside the most peaceful waters one can imagine. He has prepared a table for us that is exceeding, abundantly beyond anything we can ask or think.

We're there now. It is available now. However, this table is in the presence of our enemies in the valley of the <u>shadow</u> of death. The third verse of the 23rd Psalm says, "He leads me in the paths of righteousness"—or in the covenant paths that lead through this valley of danger, in perfect protection. This is no time to run off the covenant road onto some rabbit trail that leads out into the dark where the pitfalls and stumbling blocks can't be seen. Our road is a well-lit road when the Word is the light to our pathway and a torch before our feet.

Let's go to the fourth chapter of Mark's Gospel and see what Jesus has to say about how the devil works to steal our most precious asset— the <u>Word</u> of <u>God.</u> Remember, it was the written Word that Jesus used to totally defeat satan and drive him from His presence. Let's look at verses 14-20:

14 The sower soweth the word.

15 And these are they by the way side, where the word is sown; but when they have heard, Satan cometh immediately, and taketh away the word that was sown in their hearts.

16 And these are they likewise which are sown on stony ground; who, when they have heard the word, immediately receive it with gladness;

17 And have no root in themselves, and so endure but for a time: afterward, when affliction or persecution ariseth for the word's sake,

immediately they are offended.

18   And these are they which are sown among thorns; such as hear the word,

19   And the cares of this world, and the deceitfulness of riches, and the lusts of other things entering in, choke the word, and it becometh unfruitful.

20   And these are they which are sown on good ground; such as hear the word, and receive it, and bring forth fruit, some thirtyfold, some sixty, and some an hundred.

Jesus has revealed the five things that the devil uses against the believer to open a door to destruction. No animal ever intended to fall or walk into a trap. He had to be fooled, or baited, into it. These five things are baited traps:

1. Affliction
2. Persecution
3. Cares of this world
4. Deceitfulness of riches
5. Lusts (pressures) of other things

The word translated *affliction* in verse 17 does not mean sickness or disease. It is referring to, and means, suffering due to the pressure of circumstances. Abraham in Romans 4:16-21 considered not his circumstances but only that which God had promised. The Word is stronger than <u>any</u> circumstance. It is greater than anything satan can surround us with.

Notice Jesus said afflictions and persecutions arise for the Word's sake—not to teach us some wonderful lesson. The devil is not the teacher of the Church. The Holy Spirit is, by the Word. Now we learn from these situations, but they are not from God. The Word is from God. Everything else in the situation is from satan. Learn to separate the pressure from the problem. Jesus has already overcome the problem—whatever it is. The pressure comes when we allow the circumstances to get into our eyes. That's the bait. Don't go for it. Stay with the promises.

Persecutions are closely related to afflictions, but with a major difference. Persecution comes from being pursued. It means someone is trying to drive you away. Satan is using people to try to bring all your attention to what "they" are doing to you. He's pressing you away from the Word. He has to, because the Word pressures and drives him away.

Both of these things, afflictions and persecutions, lead or bait believers into becoming offended. Taking offense stops the work of the anointing. Without the anointing there is no removing of burdens or destroying of yokes. When people do and say things that offend you, that's the bait! Don't take it. Immediately forgive and walk away. Stay with the Word!

The cares of this world come from paying too much attention to all the stealing, killing and destroying satan is doing out there. Those cares cannot overcome the Word unless you let them get inside you and choke it. The voice of the world—CNN, evening news, e-mail gossip, etc.—delivers the bait. Don't take it. Don't let it in. Those are the cares of the world. They are not the cares of the Church.

The deceitfulness of riches sneaks in when a believer begins to see money the way the world does. When you become too busy to spend time in the Word and prayer, you step into the trap. A little at a time, the deceitfulness of riches will draw you into a place of trusting money. Tithing becomes difficult. It's a trap! Run! Run back to the Word. Lean not to your own understanding. Trust God.

Lusts of other things includes anything that brings pressure and unrest through a desire that's gotten out of hand. Usually the first thing people think of is sexual desire, and that's an example of it all right, but any lust is bait for the trap. It brings attention to the flesh. It creates the atmosphere for covetousness. It will even bring one to a place where he or she doesn't want to hear what the Word has to say about it. One example would be the lust and pressure to buy things you know you don't have the money to buy, especially when you are pressured to go in debt to get them. Another would be the desire to run around with people you shouldn't—people who gossip, backbite, etc. And of course there are many, many more examples that could be given.

You know those lusts have entered in when you don't want to be corrected by the Word. <u>It's bait!</u> <u>Don't take it.</u> If you already have, repent. NOW! Whether you want to or not. If you're already in the trap, turn loose of the bait. Grab hold of the Word of God and break free. Satan cannot hold you when you slap your own spiritual jaws, take the correction of the Word and get back where you belong on the path of righteousness—right behind your Shepherd—Jesus. He's the Savior. He's the Victor. Pull back up to the table of abundance and rejoice that no trap of the devil can hold a covenant believer.

Lay your hands on your offering seed this month and begin to call things which be not as though they <u>were:</u> "It's so good to be healed! The Word says I was, so I am. It's so good to be financially free and out of debt! The Word says I am, so I am. Thank God, I'm free from every trap.

"According to Mark 4:20, I count myself as one of those 'which are sown on good ground; such as hear the word, and receive it, and bring forth fruit, some thirtyfold, some sixty, and some an hundred.'"

I'm so excited about what all is happening all over the world in this ministry. Satan tried to bring financial pressure on us recently, but we didn't take the bait. This ministry is taking the uncompromised message of faith the world over. The Word works!

Gloria and I love you very much and we pray for you every day. Have a very merry Christmas and a wonderful new year.

Love,

Ken

P.S. Don't forget to send me your picture if you haven't already!

Gloria and I have enclosed our picture in a Christmas card to you.

"...And they shall call his name Emmanuel, which being interpreted is God with us" (Matthew 1:23). Know that His presence—and our love—are with you this Christmas season, and throughout the new year.

Love,

Kenneth and Gloria

Fellowship = Being Together to Share Mutual
Interests, Experiences and Companionship

Dear Partner

Only God Himself really knows how very important this new year is. Not only to us, but also to Him and to His dream for man. His man! The man He created to be His companion—to stand alongside Him in everything He does. Created in His image and likeness, man is the only thing God made that has the capacity to share fellowship with Him.

The attitude God desires for us to walk in is the attitude of Jesus described in Philippians 2:5-6:

> 5 Let this mind be in you, which was also in Christ Jesus:
> 6 Who, being in the form of God, thought it not robbery to be equal with God.

When you meditate on that passage and the attitude it portrays, it's clearly the attitude any loving parent desires from his children. When my children were growing up, I didn't think it robbery if they tried to act and talk like Gloria and me. What's wrong with children trying to act just like their parents? Nothing, if the parents are the right kind of people.

God's dream is to bring us, His children, to the place where we act exactly like Him instead of acting like the devil. Jesus said to the most religious people of His day in John 8:44:

> 44 Ye are of your father the devil, and the lusts of your father ye will do. He was a murderer from the beginning, and abode not in the truth, because there is no truth in him. When he speaketh a lie, he speaketh of his own: for he is a liar, and the father of it.

The only way satan has of getting anything done is to get people to act like him. The only way God has of getting anything done in the earth is to have His people act like Him. In order to protect himself, the devil lies to people through religion and tries to get God's people to think there's something blasphemous about acting and talking just like God. But if acting and talking like God were really blasphemous, Jesus would be the greatest of all blasphemers. His whole life on this earth was spent saying only what His Father said, doing only what His Father did.

Jesus didn't shamefully say, "If you've seen Me, you've seen the Father." He said those words boldly in love and faith. That's one of the major problems the high religious people had with Him. In Isaiah 53:4 we read, "Surely he hath borne our griefs, and carried our sorrows: yet we did esteem him stricken, smitten of God, and afflicted." The religious leaders told the people God had done all this to Him. They said it was punishment for the blasphemy of daring to call God His Father and act like Him.

But to call God our Father and act like Him is exactly what we are called to do. Ephesians 5:1 commands us to follow or imitate God as dear children imitate their parents. Love like He loves, speak like He speaks and act like He acts.

Now this brings us to a place where we can talk about something very important to God and to us, yet almost unheard of in the Body of Christ. That's fellowshiping with the Father. In fact, I've heard very few messages preached on the subject and have found even fewer books on it. That's really strange, and also sad, when you realize that the Word says we are called to fellowship with our Father and with the Lord Jesus.

Let's look at 1 Corinthians 1:9:

9   God is faithful, by whom ye were called unto the fellowship of his Son Jesus Christ our Lord.

Now, 1 John 1:3-4:

3   That which we have seen and heard declare we unto you, that ye also may have fellowship with us: and truly our fellowship is with the Father, and with his Son Jesus Christ.

4   And these things write we unto you, that your joy may be full.

Notice in 1 John 1:4 that fellowship with the Father and with Jesus is a source of fullness of joy. The joy of the Lord, remember, is our strength.

Let's take a look at the word *fellowship.* The word translated *fellowship* is also translated *communion,* which means "intimate familiarity." *Fellowship* is defined as "companionship; mutual association of persons on equal and friendly terms."

Ephesians 5:11 says we are to have no fellowship (mutual association on equal terms, or companionship) with unfruitful works of darkness. What, then, does that say to us who are the children of light (1 Thessalonians 5:5)? The born-again believer has everything in common with God, who is light, and nothing in common with darkness, which is the devil.

How, then, do we fellowship with God? How can we be a companion to Him? <u>Around His Word.</u> Taking time to visit with Him instead of pulling on Him with trouble and problems all the time.

Ask, "Father, is there anything I can help <u>You</u> with today? Is there anything in Your Word that You would like to <u>share</u> with me while we are together?" Then be still and just listen. A good companion is one who doesn't do all the talking.

Visit with Him about the things you enjoy. He put those desires inside you. They are part of your divine makeup. That's the reason no two of us are exactly alike. Most Christians spend all their time with God dealing with all the things they don't like. Then they visit with their earthly friends about the things they do like. <u>Talk to your heavenly Father about the good stuff.</u> Let Him enjoy it with you.

Jesus said, "I am come that they might have [and enjoy] life more abundantly." That's the reason the Apostle John said in 1 John 1:4: "These things write we unto you that your joy may be full." If you really want to get Him going, talk about what He enjoys—THE PROSPERITY OF HIS FAMILY!! "Beloved, I wish above all things that thou mayest prosper and be in health, even as thy soul prospereth" (3 John 2).

Dream His dream with Him. See yourself overwhelmingly healthy, rich, anointed and walking in His power. When you start spending time with the Father like that, you're on your exciting way to exceeding, abundantly, beyond all you can ask or think.

What are you waiting for? The door to His treasure house—His Word—is open. It's the door to His heart, and nothing would thrill Him more than to have you come on in. He loves you more than words can tell!

This is a big year for KCM. We are expanding in every direction. Our TV bill is more than $2 million a month—and growing. The cry of people overseas, "Come teach us!" is growing louder and louder all the time.

I need your prayers more than ever since I've been in this ministry. I'm stronger than I've ever been physically, but I've much more to do. Our income is more than ever, but we're spending it just as quickly as it comes in. Gloria and I are walking in more anointing than ever in our lives, but we also have more demands on us for ministry than ever before.

<u>Press in the spirit with us.</u> Together we can explode in faith in the greatest victories of soul winning, healing and deliverance the world has ever seen. We are raising up an army for God the likes of which has never been seen before. Let's press for the billion flow. Billions of dollars and billions of souls. At least five million souls will come into the kingdom of God this year through this ministry. <u>I am calling for twice that many. Together we can do it!</u>

As you sow your financial seed this month, lay your hand on it and pray. See the avalanche of people running to the light of the Word—a flowing river of people being snatched out of judgment and in to the glory of God.

Gloria and I love you very much, and we pray for you every day.

Love,

Ken

The 7th Millennium

Dear Partner

The seventh millennium has officially begun. What a time to be alive! All the years past that we've talked about it, prayed about it and wondered about it make it seem like some sort of a dream, but it's actually here.

Now what are we going to do with it? You and I as Partners in this preaching of the gospel are going to take full advantage of everything God has promised in His Word, and we're going to hit this world with a flood of the word of faith in Christ Jesus.

There's something else we <u>must</u> do <u>right now.</u>

We have a new president and vice president and a totally new kind of Congress in the United States. An even split. Who ever heard of such a thing? None of us alive today has ever seen such a thing. But that's the way things are going to be from here on out.

"<u>We've never seen anything like this before</u>" is going to become the normal, everyday thing. We will see God doing things beyond anything before, and at the same time satan will be pulling things we've never seen before.

That puts us right in the middle of everything. We must realize what that means and take our place in faith, prayer and power. We must pray for and stand in faith with the new administration, both in the White House and in the Congress. Without the prayer strength of believers, the forces of darkness will push them in their direction. We must not allow that to happen.

God is holding us, the Church, responsible for the way it all goes. We will answer to Him, because we are the ones assigned and empowered to see that God's ways and callings prevail. George W. Bush and the other leaders have their part to play, but failure or success is laid at the feet of the Body of Christ. <u>ALWAYS!</u>

To take <u>our</u> place means I must take <u>my</u> place. Every born-again believer will be held personally responsible for whether he or she did his or her part in prayer, attitude and faith.

Let's talk about prayer first. First Timothy 2:1-8 says,

1   I exhort therefore, that, first of all, supplications, prayers, intercessions, and giving of thanks, be made for all men;

2   For kings, and for all that are in authority; that we may lead a quiet and peaceable life in all godliness and honesty.

3   For this is good and acceptable in the sight of God our Saviour;

4   Who will have all men to be saved, and to come unto the knowledge of the truth.

5   For there is one God, and one mediator between God and men, the man Christ Jesus;

6   Who gave himself a ransom for all, to be testified in due time.

7   Whereunto I am ordained a preacher, and an apostle, (I speak the truth in Christ, and lie not;) a teacher of the Gentiles in faith and verity.

8   I will therefore that men pray every where, lifting up holy hands, without wrath and doubting.

Exhort is a strong word. To exhort us to <u>first</u> <u>of</u> <u>all</u> pray is to say, "This is a definite priority." For God's Word to place a <u>first</u> <u>of</u> <u>all</u> on prayer is serious business. Especially when we realize that the reason He said it is because He has given us the use of His power and authority with which to control satan's activity in every area of life on this earth. That is even more so in this new millennium.

Look at verses 2-4. Praying for those in authority has a direct effect on people being saved and taught the truth. The financial state of the nation is not controlled by politicians. It is controlled by the prayers, attitude and faith of God's people. When we don't pray, the devil controls the politicians. When we pray and use our faith, God controls those in office. The results are tied directly to what we do with what

God has commanded us to do.

Another area of this that needs to be addressed is the fact that when we are disobedient in one area of our lives, it affects other areas. By not praying first of all according to the Word, other parts of our prayer lives suffer. Things don't work the way they should.

Connect that with an attitude of unbelief, and it gets even worse. For instance, you may not have voted for George W. Bush. But, even if you don't like anything about him, that doesn't excuse you from praying for him and standing against the forces of darkness for his administration. Attitude really, really becomes important, because you can't pray and expect results when you're praying one thing and saying and acting another. The prayer of faith <u>demands</u> corresponding words and actions.

"Why, Brother Copeland, if I talk and act in faith for that person, people will think I voted for him." <u>What do you care what people think?</u> You need to be caring what God thinks.

Think about it. The seventh millennium has come. That means we're very, very close to having to face and answer to God for all these things.

We have before us the greatest opportunity ever offered to any generation. It's time to completely lay our lives on the line and go for God's best of everything. We will win more souls this year than all the years of this ministry put together. I am spending this time before God in renewing my commitments and consecration to Him and to His Word—to get totally in line with His will for this ministry and for our personal lives.

Hebrews 12:1 says it best: Lay aside every weight and the sin which does so easily beset us and <u>RUN THE RACE!</u> But do it looking to Jesus and nowhere else. By doing our part God will have His way, and His glory will manifest in every area of our lives—including the politics of this nation and also the world.

As you sow your seed this month, <u>stand with us</u> in faith financially. We are moving out in outreaches worldwide. <u>More</u> of everything—

especially TV and Internet. That, of course, calls for Gloria and me to go even more. Your prayers are vital to everything we do. In turn, we are praying and believing with you for the greatest of all harvests ever in your life.

We love and appreciate you more than you know.

Love,

Ken

We are grateful to the Lord for the friendships of so many anointed ministers of the gospel who love and serve the Lord, and minister alongside us.

Take Your Stand! This Is the Year of the Turnaround

Dear Partner

In last month's letter we talked about the authority of the believer. Let's go on a bit further into it this month.

In the book of Genesis, chapter 1, verses 26-28, God created man— not his body—him. Seven times before the 26th verse, the scripture says, "And God said...and it was," making it very clear that the saying was the creating.

The eighth time it says "And God said...", it tells of the creation of man. It is no different here. The saying was the creating. God did not say He was going to make man and then do something else to create him. The saying was the creating. The reason this is so important is because man was created with words of dominion. Let's look at it.

26   And God said, Let us make man in our image, after our likeness: and let them have dominion over the fish of the sea, and over the fowl of the air, and over the cattle, and over all the earth, and over every creeping thing that creepeth upon the earth.

27   So God created man in his own image, in the image of God created he him; male and female created he them.

28   And God blessed them, and God said unto them, Be fruitful, and multiply, and replenish the earth, and subdue it: and have dominion over the fish of the sea, and over the fowl of the air, and over every living thing that moveth upon the earth.

God did not create Adam and then appoint him as His manager. He created Adam to rule. It is man's nature to rule the same as it is God's nature to rule.

When God spoke in verses 20-21 and created the fish of the sea, the image, or pattern, for those fish was inside God. So when He spoke and released His creative power, they came into being exactly as God had designed and planned them. Remember, Jesus called the Word of God the seed of God. The life and image in the seed produces after its own kind.

However when God created man, the image was not just something He had planned. The image of Adam was God Himself. In Adam God reproduced Himself. So the authority with which Adam was created was God's authority. God didn't just give it to him or confer it upon him. Adam was created with it. He was created with words of dominion.

Now this brings up the question, "What happened to Adam when he sinned?" He was "born again" in every sense of the word. He was born from life to death. His spirit was separated from God's Spirit and joined unto the fallen angel satan. Adam took satan's corrupted nature of spiritual death. Satan became his father.

Let's look at Ephesians 2:1-3:

1   And you hath he [made alive], who were dead
     in trespasses and sins;
2   Wherein in time past ye walked according
     to the course of this world, according to the
     prince of the power of the air, the spirit that
     now worketh in the children of disobedience:
3   Among whom also we all had our conversation
     in times past in the lusts of our flesh, fulfilling
     the desires of the flesh and of the mind; and
     were by nature the children of wrath, even
     as others.

Notice in that third verse the phrase "were by nature the children of wrath." Adam received the nature of his father, the devil, lodged into his spirit, and we received it from Adam. Look at it again in John 8:44:

44   Ye are of your father the devil, and the lusts
      of your father ye will do. He was a murderer

from the beginning, and abode not in the
truth, because there is no truth in him. When
he speaketh a lie, he speaketh of his own: for
he is a liar, and the father of it.

I wanted you to see that when Adam took satan's word and acted
on it, he changed from the image of God to the image of his new father.

What I am about to show you now from the Word, religious
people have never even heard, much less believed. First let's look at
2 Corinthians 4:4:

4   In whom the god of this world hath blinded
        the minds of them which believe not, lest the
        light of the glorious gospel of Christ, who is
        the image of God, should shine unto them.

Notice in the last part of that verse the words "Christ, who is the
image of God." Now let's look at Hebrews 1:1-3.

1   God, who at sundry times and in divers
        manners spake in time past unto the fathers
        by the prophets,
2   Hath in these last days spoken unto us by
        his Son, whom he hath appointed heir of all
        things, by whom also he made the worlds;
3   Who being the brightness of his glory, and the
        express image of his person, and upholding all
        things by the word of his power, when he had
        by himself purged our sins, sat down on the
        right hand of the Majesty on high.

Again look at verse 3. Jesus is the express image of God's person.
Now from verse 6 through verse 12 are the words God spoke when
He raised Jesus from the dead. Notice carefully that they are words of
dominion. Satan lost his authority over God's work when Jesus, the last
Adam, was raised up—born from the dead the express image of God.
Now look at Colossians 1:15.

15   Who is the image of the invisible God, the
        firstborn of every creature.

Here Jesus is called the image of God, but He is also called the
firstborn of every creature. That tells us that is a new creation. God
could not go back to the dust of the earth and create another Adam. In
the first place, satan had become the ruler of the dirt. And in the second
place, the dirt was cursed. But now with the resurrection of Jesus, God
reproduced Himself again. A new creation!

Now, here comes the hallelujah part. Second Corinthians 3:17-18:

17   Now the Lord is that Spirit: and where the
        Spirit of the Lord is, there is liberty.
18   But we all, with open face beholding as in a
        glass the glory of the Lord, are changed into
        the same image from glory to glory, even as by
        the Spirit of the Lord.

And Romans 8:29:

29   For whom he did foreknow, he also did
        predestinate to be conformed to the image of
        his Son, that he might be the firstborn among
        many brethren.

The word *predestinate* in Romans 8:29 is referring to before the
foundation of the world. God decided then that His family would be in His
image, and there's no way satan or Adam or anyone else can change that.

Let's go a step further with this. He created Adam with His Word.
He raised Jesus with His Word. First Peter 1:23 says we are born again
"not of corruptible seed, but of incorruptible, by the Word of God."
Then 2 Peter 1:4 says, "Whereby are given unto us exceeding great and
precious promises: that by these ye might be partakers of the divine
nature, having escaped the corruption that is in the world through lust."
We are partakers of the divine nature. That nature is one of authority
and dominion—not that of weaklings subject to death and fear and all
that goes with it.

The Word says that Jesus sat down at God's own right hand with authority far above <u>all</u>. Look at Ephesians 1:19-23:

19 And what is the exceeding greatness of his power to us-ward who believe, according to the working of his mighty power,

20 Which he wrought in Christ, when he raised him from the dead, and set him at his own right hand in the heavenly places,

21 Far above all principality, and power, and might, and dominion, and every name that is named, not only in this world, but also in that which is to come:

22 And hath put all things under his feet, and gave him to be the head over all things to the church,

23 Which is his body, the fulness of him that filleth all in all.

Brother, that's authority. Not just a bit above but <u>far</u> above.

But wait a minute. Hebrews 10:13-14 says He sat down "<u>expecting</u> till His enemies be made His footstool." How could He expect that if His Body in this earth didn't have the authority to bring His enemies, satan and his demons, under His feet?

The 23rd verse of Ephesians 1 says it boldly: "Which is his body, the fulness of him that filleth all in all." He's the head. We're the Body of Christ. His feet are on the body. A footstool is entirely different than a pillow. The Body—every born-again believer—has His authority. It was not conferred upon you. You were born with it. Even more, you were born by it. There are no spiritual birth defects. You were born again by <u>in</u>corruptible seed in the <u>image</u> of Jesus, <u>who is the express image of God.</u>

Finally this. Release the authority that's inside you the same way God does. Put His mighty, creative Word into your heart and release it with your mouth. You have the authority to do so in Jesus' Name. Then cast down every other <u>image</u> that tries to say anything contrary to the <u>image of Jesus</u> that's in you (2 Corinthians 10:3-6). Think authority.

Speak authority. Act with authority. After all, you don't just have authority, you are His authority in this earth under Jesus, who is His authority in heaven.

As you sow your financial seeds of faith this month, do it with a sense of authority. Tell it, "Go! Bring in souls." Ten million in 2001 through this ministry. Command satan to keep his hands off of it and off your harvest. Then with that same authority, command your harvest to come into your storehouse NOW! Money thou art loosed. NOW! It has to obey.

But right here is where the image of God in you is so important. You're not just you any longer. You are born of God. You're one spirit with Jesus, and you're a Covenant Partner with Gloria and me and this ministry. A million Partners standing strong for one another.

This is the turnaround year. Everything going the wrong way must turn around. But it won't until you tell it to. God has already spoken. Now it's your turn.

Gloria and I love you and pray for you every day.

Love,

Ken

If Not Me, Who? If Not Now, When?

Dear Partner

Here it is, April 2001 already. Where did the year 2000 go? It was a big year for the kingdom of God—one in which more people came to know Jesus as Lord than any year in history. In a lot of ways it was also a tough year that had to be overcome by faith. Still, it seems as if it went by in a blur.

2001 has started off the same way. Three months of it are already gone. Time is becoming shorter in more ways than one. I am determined not to wind up desiring to have done more of the will of God in my life. I am determined not to let the time slip by me because my commitment was not what it should have been. Of course the way to avoid that is to do what I know to do and act on God's Word <u>NOW</u>—not tomorrow!

We <u>must</u> train ourselves to be more instant in season and out. We certainly want God to do what we ask Him to do instantly, on the spot, right now.

I believe one of the major reasons we don't receive quickly is because we don't give quickly. <u>I'm not talking just about money here,</u> but about anything God asks us to do. Remember, it's not a matter of God doing something. He's already done everything. Jesus has already gone to the cross. Our every need has already been provided <u>by our covenant</u> in His Name and in His Blood.

Hebrews 4:3 says the works were finished before the foundation of the world. Our problems lie not with God not acting or doing for us, but in our failure to receive. And our receiving is a mirror image of our giving. If we are slow to pray, then we are also slow to hear from heaven. If we are slow to forgive, then we are also slow to receive forgiveness. When we are slow to obey God when He asks us to give money or things, then we are also slow to receive the harvest.

Let's look at Mark 4:24:

24   And he said unto them, Take heed what ye hear: with what measure ye [measure], it shall be measured to you: and unto you that hear shall more be given.

There it is. With what measure you measure, it shall be measured back to you. If you measure out in slow teaspoons, even if you receive a hundredfold, it will come in slow teaspoons. Buckets for buckets. Dump trucks for dump trucks. God is not the one doing the measuring, we are.

Another part of this has to do with our honoring God. He is God—not just God, but the Most High God! I have learned to honor Him and being quick to obey Him must be for a much greater purpose than just because I want a quick response or harvest. He deserves better than that. In fact, He deserves far more than anyone could ever give. However, He doesn't see it that way because He loves us so much. To Him, our being quick to obey and quick to love Him is the greatest thing there is. After all, being quick to respond to someone is an act of love.

So, my prayer recently has been "Father, please show me all the areas of my life where I'm slow to act and slow to receive." In praying this, I realized that recognizing those areas in which I'm receiving more slowly than I should shows me what I should be concentrating on first. That then leaves two things to do. First, get wisdom, because wisdom is the principal thing. Let's look at 1 Corinthians 2:7 and James 1:5-6:

But we speak the wisdom of God in a mystery, even the hidden wisdom, which God ordained before the world unto our glory (1 Corinthians 2:7).

If any of you lack wisdom, let him ask of God, that giveth to all men liberally, and upbraideth not; and it shall be given him. But let him ask in faith, nothing wavering. For he that wavereth is like a wave of the sea driven with the wind and tossed (James 1:5-6).

Begin praying in the spirit and know that you are praying the perfect wisdom of God. Pray also that you interpret. Now the interpreting may come as spoken words. It may come as an inner knowing or it may come as a strong conviction. Over time, all of the above will probably be involved in receiving wisdom from God.

Remember, I said there were two things to do. The second one is to fill your mouth with what you desire to become in Christ Jesus. "I thank God that I'm always quick to hear His voice, quick to obey and quick to receive. I'm a forgiver not a condemner, therefore I'm quick to repent, quick to forgive and slow to anger. I honor the Most High God in all that I do and with all that I have. I confess these things in Jesus' Name and I believe I receive."

Now take the time to listen. Listen to your heart. Speak your desire in faith (Mark 11:23-24), then listen for the Master's voice.

It may take a while for the results to bring big changes, but the changing will begin when you begin. Then the more you confess the Word and listen, then act on what you hear, the faster things will start to change. It will come to pass.

Partner, you and I have a huge job to do and we are going to get it done. All of it!

We're not going to come up short and leave anything lying on the table that belongs to us. We will not arrive at the end of this year suddenly realizing 2001 went by without us doing what we should have done in 2000 or 2001. No sir!

God is moving and we're moving with Him. You can have His best and His all—go for it!

Gloria and I love you and pray for you every day. We've brought a number of new people in to Partner Services to serve you and pray for you. We're expanding this ministry far and wide in order to obey all the Lord Jesus wants done and also to make your life a greater joy while you're still on this earth.

As you sow your seed this month, do so with the realization that Gloria and I appreciate you and your prayers and your financial support of this ministry with all our hearts. We have the best Partners in all the world. You're One in a Million!

Love,

Ken

Righteousness Speaks!

Dear Partner

The boom is on!

I remember when I was a small boy in West Texas there were oil "boom towns." One day there would be a small, sleepy little town with almost empty streets, and a few days later the same town would be so full of people it was almost impossible to walk down the sidewalks, or anywhere else for that matter. Suddenly there was not enough of anything anywhere in town. Why? Because someone struck oil someplace nearby. A treasure had been discovered and everyone from far and near wanted a piece of it.

Much the same thing is happening today. Only this time people are discovering Jesus and His Word. They are finding out about what He's done for them. They are learning how to use their faith and develop their prayer lives. They are tapping in to the real treasures of life and the wisdom of God.

Our website is booming. Cfaith.com is booming. Everything is flowing and overflowing with the power and presence of God. I'm so glad we spent 1999 and 2000 getting ready for this. It was expensive but well worth it.

I want to talk to you this month about the Righteousness of God. Creflo Dollar and I just finished a two-week study on the daily *Believer's Voice of Victory* broadcast on the subject of the Righteousness of God. The broadcasts will air this month starting Monday, May 14, and continuing through Friday, May 25. <u>Please don't miss a single program.</u> There are some moments of anointing during those broadcasts that are explosive.

Let's look at John 11:1-4.

    1   Now a certain man was sick, named Lazarus, of

Bethany, the town of Mary and her sister Martha.

2 (It was that Mary which anointed the Lord with ointment, and wiped his feet with her hair, whose brother Lazarus was sick.)

3 Therefore his sisters sent unto him, saying, Lord, behold, he whom thou lovest is sick.

4 When Jesus heard that, he said, This sickness is not unto death, but for the glory of God, that the Son of God might be glorified thereby.

This is the account of Jesus raising Lazarus from the dead. For the sake of space let's go down to verses 38-40.

38 Jesus therefore again groaning in himself cometh to the grave. It was a cave, and a stone lay upon it.

39 Jesus said, Take ye away the stone. Martha, the sister of him that was dead, saith unto him, Lord, by this time he stinketh: for he hath been dead four days.

40 Jesus saith unto her, Said I not unto thee, that, if thou wouldest believe, thou shouldest see the glory of God?

What was happening when Jesus groaned within Himself, or in His spirit? He was going beyond Himself as a man and connecting with the Life Giver Himself—the Spirit of the Living God.

The same thing is available to us in Romans 8:26: "Likewise the Spirit also helpeth our infirmities: for we know not what we should pray for as we ought: but the Spirit Himself maketh intercession for us with groanings which cannot be uttered."

The difference is, of course, the Spirit and Jesus were working together 100 percent. Jesus' mind had not been darkened by sin. However, He had to do the same thing we must do, and that's depend on the Holy Spirit completely.

Look again at verse 39. He said, "Take ye away the stone." That was a righteousness consciousness speaking. No fear of failure. Total faith in God and His willingness to manifest His glory.

Now look at what Martha said. "Oh, Lord, he stinks by now." Everybody knows you can't raise someone from the dead after they have begun to stink!

Oh really? Get one that hasn't even cooled off yet and see what you can do with it! The natural mind speaks from a sin consciousness— always based in fear of failure and ever wondering whether or not God will do anything. Not only that, but a sin—fear—consciousness always has an excuse ready to explain why God can't or won't manifest Himself.

Can't you just see the picture? Martha is clinging to Jesus' arm, hoping something might happen but afraid it won't. She's afraid for His reputation and hers. And then it happens! A roar comes from the deepest part of Jesus' inner being—the same place from whence He groaned a few moments before: "Lazarus, COME FORTH!"

Can't you just hear her thoughts? *Lord! Not so loud! What if he doesn't come forth?* What she didn't realize was that it was not just Jesus *the man* who had spoken. Righteousness had spoken! God and man together spoke as one. Man right with God and God right with man. Death had to bow its knee, and Lazarus came forth.

Let's look now at three places in Scripture. First, Romans 10:6: "But the righteousness which is of faith speaketh...." Second, Hebrews 10:1-2:

1 For the law having a shadow of good things to come, and not the very image of the things, can never with those sacrifices which they offered year by year continually make the comers thereunto perfect.

2 For then would they not have ceased to be offered? because that the worshippers once purged should have had no more conscience of sins.

Then, Hebrews 1:3:

> 3   Who being the brightness of his glory, and the
>   express image of his person, and upholding all
>   things by the word of his power, when he had
>   by himself <u>purged our sins,</u> sat down on the
>   right hand of the Majesty on high.

Jesus purged our sins! That's a fact. Not a promise. Therefore, according to Hebrews 10:1-2, we should have no more <u>sin consciousness.</u> Therein lies the area of problem. We have been highly developed in sin consciousness and have done almost nothing to develop a righteousness consciousness.

Let's go to 2 Corinthians 5:17-18:

> 17   Therefore if any man be in Christ, he is a new
>   <u>creature:</u> old things are passed away; behold,
>   all things are become new.
> 18   And all things are of God, who hath reconciled
>   us to himself by Jesus Christ, and hath given
>   to us the ministry of reconciliation.

Now connect that with verse 21. He who knew no sin was <u>made</u> to be sin for us that we might be <u>made</u> the righteousness of God <u>in Him.</u> Righteousness is not something that grows up and becomes. It is a gift you received the moment you accepted Jesus as your Lord and Savior.

You cannot buy a Volkswagen and hope it will grow up and become a Cadillac. One was <u>made,</u> or manufactured, a Volkswagen, and one was <u>made,</u> or manufactured, a Cadillac.

You were <u>re-created</u> in Christ Jesus—<u>MADE</u> the righteousness of God. When you pray or groan in the spirit, edifying or building up <u>yourself,</u> and then speak to sin, sickness, demons or fear, it's not just you speaking. <u>The Righteousness of God is speaking.</u>

Jesus has given us the right to speak His Word in His Name and in His Blood. Your mind may try to hold back in fear, but step out of your flesh and mind and boldly declare, "I am the righteousness of God in Jesus' Name! I'm supposed to prosper. I'm supposed to be healed. I'm supposed to be debt free. It's my right in the kingdom of God. Remember: "Seek ye <u>first</u> the kingdom of God and <u>His</u> <u>Righteousness</u> and all these things will be added unto you."

This is only a touch on this wonderful subject. Don't miss those broadcasts May 14-18 and 21-25.

Start right now a campaign of faith to develop a righteousness consciousness. Say it out loud: "I have been made the righteousness of God in Christ Jesus. He was <u>made</u> sin with my sin, and I was <u>made</u> the righteousness of God with His righteousness!"

<u>We are going to get this powerful message out to the world!</u> As you sow your financial seed this month, lay your hand on it and shout, "Righteous seed for a righteous cause. Go, Brother Copeland, to the four corners of the earth!" That's exactly what we are doing.

Thank you from the bottom of our hearts for being our Partner. Gloria and I love you and pray for you every day.

Love,

Ken

P.S. Please pray 1 Peter 3:12: "The eyes of the Lord are over the righteous and His ears are <u>open</u> to their prayers (for Kenneth and Gloria)."

P.P.S. Read Matthew 5:6; Romans 3:21-22, 4:22-25, 5:17, 10:10; and 1 Corinthians 1:30.

Take the Step of Faith and Take Your Place

Dear Partner

How many times have all of us heard: "Well, the reason he's so hard to get along with is because he doesn't know who he really is. He's just trying to find himself"? In one way or another that's the world's excuse for almost all bad behavior, especially in young people.

Actually, they are right without really knowing it. However, the real answer to the "Who am I?" question does not come from rebellious behavior. It comes from learning what God has to say about our identity in His Word. Even those who don't know Jesus as their Lord can find out who they are and who they can be by going to God and simply asking.

Once we find out who we are in Christ Jesus, the next step is to take our place. Without that step of faith of entering in to what belongs to us, the reality and enjoyment of what God has supplied for us here on earth will not be realized—at least not in fullness.

Let's begin with Hebrews 1:1-8:

1   God, who at sundry times and in divers manners spake in time past unto the fathers by the prophets,

2   Hath in these last days spoken unto us by his Son, whom he hath appointed heir of all things, by whom also he made the worlds;

3   Who being the brightness of his glory, and the express image of his person, and upholding all things by the word of his power, when he had by himself purged our sins, sat down on the right hand of the Majesty on high;

4   Being made so much better than the angels, as he hath by inheritance obtained a more excellent name than they.

5   For unto which of the angels said he at any

time, Thou art my Son, this day have I begotten thee? And again, I will be to him a Father, and he shall be to me a Son?

6 And again, when he bringeth in the first begotten into the world, he saith, And let all the angels of God worship him.

7 And of the angels he saith, Who maketh his angels spirits, and his ministers a flame of fire.

8 But unto the Son he saith, Thy throne, O God, is for ever and ever: a sceptre of righteousness is the sceptre of thy kingdom.

Read verse 2 again. Notice God has spoken to us by appointing His Son heir of all things. That speaks to us loud and clear, because when Jesus was made to be sin for us (2 Corinthians 5:21) He was separated from the Father. Then when He was raised up, He had to be appointed heir—He had to become heir by right of covenant.

Romans 8:16-17 says we are joint heirs with Christ. How? The very same way He was—by promise or by covenant! Galatians 4:7 says, "Wherefore thou art no more a servant, but a son; and if a son, then an heir of God through Christ."

Notice the phrase "through Christ." When we received Jesus as Lord of our lives, whatever He received when He was raised from the dead became ours. He was appointed heir, and we were appointed joint heirs. Not subheirs. JOINT HEIRS! Joint means joined. Everything that belongs to Him belongs to us. NOW! Here on this earth. Not after we die and go to heaven.

That's what Philippians 4:19 is all about. God is speaking to joint heirs when He says, "I will supply all your need according to My riches in glory!" Heaven is already ours and it's ours here—where we need it.

Now look again at verse 5 of Hebrews 1: "I will be to him a Father, and he shall be to me a Son." Compare that with 2 Corinthians 6:17-18: "...I will receive you and will be a Father to you and you shall be my sons and daughters saith the Lord Almighty."

Let's look at it from another place. Romans 4:13: "For the promise, that he should be the heir of the world, was not to Abraham, or to his seed, through the law, but through the righteousness of faith." Now verse 16: "Therefore it is of faith, that it might be by grace; to the end the promise might be sure to all the seed...." We are the seed of Abraham.

Galatians 3:29 says if we belong to Christ, then we are Abraham's seed and heirs according to the promise. Actually the whole world belongs to us—not to the devil! He's a thief. He does not own anything. He ruled over it through Adam, but the last Adam—Jesus—took it back. It's His! And through Him, it's ours!

Look now at what Hebrews 1:13-14 says. The angels are ministering spirits sent forth to minister *for,* not *to,* heirs. That's us—you and me. Their ministry is for us the same as it is for Jesus.

How? Well, look at verse 4. He by inheritance, or covenant appointment, obtained a more excellent, or powerful, Name than the angels. His Name has authority over the angels. Where is that powerful Name now? Is it just in heaven?

For the answer, let's look at Acts 4:12: "Neither is there salvation in any other: for there is none other name under heaven given among men, whereby we must be saved." It's under heaven. It's in the earth. It has been given to us.

Ephesians 3:15 says the whole family both in heaven and in earth has been named after Him. That Name did not lose one bit of its divine power and authority when it was given to us. Peter said in Acts 3:16 that faith in the Name of Jesus made the man at the Beautiful gate rise up strong and walk.

"Yes, Brother Copeland, but that was an apostle."

That had absolutely nothing to do with it according to verse 12: "And when Peter saw it, he answered unto the people, Ye men of Israel, why marvel ye at this? or why look ye so earnestly on us, as though by our own power or holiness we had made this man to walk?" That Name and its authority was not given just to apostles. It's yours and mine if we release faith in it the way Peter did. Then, just to really clinch the deal, Peter himself wrote in 2 Peter 1:1, "...to them who have received like precious faith with us...through our saviour Jesus Christ." Not only did we receive His Name, we also received Jesus' faith.

Peter's faith and our faith are exactly the same, because it comes from the same place in the same way—from receiving Jesus as our Lord and Savior. He is the author and finisher, or developer, of our faith. Peter then went ahead and explained in verse 4 that it was all by exceeding great and precious promises, or by right of covenant in the blood of Jesus.

We are joint (joined) heirs in His righteousness—the ability to stand in the presence of Almighty God without guilt or shame, inferiority or condemnation (Romans 3:21-26, 5:15-19). Jesus said in Luke 12:32 that it gives our Father great pleasure to give us the kingdom—the whole thing! First Corinthians 3:21 and 2 Peter 1:3 say all things are ours!

In closing, I want to point out that what we read in Hebrews 1 had been prophesied in Psalm 2:6-8. Psalm 2:8 says: "Ask of Me, and I shall give thee the heathen [those who do not know God] for thine inheritance." Remember now, whatever belongs to the Heir also belongs to us through Him.

Gloria and I have received a stronger than ever calling and anointing to take this message to the heathen, lost, sick and dying world. We have accepted it with great joy and anticipation. Our faith to go is greater than it's ever been. As our Partner, your part of this anointing is available to you. Receive it and walk in it. Witness—preach—lay hands on the sick, expecting the greatest anointing to win souls you've ever seen. Command the devil to take his hands off and expect the ministering spirits (angels) to manifest themselves according to Psalms 91 and 103.

That anointing has come on me right now while I'm writing this letter. Receive! Your healing. Your deliverance. Your miracle of financial breakthrough, freedom from debt, ministry anointing...whatever you need, receive it now.

Pray for Gloria and me and also for our, your and my, other Partners.

We are <u>all</u> praying for you. We are the biggest Holy Ghost Gang on earth.

Gloria and I love you very much.

Love,

Ken

From the Valley of Battle to the Valley of Blessing

Dear Partner

As I write this letter I'm only three days away from leaving for Micronesia to do a meeting with Jerry Savelle. Micronesia is an island republic in the South Pacific between the Marshall Islands and the Solomons. God is doing great and mighty things in the islands of the world, and we are expecting Him to make Himself known in Kosrae in a big way.

Our expectation has been greatly intensified by something that happened a few days ago after praying with Richard Roberts, Jerry Savelle and Bishop Keith Butler. The four of us gathered together on a conference telephone call to agree together concerning our finances. All four of our ministries have been stretched to what looked like the breaking point. Also, all four of us had checked our lives and ministries to make sure everything was clean and in order before God.

Then as we prayed, the Lord spoke by the Holy Ghost and said, *This is not an attack on you personally. It's an attack on Me. I have raised the outpouring of My Spirit and glory to a new level, and satan has moved to try and stop it. You and others who are on the front lines are feeling the pressure of it. Stand fast in your faith. It's My battle and your victory!*

We all four shouted in an explosion of joy and anointing! I immediately turned in my Bible to 2 Chronicles 20:14-17:

14   Then upon Jahaziel the son of Zechariah, the son of Benaiah, the son of Jeiel, the son of Mattaniah, a Levite of the sons of Asaph, came the Spirit of the Lord in the midst of the congregation;

15   And he said, Hearken ye, all Judah, and ye inhabitants of Jerusalem, and thou king Jehoshaphat, Thus saith the Lord unto you, Be not afraid nor dismayed by reason of this great

multitude; <u>for the battle is not yours, but God's.</u>

16 Tomorrow go ye down against them: behold, they come up by the cliff of Ziz; and ye shall find them at the end of the brook, before the wilderness of Jeruel.

17 Ye shall not need to fight in this battle: <u>set yourselves,</u> stand ye still, and see the salvation of the Lord with you, O Judah and Jerusalem: fear not, nor be dismayed; tomorrow go out against them: for the Lord will be with you.

I read that and we all shouted again. <u>Remember now, all of this includes you, my Partner.</u> We stand together in it. God can't bless Gloria and me without blessing you at the same time.

As I continued reading, my eyes fell on the 22nd verse.

22 And when they began to sing and to praise, the Lord set ambushments against the children of Ammon, Moab, and mount Seir, which were come against Judah; and they were smitten.

When they began to sing and praise, God moved, and that changed everything. Let's look at verses 23 through 26:

23 For the children of Ammon and Moab stood up against the inhabitants of mount Seir, utterly to slay and destroy them: and when they had made an end of the inhabitants of Seir, every one helped to destroy another.

24 And when Judah came toward the watch tower in the wilderness, they looked unto the multitude, and, behold, they were dead bodies fallen to the earth, and none escaped.

25 And when Jehoshaphat and his people came to take away the spoil of them, they found among them in abundance both riches with the dead bodies, and precious jewels, which they stripped off for themselves, more than

they could carry away: and they were three days in gathering of the spoil, it was so much.

26 And on the fourth day they assembled themselves in the <u>valley of Berachah;</u> for there they blessed the Lord: <u>therefore the name of the same place was called, The valley of Berachah, unto this day.</u>

Look at the 26th verse again. They gathered in the valley of Berachah. *Berachah* means "blessing." That day, the Valley of Battle became the Valley of Blessing.

Notice that verse says the place was called the Valley of Blessing until this day. Later that same day I shared all this with Billye Brim. You know how Billye shouts and praises God. She said, "Brother Copeland, only a few days ago I was in that very valley in Israel. There is an ancient building still standing with the words on the side 'The Valley of Blessing.' It is still called the Valley of Blessing." That valley was the Valley of Battle for only a few hours, but it's been the Valley of Blessing for thousands of years!

After that phone call, I was sitting here in my study in God's presence, just worshiping Him and taking in all that had just happened, when He said, *How much does it cost your ministry to bring a soul into the kingdom?*

I said, "About a dollar per person."

He said, *How much money have you and Gloria asked and believed for?*

I said, "A hundred million dollars!"

Then He reminded me of something He had said to me several years ago. He said when this ministry was in the thousand flow, we were winning thousands. When we pressed into the million flow, we were winning millions. And that's when He demanded that we release our faith for the billion flow. There are five billion people on earth going to hell, and that's an unacceptable casualty rate.

Then He took me back to a day in Little Rock, Arkansas, that changed my life and ministry. He had been talking to me about radio and television, and the cost of it all had about staggered my faith. He said, *Don't seek ways to get the money in. Seek ways to get the Word out. The money, then, will come.* I'll never forget how that released my faith.

As I was remembering all this, He said, *Make an adjustment in your believing from dollars to souls. Change your confession from 100 million dollars to 100 million souls, and the money and everything else it takes to bring them in will come.*

I saw it. Go from the Valley of Battle to the Valley of Blessing.

Gloria and I began immediately sowing our seed for 100 million souls. Our faith leaped forward with a renewed strength. I saw a new and more powerful reason to be healed. Not just to be rid of pain, but to be strong and able to go to preach, teach and minister all over this world and bring in a record harvest of souls—100 million of them.

People are God's reason for doing everything He does. He has no other motive. He loves people. All people. He's not willing that any should perish.

I'm not either. We are going after them with everything we have. This ministry is ready for this assignment. Everything must be stepped up, geared up and turned wide open. Jesus is coming very, very soon, and we're going to get our part done.

Take hold with us in this and begin to shout with us for 100 million souls. You're a vital part of it all. This anointing that's come is there for you as well as for us. Adjust your faith and confession from whatever you're believing for to a harvest of people receiving Jesus as Lord and Savior. As you reap His harvest, He will reap yours.

A hundred million looks like an impossible number, but it isn't. All of us together can do it in the power of the Spirit of God. As you sow your financial seed this month, dedicate it to the 100 million for the kingdom. Jesus said this battle is His and the victory ours.

Lay your hand on your seed and on this letter and shout the victory.

Those 100 million souls are ours. All we have to do now is go into all the world and bring them in. Together we can do it.

Gloria and I love you and pray for you every day.

Love,

Ken

Because of your faithfulness, we have been able to take this message of faith into parts of the world where others said we couldn't go. Nothing is going to stand in our way of doing whatever God calls us to do.

Get on the Giving Side!

Dear Partner

I am especially excited as I write this letter because of good news reports and testimonies of breakthroughs that are happening to our Partners.

A man I have known for many years came <u>running</u> up to me this morning with a smile on his face and a shout in his voice as he told me how God had awakened him in his hotel room, speaking to him. God told him to get up and go home immediately: *Someone is coming this morning to buy your business.* He obeyed and in a few hours a multimillion dollar sale was closed.

It doesn't take God long to do things if we listen to and obey Him. Don't turn loose of your faith, and don't turn loose of your dream. There's a time for everything, and it's breakthrough, harvest time right now.

In this month's letter I want to share something with you that I received a few weeks ago in Kosrae, Micronesia. That's an island in the South Pacific where Jerry Savelle and I had a meeting together—a very good meeting I might add.

Preachers were there from different islands of the Pacific. Some came from close by, and some from very distant island countries, but they were all so very hungry for the Word of God. They refused to miss a service, even when they had to sit in a downpour of tropical rain to get it. It was great, and God certainly did not disappoint them, or us.

Let's look at John 3:16-17. Read very slowly and carefully:

16   For God so loved the world, that he gave his only begotten Son, that whosoever believeth in him should not perish, but have everlasting life.

17   For God sent not his Son into the world to condemn the world; but that the world through him might be saved.

God is a giver. He is not a taker. Had He been a taker, He would <u>not</u> have given Jesus, because Jesus was the best He had. Takers never give their best for fear of losing or diminishing what they have. God gave His very best. He gave Himself.

During that meeting in Kosrae, the Lord instructed me to tell the people to "get on the giving side." The scripture He gave me was Matthew 25:31-40. Let's take a look at it:

31   When the Son of man shall come in his glory, and all the holy angels with him, then shall he sit upon the throne of his glory:

32   And before him shall be gathered all nations: and he shall separate them one from another, as a shepherd divideth his sheep from the goats:

33   And he shall set the sheep on his right hand, but the goats on the left.

34   Then shall the King say unto them on his right hand, Come, ye blessed of my Father, inherit the kingdom prepared for you from the foundation of the world:

35   For I was an hungered, and ye gave me meat: I was thirsty, and ye gave me drink: I was a stranger, and ye took me in:

36   Naked, and ye clothed me: I was sick, and ye visited me: I was in prison, and ye came unto me.

37   Then shall the righteous answer him, saying, Lord, when saw we thee an hungered, and fed thee? or thirsty, and gave thee drink?

38   When saw we thee a stranger, and took thee in? or naked, and clothed thee?

39   Or when saw we thee sick, or in prison, and came unto thee?

40   And the King shall answer and say unto them, Verily I say unto you, Inasmuch as ye have done it unto one of the least of these my brethren, ye have done it unto me.

In verses 35-36, He said to those on His right hand:

I was hungry and you *gave*...
I was thirsty and you *gave*...
I was a stranger and you *gave* me shelter
I was naked and you *gave*...
I was sick and you *gave* me your time
I was in prison and you *gave* me of yourself by coming to me.

The right side of God is the giving side. Now look at verse 34. Those on the giving side were blessed, or empowered to prosper. They inherited the kingdom, or a better, more scriptural way of saying it is, they inherited God and all He has.

Getting on the giving side is living the giving lifestyle. To live on the giving side is to live to give. When giving is a lifestyle, a person does not give only when he or she is asked to. Nor do they just give at church. They live to improve and prosper the lives of everyone with whom they come into contact. Jesus said they gave even to the least—not just to important projects. They gave of their homes, their time, their food, their water, their money and themselves. On the other hand, the goats gave <u>nothing.</u> They are the takers and keepers.

Think this through with me.

The Giver gives

> When times are good,
> When times are bad,
> When he has it to give,
> When he doesn't have it to give.

The Giver's lifestyle is to prosper all with whom he comes into contact.

The Taker takes

> When times are good,
> When times are bad,
> When he has,
> When he has not.

The Taker's lifestyle is to take and keep from all with whom he comes into contact.

Now look at verse 41: "Then shall he say also unto them on the left hand, Depart from me, ye cursed, into everlasting fire, prepared for the devil and his angels." The Takers and Keepers inherit the devil and his darkness. That's not just at Judgment Day. That's every day. While the Taker walks in need and darkness, the Giver walks in his inheritance of light and blessing. For the Giver, Ephesians 6:8, then, comes shouting through: "Knowing that whatsoever good thing any man doeth, the same shall he receive of the Lord, whether he be bond or free."

Shout it out loud right now with me: "I'm on the giving side! I'm a sheep, not a goat! I'm blessed of My heavenly Father, and I am His heir, joint heir with the greatest of all givers, Jesus, my Lord and Savior!"

When you sow your financial seed this month, bless it before you send it. Take a few minutes to pray over it. See it going all over the world sending the word of faith to the far corners—near and wide. Help Gloria and me believe 100 million souls into the kingdom of God.

You are a giver, not a taker. You are blessed—not cursed. We are Partners in God's very best.

Pray for Gloria and me. We are going, going, going. Preaching, preaching, preaching.

Come get into every meeting you can. The anointing is increasing every day. Especially the prophet's anointing.

Gloria and I love you and pray for you every day.

Love,

Ken

First Words!

Dear Partner

I want you to know how very much you are loved and appreciated.

A few days ago, my daughter Kellie began talking about how, when she was a child, she thought our Partners were some of our family members. Gloria and I talked about our love for all of you so much that the kids thought we were kinfolk. <u>We are!</u> While she was telling us these things, I became determined to let you know what a major part of our lives you really are.

The Apostle Paul said to his partners in Philippians 1:7, "I have you in my heart." I know how he felt. When you pray for someone every day—and sometimes all day—that person becomes a living part of your life. That's the way it is with Gloria and me and the rest of our family concerning you. You'll never be without love and prayer ever again.

I want to share with you something that the Lord has been teaching me about and training me on for the past couple of months. It's about the vital importance of <u>first words.</u> These are the words that jump out of your mouth instead of being thoughts and then spoken. The words that explode out when sudden pain strikes. The blast, and sometimes whole strings, of words that come when you are startled or suddenly frightened.

These are also the first words spoken when someone irritates you or makes you angry. Proverbs 15:1 says, "A soft answer turneth away wrath: but grievous words stir up anger." Are your first words soft in the face of strife or do they stir up more anger?

Most people think there's nothing that can be done about these kinds of word reactions but there is.

<u>First words are the words that set the course and direction for what happens next and by whom.</u> If your first words are God's words, then what happens next will be in your favor. If they are words of doubt,

unbelief, profanity, or the like, the course is set for destruction.

The devil and his crowd are always ready to carry out words that open doors for them. Speak the devil's word, and he will move in and take over—to steal, kill and destroy.

What can we do to keep God's words ever at the door of our lips? The very first thing is pray the simple but powerful prayer David prayed in Psalm 141:3, "Set a watch, O Lord, before my mouth; keep the door of my lips."

Remember, the Apostle James said that the tongue cannot be tamed with natural power (James 3:6-8). To do this takes the supernatural power of God and His Word—especially when it comes to first words. <u>Ask to be made always aware of your words.</u> Ask the Holy Spirit to train you by opening your ears to what is coming out of your mouth. What you say all the time is most likely what will come out under stress.

The next thing to do is begin to flood your spirit with God's words and His ways of doing things. This is done primarily in two ways. First, listen to at least one complete tape a day—and not just when you're busy doing something else. Take the time to <u>listen and study.</u> Give some quality time to the Word of God.

Second, train yourself to speak to God the <u>very first thing</u> each morning. The moment your eyes open from sleep say out loud, "This is my healing day. This is my day to receive." Then begin to praise God and thank Him for the abundance of all things. That sets the course for the day.

Even when you wake up during the night, <u>make your first words to God in praise.</u> If you lay down for only a few minutes, <u>when you open your eyes,</u> praise God! You and the Holy Spirit are training you to bring your faith into the <u>NOW.</u>

God is not the Great God who was. He is not the Great God who will be some day. <u>He is the Great I Am! NOW!</u> Faith is NOW. Always. The past is the past. The future is hope, and without faith, hope has no substance.

Faith is always <u>NOW.</u> Too much of the time we step out in faith for something, and then begin to look for it to happen out in the future. Keep it <u>today.</u>

When your first words are faith and praise, the rest of the day you'll be a whole lot less likely to say anything against your words of faith and receiving. Your <u>first words will begin to be your all-day words.</u> Very soon they will be the words right at the top of your spirit and your mind. That's what will happen when there's no room for anything else.

Read these words of Jesus very carefully and then meditate on them for the rest of the day today: Luke 6:43-49 then Matthew 12:36-37.

Luke 6:43-49:

43   For a good tree bringeth not forth corrupt fruit; neither doth a corrupt tree bring forth good fruit.

44   For every tree is known by his own fruit. For of thorns men do not gather figs, nor of a bramble bush gather they grapes.

45   A good man out of the good treasure of his heart bringeth forth that which is good; and an evil man out of the evil treasure of his heart bringeth forth that which is evil: for of the abundance of the heart his mouth speaketh.

46   And why call ye me, Lord, Lord, and do not the things which I say?

47   Whosoever cometh to me, and heareth my sayings, and doeth them, I will show you to whom he is like:

48   He is like a man which built an house, and digged deep, and laid the foundation on a rock: and when the flood arose, the stream beat vehemently upon that house, and could not shake it: for it was founded upon a rock.

49   But he that heareth, and doeth not, is like a man that without a foundation built an house upon the earth; against which the stream did

beat vehemently, and immediately it fell; and the ruin of that house was great.

Matthew 12:36-37:

36   But I say unto you, That every idle word that men shall speak, they shall give account thereof in the day of judgment.

37   For by thy words thou shalt be justified, and by thy words thou shalt be condemned.

<u>The first words come from what's in your heart in abundance.</u> They are words that build the foundation of faith. They are the words by which you are made righteous or by which you are condemned. What you set as the main course of life will come from first words of faith, hope and love.

Thank You, Jesus, for a hundred million souls! Today! You and I can get this done, Partner. Together we can and will accomplish everything Jesus, our Champion and Lord, has asked us to do.

Pray over your seed and agree with Gloria and me.

Anaheim was marvelous in our eyes. It was the work of the Lord. Many people received from God, including <u>many</u> souls saved, healed, filled with the Spirit and blessed financially. God is moving and you and I are right in the middle of it all.

Gloria and I love you and pray for you every day.

Love,

Ken

Recessions, Slow-Downs, Economic Downturns Do
Not Belong to the Righteousness of God!

Dear Partner

I am writing this letter from our prayer cabin in Arkansas. Gloria and I came up here to rest a day or two after the Southwest Believers' Convention in Fort Worth. The West Coast and Southwest Conventions both were great meetings. Every service was an experience in itself.

Many times during both meetings, Gloria and I expressed our desire that all of our Partners could be in those services and receive what we were all receiving. Every speaker was anointed beyond what I had seen them under before, and I have known each of them for a very long time and have heard them preach many, many times. It was heaven come down. I hope you didn't miss it. If you did, be sure and get the tapes.

I want to share something in this letter that I received during Southwest that has really helped me.

The Lord reminded me that recessions, slow-downs or economic downturns do not belong to the righteousness of God, therefore we should never join in on them with the world. From Matthew 6:24-34, Jesus said five different times in 10 verses, "take no thought," or don't even think about the things you need to eat and wear, etc. All of that is our heavenly Father's responsibility. He'll take care of it if we follow through with what He said in verse 33: "But seek ye first the kingdom of God, and his righteousness; and all these things shall be added unto you."

The righteousness of God and the kingdom of God do belong to us, and that's what should occupy all of our thinking. In other words, think or take thought about what does belong to us—God's kingdom and all that's in it—instead of taking even one thought about what does not belong to us—the world and its curse of poverty, sickness and all that comes under the law of sin and death. Remember Romans 8:2: "For the law of the Spirit of life in Christ Jesus hath made me free from the law of sin and death."

In order to not take thought about one thing, one has to fill his thoughts with something else. In verse 31, Jesus gave us the basic key to controlling our thought lives. He said, "Take no thought <u>saying</u>."

By putting a thought in your mouth and then speaking it, you <u>take</u> that thought. Once the thought becomes spoken words, it has been activated—especially when a born-again believer takes a thought and says it. We are the righteousness of God. We have the God-given <u>right</u> to speak and expect.

During Southwest, I was ministering along these lines and the Spirit of God said, *Tell the people to stop repeating what the media says about the economy, and start saying what I said about it. The economy the media is talking about is the world's economy. My people are free from that system and its way of doing things. My kingdom is higher than that kingdom. It is separate from that kingdom and operates in the law of the Spirit of life in Christ Jesus.*

Remember in Philippians 4:19 I said I meet your needs according to My riches in Glory by Christ Jesus? Notice that both of those scriptures, Romans 8:2 and Philippians 4:19, are by Christ Jesus—by His Anointing. You belong to Christ Jesus, and everything He has in heaven belongs to you on the earth. Put the profile of the prosperous believer—Psalm 112—in your mouth and keep it there. It belongs to you. Receive it!

When He said that, I immediately went to Psalm 112. Then He pointed out something in that Psalm that I had never seen before. Let's look at it now.

1   Praise ye the Lord. Blessed is the man that feareth the Lord, that delighteth greatly in his commandments [covenant promises].

2   His seed shall be mighty upon earth: the generation of the upright [the righteousness of God in Christ Jesus] shall be blessed.

3   Wealth and riches shall be in his [the righteous'] house: and his righteousness endureth for ever.

4   Unto the upright [the righteous] there ariseth light [answers of wisdom] in the darkness: he

[the righteous] is gracious, and full of compassion, and righteous.

5   A good man [the righteous in Christ] showeth favour, and lendeth [Ephesians 6:8]: he [the righteous] will guide his affairs with discretion [good judgment].

6   Surely he [the righteous] shall not be moved for ever: the righteous shall be in everlasting remembrance.

7   He [the righteous] shall not be afraid of evil tidings: his [the righteous'] heart is fixed, trusting in the Lord.

8   His [the righteous'] heart is established, he [the righteous] shall not be afraid, until he [the righteous] see his desire upon his [the righteous'] enemies.

9   He [the righteous] hath dispersed, he [the righteous] hath given to the poor; his righteousness <u>endureth for ever;</u> his [the righteous'] horn [supply of plenty] shall be exalted with honour.

10   The wicked shall see it, and be grieved [the devil can't do anything about it]; he shall gnash with his teeth, and melt away: the desire of the wicked shall perish.

That's the way the Lord read that Psalm to me. When I read it that way, <u>out loud,</u> it literally filled my being with power and well-being. Do that now. Read it aloud and take the thought. Receive it. You're the righteousness of God in Christ Jesus. It belongs to <u>you.</u> Jesus paid for it with His precious blood.

What you and I are doing right now is what is outlined in Romans 5:17, "For if by one man's offence death reigned by one; much more they which <u>receive</u> abundance of grace and of the gift of righteousness shall reign in life by one, Jesus Christ." We are <u>receiving</u> abundance of grace and the free gift of righteousness. That puts us in a reigning position over all lack, debt, sickness and all the law of sin and death. We live in the life cycle—not the cycles of sin and death.

Before you send your seed-faith offerings this month, lay your hands on them and speak the profile (Psalm 112) over them. Your harvest is produced by the Word of the kingdom.

Pray for Gloria and me. We're ministering overseas a lot between now and the end of the year.

We love you and pray for you every day.

Love,

God Takes Care of His Own

Dear Partner

My, a lot of things have happened in the past few days. As I write this letter, it's been seven days since the terrorist attack against the World Trade Center and the Pentagon. It's amazing how the whole world can change in one day.

A lot of questions have come up about all of this, and it's <u>very</u> important to keep our thinking straight. The way we do that is to stay on the Word. God <u>never</u> changes and His Word still says the very same things.

<u>He still moves by faith! Faith still moves Him.</u> The key issue is in our receiving. God always does His part.

The first question most people ask is, "Why did God let this happen?" Another is, "Has God lifted His hand of protection?"

It is very important to keep the answers to these, and other questions like them, in proper perspective. The answer to both these questions is the same. God did not lift His hand of protection. <u>It was pushed away</u> by people, even Christians, who did not want Him in their affairs.

Let's take a closer look at what got hit. It was called the World Trade Center. No god can rise above God and stay there for any length of time. He is the <u>Most High God.</u>

Of course, money is the world's god. We expect it to be, because the <u>love</u> of money is the root of <u>all</u> evil. But when money or anything else becomes god in the lives of His children, it will come down. The World Trade Center represented the money god.

One of the most disastrous things Christian people have ever done in this country was to support and vote for immoral people because of money. Abortion was not the main sin. It was the result of the main sin. Pornography and all the other terrible sins running loose in this country are not the main cause. They are sins of the flesh. As bad as they are, they are not as disastrous as <u>spiritual adultery</u>.

The main sin was to knowingly vote into power the people who not only commit these sins themselves, but who open the political doors and make it possible through the courts for them to continue. At the same time, the politicians have for years arrested, jailed, fined and brought reproach upon people for praying in government buildings and displaying the Ten Commandments. And it was money-voting Christians who put those politicians in office.

These are the reasons that for the past six to eight years, God's main thrust has been on His prospering His own—separating us from the world's money system so that we look to Him, and Him only, for our money and all that goes with it. He is <u>our</u> source. Especially in times like these.

The god of the terrorists is nowhere near as "terrible"—as worthy of genuine reverence and holy fear—as our God! Our God is the Most High God. Our God holds all the stars in place. Our God is the Great Deliverer, Savior, Healer, Lord of the Universe. Those that have attacked His people have attacked Him.

We are about to see Him in a way we've never seen Him before— the Great Jehovah—the Almighty. However, you and I know Him as Lord and Savior, full of mercy and compassion.

The great thing about Him is—IT IS NEVER TOO LATE WITH HIM! It's never too late to repent. James 4:8 says, "Draw nigh to God, and he will draw nigh to you." People all over this country are drawing nigh to Him, and it's up to us to help them break through to His way of life and victory through Christ Jesus.

Another question people ask about tragedies such as this is, "Why did God tell some to get out and didn't tell others?" There was not a person in those buildings that God did not warn! God is no respecter of persons. Jesus said in Matthew 5:45, "He maketh his sun to rise on the evil and on the good, and sendeth rain on the just and on the unjust."

There were three classes of people in those buildings:

1. Those who had no ear to hear at all,
2. Those who heard in some form and did not obey, and
3. Those who heard and either did not go there or got out.

Pastors with whom we have spoken who have taught their churches the word of faith and commitment—whose members either worked in the WTC or were supposed to be there for some reason or another—told us of instance after instance in which those members were not there. Or, as in the case of one man, they just walked out right through the middle of it all without being touched.

<u>Many</u> were simply late to work for one reason or another. One man's young child suddenly became hungry on the way to school, and he decided it would be good for them to stop and have breakfast together. He worked in the WTC and missed the whole terrible thing.

One of our Partners, Pastor Dan Stratton, whose office is in ground zero was in the home of a friend praying instead of going to the office that morning. The great testimonies go on and on. "But Brother Copeland, what about those firefighters and police officers who died?" <u>They sacrificed their lives!!</u>

What about the future? Your future and mine is the same. Our future is Jesus! Our job is the same: Go into all the world and preach the gospel to every creature. Jesus—His love, His blood, His Word, His victory—is still the answer.

What about the country's future? That depends on you and me.

<u>Jesus is the Superpower,</u> not the USA or any other nation. The Body of Christ is His superpower in this earth. We must stand tall in His Word before this hurting and fearful people. We must pray, especially in the spirit, for our president and his cabinet.

We must, as never before, sow our money, time and effort into the preaching of the Word. We must sow in faith, aiming and claiming our harvest of total victory over terrorism. Isaiah 54:14-17 declares our victory over oppression, fear and terror, but that victory is rooted in being established in the righteousness of God in Christ Jesus.

We must pray and believe God for our military. Psalm 91 is the promise of God for all who go in harm's way. It is also the believer's shield in times of trouble.

Father, I pray right now for all my Partners in the Name of Jesus. I plead the blood of Jesus over us all for protection against every evil spirit, every evil person, every evil thing and every evil plan of the devil.

Together we bind you, satan, according to the written Word of God. Take your hands off God's property!

Thank You, Heavenly Father, for being so real and so close to us right now. Thank You, Jesus, for my Partners.

As you sow your victory seeds this month, take your offering in your hands and read Psalm 91 and Isaiah 54:14-17 out loud and believe it with all your heart.

<u>God is not through with the United States of America yet! Let's rise up in faith and win. The victory is ours, the battle is the Lord's!</u>

Gloria and I love you and pray for your complete victory every day.

Love,

Ken

The Lord is my helper. I will not
fear what man shall do to me!

Dear Partner

Take a look around you and almost all you see and hear is *fear.* That's
what "terror-ism" is. Terrorism is an organized form of oppression that
uses fear as a weapon. Its goal is to terrify to the point that a person, or
a people, cannot resist.

The definition of *oppression* explains the use of terror as a weapon
or tactic: Oppression is the spoiling or taking away of men's goods or
estates by terror or force, without having any right thereto, by working
on the ignorance, weakness or fearfulness of the oppressed.

In light of that definition, we can better understand Acts 10:38:
"How God anointed Jesus of Nazareth with the Holy Ghost and with
power: who went about doing good, and healing all that were oppressed
of the devil; for God was with him."

We, the Body of Christ, must be the ones standing tall in the middle
of all this, not being ignorant, weak or fearful. We have the Word of
God. We're strong in the Lord and in the power of His might (Ephesians
6:10). And we've been delivered from fear. Yes, DELIVERED!

Let's look at Hebrews 2:14-15:

> 14   Forasmuch then as the children are partakers
>   of flesh and blood, he also himself likewise
>   took part of the same; that through death
>   he might destroy him that had the power of
>   death, that is, the devil;
> 15   And deliver them who through fear of death
>   were all their lifetime subject to bondage.

Notice that the fear of death is the fear. That's the master fear
from which all other fears come. All worry, phobias, etc., stem from the
fear of death. But we can see from the above verses that we have been

delivered from the source of terror and its oppression. We are no longer subject to it. In fact, we have been set free from the spiritual laws in which sin and death operate.

Let's read Romans 8:2.

> 2   For the law of the Spirit of life in Christ Jesus hath
>   made me free from the law of sin and death.

That's shouting ground, brother!

Terror—and all that it is supposed to do—<u>cannot</u> work on you and me if we take a strong stand on the Word, in the blood of our righteous covenant in the Name of Jesus!

There is a difference between putting fear down or controlling it, and being delivered from it.

For instance, a champion bull rider in a rodeo makes his living doing something that's very scary to those who watch him ride. Through training and practice, riding a huge, mean animal is no longer fearful to him. He has put that fear down in that part of his life.

At the same time, that supposedly fearless cowboy may be worried sick about his finances or his family, or something else about which he's very much afraid.

On the other hand, that same man, by taking advantage of what Jesus and His Blood have done for us, could have all fear cast out. GONE! Gone from *every* area of his life. That's far greater than just putting fear down through natural means.

Training, logic, and the like, are good, but they are not complete. Fear is a spiritual force and must be dealt with by the spiritual weapons of our warfare which are not carnal, but powerful through God for the pulling down of strongholds (2 Corinthians 10:4)—especially, the stronghold of fear.

Now notice 2 Timothy 1:6-7:

6   Wherefore I put thee in remembrance that thou stir up the gift of God, which is in thee by the putting on of my hands.

7   For God hath not given us the spirit of fear; but of power, and of love, and of a sound mind.

There are several things to act on in these verses.

1.   The gift of <u>God</u> is in us *now.* However, we must stir up that gift. <u>God</u> is Love, and perfected love casts out fear (1 John 4:18). Love (He) doesn't put fear down or control it. Love (He) casts it <u>OUT!</u>

2.   Fear is a spirit. It must be dealt with as a living thing that does not belong to us. It does not come from God, and it's not *OK.*

3.   We have been given the gift of God—and remember, <u>God is Love!</u>

We've been given the gift of *power...love...*and a *sound mind.* A fear-filled mind is not a sound mind.

"Well, Brother Copeland, what can I do about this?"

For one thing, you can turn off the news media. Fear is the media's stock in trade. Without fear they couldn't exist.

Another thing is, you can turn on the word of faith—especially the word of God's love. Major on the word of His love. Read the book of 1 John over and over until the revelation of God's love overflows your cup. Then, every time fear or anything fearful comes along, say out loud, "That's under the curse and I'm redeemed from the curse of fear."

In Deuteronomy 28:66-67, the curse of the law says this:

66   And thy life shall hang in doubt before thee; and thou shalt fear day and night, and shalt have none assurance of thy life:

67   In the morning thou shalt say, Would God it

were even! and at even thou shalt say, Would
God it were morning! for the fear of thine
heart wherewith thou shalt fear, and for the
sight of thine eyes which thou shalt see.

But, then, Galatians 3:13 states that we've been delivered from that
curse: "Christ hath redeemed us from the curse of the law, being made a
curse for us: for it is written, Cursed is every one that hangeth on a tree."

Just shout it out loud—*right in fear's face:* "I've been <u>delivered</u> from
you by the blood of Jesus!"

One final note: Being fearful is far more serious than Christians
have taken it. But Revelation 21:8 puts it in its rightful place...

8   But the fearful, and unbelieving, and the abomi-
         nable, and murderers, and whoremongers, and
         sorcerers, and idolaters, and all liars, shall have
         their part in the lake which burneth with fire
         and brimstone: which is the second death.

Notice in this horrible list what is in first place.

As you prepare your financial seed for sowing this month, take it in
your hand, go before the Lord and pray this:

"Lord, Jesus, I bring my seed before You as an offering for Your work.
I sow it as a seed of love toward the complete casting out of all fear in
my life. You suffered, died and rose from the dead, so I could have a
fear-free life. With this offering I stir up the gift of God in me. According
to Hebrews 13:6, I boldly declare, *The Lord is my helper, and I will not
fear what man shall do unto me.*"

Gloria and I love you very much, and we pray for you every day.

Love,

PS. We have Received OUR orders from heaven concerning our part of This war. We LAUNCHED AN All-out campaign Against fear Oct. 18, 2001, IN Washington D.C. We will pull its strong holDs DOWN By The power IN the WorD, The NAme, the Blood of Jesus. This is what I was BORN to Do! Together we will Do it! Ken

No Fear Here!

Dear Partner

In our campaign against fear, let's look at something that happened in the ministry of Jesus. I know you remember when Jairus, ruler of the synagogue, fell down at Jesus' feet and said, "My little daughter lieth at the point of death. I pray thee, come lay thy hands on her that she may be healed; and she shall live. <u>And Jesus went with him</u>" (Mark 5:23-24).

Now, on the way, the woman with the issue of blood stopped Jesus by touching the border of His garment. As Jesus was ministering to her, one came from Jairus' house and said, "Your daughter is dead." When Jesus heard that, He immediately said to Jairus, "<u>Fear not!</u> Believe <u>only!</u> And she <u>shall</u> be made whole."

The first thing Jesus dealt with was fear. He made it very clear that fear and faith won't mix. He also made it clear that what He was there to do would work if fear was not there to stop it.

What Jesus has given us by His great sacrifice always works— salvation, healing, deliverance, peace, and all that goes with it—every time, when fear is not there to stop it.

Let's look at it from another angle. The Word. Everything we receive from heaven comes through the Word. We were born again not of corruptible <u>seed</u> but incorruptible, by the Word of God which is alive forever. He sent His Word and healed us. In fact, Jesus is the Word manifested. Now with that in mind, let's look at Mark 4:20: "And these are they which are sown on good ground; such as hear the word, and receive it, and bring forth fruit, some thirtyfold, some sixty, and some an hundred."

The Word producing one hundredfold is the will of God for everyone who will hear the Word and receive or believe it.

Remember though, Jesus said believe <u>only.</u> Now let's read 14-19:

14   The sower soweth the word.

15   And these are they by the way side, where the word is sown; but when they have heard, Satan cometh immediately, and taketh away the word that was sown in their hearts.

16   And these are they likewise which are sown on stony ground; who, when they have heard the word, immediately receive it with gladness;

17   And have no root in themselves, and so endure but for a time: afterward, when affliction or persecution ariseth for the word's sake, immediately they are offended.

18   And these are they which are sown among thorns; such as hear the word,

19   And the cares of this world, and the deceitfulness of riches, and the lusts of other things entering in, choke the word, and it becometh unfruitful.

Jesus brought out five things that satan uses to stop the Word. He doesn't have anything else to work with:

1. Affliction—pressure
2. Persecution—to pursue or to chase after
3. Cares of this world—care (division, distraction, worries)
4. Deceitfulness of riches—money is the answer to my <u>worries</u>
5. Lusts of other things—desires that cause pressure, especially from "I may never have enough."

Look very carefully at all these things. All five of them depend on fear to work. On the other hand, a revelation of God's great love for you will defuse everything the devil has to use to stop the Word. <u>If he cannot stop the Word, he can't stop you!</u>

What difference does it make what terrible (<u>terri</u>-ble) thing some bigot or racist says about you or to you? When your heart and mind are filled with how much God loves you and cares for you, you don't even hear it. You just have compassion for that person because Jesus loves him and wants very much to save and deliver him. Philippians 4:6

is the answer to the cares of this world, along with what Jesus said in Matthew 6:30-33:

Philippians 4:6:

> 6   Be careful for nothing; but in every thing by prayer and supplication with thanksgiving let your requests be made known unto God.

Matthew 6:30-33

> 30   Wherefore, if God so clothe the grass of the field, which to day is, and to morrow is cast into the oven, shall he not much more clothe you, O ye of little faith?
> 31   Therefore take no thought, saying, What shall we eat? or, What shall we drink? or, Wherewithal shall we be clothed?
> 32   (For after all these things do the Gentiles seek:) for your heavenly Father knoweth that ye have need of all these things.
> 33   But seek ye first the kingdom of God, and his righteousness; and all these things shall be added unto you.

Also, 1 Peter 5:6-7:

> 6   Humble yourselves therefore under the mighty hand of God, that he may exalt you in due time:
> 7   Casting all your care upon him; for he careth for you.

Your heavenly Father is filled with desire to exalt you and take care of all your needs because He cares for you so much.

Now we're back to what Jesus said to Jairus: "Fear not. Believe only." Mark 4:19 says these fear weapons must enter in one's heart before they can choke the Word. Love and faith block the door. First John 4:16-19 must become the guard over our hearts and mouths:

> 16   And we have known and believed the love that God hath to us. God is love; and he that dwelleth in love dwelleth in God, and God in him.
>
> 17   Herein is our love made perfect, that we may have boldness in the day of judgment: because as he is, so are we in this world.
>
> 18   There is no fear in love; but perfect love casteth out fear: because fear hath torment. He that feareth is not made perfect in love.
>
> 19   We love him, because he first loved us.

We <u>must</u> meditate and confess these verses until they come flying out our mouths at the very mention of fear of any kind. My God loves me and I love Him! He has commanded me to love, and I obey His command! I have not been given a spirit of fear but of power, <u>LOVE</u> and a sound mind.

You will notice as you do this, Love released begins to flush all fear out of you. Stay with it until it's <u>gone.</u> Then when fear tries to get back in, resist it in Jesus' Name and watch it flee. Talk back to the fear merchants on TV: "No! We won't have it that way! I fear no evil! The Most High God is my Father and He loves and cares for me." Psalm 27:1 says, "The Lord is my light and my salvation; whom shall I fear? the Lord is the strength of my life; of whom shall I be afraid?"

NO FEAR HERE!!

As you sow your seed-faith offering this month, lay your hands on it and pray aloud, "I am a fearless giver. God is my source. There's a whole lot more where this came from—heaven!"

Also pray for Gloria and me and all of us at KCM around the world. We have attacked fear on all fronts. It is a very big job, but together we can do it. We love you and have you in our hearts. All of us pray for you every day.

Love,

Ken

Oh, yeah, I got so excited I almost forgot—HAPPY—NO FEAR HERE—
NEW YEAR!—KC

A.W. and Vinita Copeland with Kenneth in June, 1939, Abilene, Texas. Kenneth was 3 1/2 years old.

Jesus said—I Will Not Leave You as Orphans!

Dear Partner

Let's begin our time together this month by going to Ephesians 2:11: "Wherefore remember, that you being in time past Gentiles...." For the definition of *gentile*, look at the first three verses of chapter 2:

1 And you hath he quickened, who were dead in trespasses and sins;

2 Wherein in time past ye walked according to the course of this world, according to the prince of the power of the air, the spirit that now worketh in the children of disobedience:

3 Among whom also we all had our (manner of life) in times past in the lusts of our flesh, fulfilling the desires of the flesh and of the mind; and were by nature the children of wrath, even as others.

In other words, a gentile is a person without a covenant with God—one who doesn't know or have any relationship with God.

Now look at verse 12: "That at that time ye were without Christ, being aliens from the commonwealth of Israel, and strangers from the covenants of promise, having no hope, and without God in the world." That is a horrible thought! I would never allow myself to remember those days if the Word didn't tell me to do so. However, today you'll be glad you did.

Verse 12 describes a spiritual orphan. The dictionary says an orphan is one who has no parents or friends. A child without parents has to begin life with no advantages whatsoever. He has no one's wisdom from which to draw—no one to teach and encourage him. He has to learn everything the hard way. Everyone takes advantage of his lack of knowledge, leaving him on the short end of everything. In most cases, this all leads to a bitterness in life at a very young age.

Remember the stories we heard in childhood about little orphan children and how sad they were? The orphan's home was always a hard place run by a wicked, old lady and a mean, little, stingy man who hated children. The daily dream of all the children was to be adopted by a loving family and live in a warm and loving home. People would come and look the children over and for one reason or another turn the children down, leaving them once again to go to their dreary dorm room after a scant supper of bread and water, or less. What a <u>hopeless</u> picture those stories and old movies painted. That's the situation verse 12 describes—<u>without hope and without God in the world.</u>

YEAH, BUT NOW READ VERSE 13:

"But now in Christ Jesus...."

"What [people] is there so great who has God [Love] so nigh unto them..." (Deuteronomy 4:7).

Now let's go to John 14:17-18: "Even the Spirit of truth; whom the world cannot receive, because it seeth him not, neither knoweth him: but ye know him; for he dwelleth with you, <u>and shall be in you.</u> I will not leave you <u>comfortless:</u> I will come to you." In verse 18, the English word *comfortless* was used to translate a Greek word meaning "orphans." <u>Jesus said, "I will not leave you as orphans."</u>

Now we're getting to the heart of what God has really done for us through the shed blood of Jesus. Romans 8:14-16 gives us even more understanding:

14   For as many as are led by the Spirit of God, they are the sons of God.

15   For ye have not received the spirit of bondage again to fear; but ye have received the Spirit of adoption, whereby we cry, Abba, Father.

16   The Spirit itself beareth witness with our spirit, that we are the children of God.

We are no longer spiritual orphans! <u>We've been adopted!</u> Can't you just see that little brother and sister running and shouting as they leave the old, dreary orphanage with their lovely, new, happy, wonderful parents? "We have a father and mother who chose us! We're free!"

That's the spirit of adoption whereby we cry, shout and rejoice, "I have a Father! I have a Daddy who loves me so much that He shed His own Blood in order to covenant me into His very own family. Everything He has is now mine because He loves me so much." (See John 16:15.)

Let's go once again to Romans 8:15: "For ye have not received the spirit of bondage again to fear; but ye have received the Spirit of adoption...." The spirit of adoption has delivered us from the spirit of fear and bondage. Hebrews 13:5-6 *(The Amplified Bible),* describes the bold confidence of the adopted:

> 5 Let your character or moral disposition be free from love of money [including greed, avarice, lust, and craving for earthly possessions] and be satisfied with your present [circumstances and with what you have]; for He [God] Himself has said, I will not in any way fail you nor give you up nor leave you without support. [I will] not, [I will] not, [I will] not in any degree leave you helpless nor forsake nor let [you] down (relax My hold on you)! [Assuredly not!]
>
> 6 So we take comfort and are encouraged and confidently and boldly say, The Lord is my Helper; I will not be seized with alarm [I will not fear or dread or be terrified]. What can man do to me?

By now you should be running around the room, dancing and shouting, "I've been adopted! I have a Father! I've got brothers and sisters I've never even met! I am loved, I have a Savior, and we're all rich, rich, rich!"

Under Jewish law, an adopted child is equal in every way to the firstborn and enjoys all the inheritance and privileges thereof. Jesus is the Firstborn from the dead. He is Lord, Head of the Church. He sits at the Father's right hand in all authority and power.

We've been raised up with Him and we've been made to sit with Him in heavenly places. We are joint, or equal, heirs with Him. We've been given His all-powerful Name with which to command authority over all principalities and powers. We've been made the righteousness of God in Him. Not just righteous *before* God but the Righteousness *of* God IN HIM!

Love did all this. And He did it for you. He loved you more than His own life. He gave Himself for you and is still giving Himself for you.

Fix your mind on these things. Think about them all day long, every day. Every time some fear thought tries to get in, shout at it—"NO! My Father loves and cares for me and I have no fear of that. You cannot come here. There's no fear here! Jesus and I take our stand against you sin, sickness, demons, poverty, lack and fear. I have a Father! I've been chosen—BY THE MOST HIGH GOD! Leave my presence now!"

As you sow your financial seed this month, lay your hand on it and worship your Father and your God and remind the devil: "I am a fearless giver. I refuse to partake in the world's fear and hard times."

Take a stand of agreement with Gloria and me. We are increasing every outreach of this ministry in the war against fear. This is the most exciting time of our lives even though it is wartime. Wartime means victory-in-Jesus time. He is coming so soon. Let's get this job done and fill our Father's house with newborn children.

Together we can and will get it done.

We love you and pray for you every day.

Love,

P.S. You ARE our Valentine! We love and care about you very much!
Ken & Gloria

Fear Is Down! Faith Is Up!

Dear Partner

Oh, how Gloria and I love and care for you. Your faithfulness to pray and give never ceases to bless and thrill me, especially when I think about all of the hard and difficult places we would not have made it through had you not been there praying and standing with us. I am eternally grateful to the Lord Jesus for divinely connecting us together in His love.

The years 2000 and 2001 were big years spiritually, but very hard years financially. 2002 is already a breakthrough year. The gifts of the Spirit are being manifested more clearly and with greater power than ever before in this ministry. Our finances are on the rise once again, and what's most important, more souls are coming to Jesus than ever before.

Fear is down! Faith is up! And thank God, He always causes us to triumph.

I want to remind you of a couple of things we have learned from the Word about being delivered from fear. First, as believers, <u>we don't cope with fear, we attack it.</u> Hebrews 2:14-15 tells us that through His death on the cross Jesus has delivered us from fear.

Secondly, perfected love casts out fear. As we meditate on the fact that God is Love, and on how much He loves us, His love begins to rise within our inner man until it <u>flushes out all fear.</u> Then, as we walk in that love, it grows and penetrates every area of our lives. Faith, then, which works by love, has no fear interfering to stop the things Jesus has given us. Nothing can stop faith when there is no fear. All things are possible to him who <u>believes.</u>

Today, let's take a look at fear-based prayers.

Fear is the <u>spirit connector</u> to disaster and death the way faith is the spirit connector to salvation and life. Let's go first to Job 1:4-5:

> 4   And his sons went and feasted in their houses, every one his day; and sent and called for their three sisters to eat and to drink with them.
>
> 5   And it was so, when the days of their feasting were gone about, that Job sent and sanctified them, and rose up early in the morning, and offered burnt offerings according to the number of them all: for <u>Job said,</u> It may be that my sons have sinned, and cursed God in their hearts. <u>Thus did Job continually.</u>

Notice Job's fear-based confession in verse 5: "It may be that my sons have sinned and cursed God...."

This confession, based on fear instead of faith, drove Job to make sacrifices <u>continually,</u> instead of making them once in faith and then filling his mouth with faith in God's promises in the blood of those sacrifices. That was the basis for the conversation between God and satan.

God did not bring disaster on Job, nor did He authorize satan to do so. Job did! In verse 11, satan tried to get God to touch everything Job had, but God refused. Look at verse 12, and notice the word *behold:*

> 12   And the Lord said unto Satan, Behold, all that he hath is in thy power; only upon himself put not forth thine hand. So Satan went forth from the presence of the Lord.

Behold means to look and see. Job had broken the covenant Hedge about himself through fear-based prayers and worry-filled confessions of fear.

Now, let's look at Job 3:25-26:

> 25   For the thing which I greatly feared is come upon me, and that which I was afraid of is come unto me.
>
> 26   I was not in safety, neither had I rest, neither was I quiet; yet trouble came.

Verse 26 is a real eye-opener. Job thought he was being a responsible father by worrying day and night about his family, not realizing that the truly responsible thing to do was to roll all the <u>care</u> over on God who <u>cared</u> for him and with whom he had covenant.

It is an act of pride to try to carry your own cares. First Peter 5:5-7 says,

5   God resisteth the proud, and giveth grace to the humble.

6   Humble yourselves therefore under the mighty hand of God, that he may exalt you in due time:

7   Casting all your care upon him; for he careth for you.

This is exactly what Jairus did in Luke 8:49-50, when he was told, "Thy daughter is dead; trouble not the master." When Jesus heard that report, He said, "Fear Not! Believe only! And she <u>shall</u> live!"

<u>Fear tolerated contaminates faith.</u> Faith and fear in the same prayer, or trying to believe and entertain fear at the same time, brings disastrous results. Notice that Jesus did not say to Jairus, "Let me get rid of the fear for you." No, that responsibility belonged to Jairus. Jairus simply obeyed. He refused fear and cast <u>all</u>—everything—onto Jesus.

Fear Not! Love is here!

So, had Job made his sacrifice according to what God had taught him and said, "Amen! So be it! That settles it! The care is now in the Hands of my covenant Father. He cares for me and He cares for my family..." then every time satan tried to bring up those fears, had he said, "I cast down that imagination and I refuse to touch it in my thought life. I choose to think on whatsoever things are true, whatsoever things are honest, just, pure, lovely, of a good report—I think about my covenant with my God and how much He loves me..." <u>then began to praise and worship, instead of worrying,</u> things would have been very different. Job could have spent the next nine to 12 months in peace instead of disasters.

Jairus, however, obeyed, and as a result, experienced the Glory of

God (Love) in the place of death.

Consistent faith in God is Love is the key to John 10:10, where Jesus said, "I have come that you might have life and have it more abundantly." Constantly and consistently believing Love = God casts out all fear. And fear that is cast out is gone. Not just coped with or put under control in one or two areas of life. GONE! Fleeing from you!

Faith, then, which works by love is free to receive every need met according to Love's riches in Glory by Christ—the anointed Jesus, through His Anointing.

Read this letter several times. Look up the scriptures for yourself. Everywhere you read *God,* replace it with *Love.* "The Love of Love Himself has been shed abroad in Your heart by the Spirit of Love...." That Love (God) will *immediately* begin rising up inside you. Stay with it until the joy of Love explodes. That's your strength. That's who you are! A fearless child of the Most High God. Love Himself!

Gloria and I need you to stand with us and believe with us to take this Word to a fearful, terrified world. People are afraid, and they're looking for answers. That's why we've enclosed a set of cards for you to have on hand to help you minister to those around you who are trapped in fear. The Word-based principles listed on these cards will lead people out of *fear* and in to *Love.*

So, study these cards. Keep one for yourself and pass the other one along—or pass them both along.

I tell you, Gloria and I have never before been this excited about any calling we have received. The whole ministry is afire with fearless, abounding love. Together, we can—and will—preach it far and wide with signs following.

We love you and hold you in our hearts. We pray for you every day.

Love,

Ken

God Is Love
Love Is God

Dear Partner

I know you remember how, a few years ago, we renewed our minds to the true meaning of the word *Christ*. We translated the Greek word *Christ* into its English counterpart, "The Anointed One and His Anointing." *Translate and meditate* was the phrase I heard the Spirit of God say. When we began to do that, it opened up the entire New Testament in a way we had never seen before. In fact, I still read the word *Christ* that way, and always will.

The reason it was so important to translate and meditate *Christ* is because its meaning had been lost to English-speaking people. Very much in the same way, there's almost no meaning to the English word *God*. It came into English from the German word *Gott* and even when properly translated, its meaning sheds no real light on who He really is.

The dictionary simply defines *God* as "the Supreme Being; the eternal and infinite Spirit, the creator and sovereign of the universe." That, of course, is all true, but *God* can mean just about anything in the minds of people. To some, it represents some object or idol.

In fact, the dictionary definition is no real help in understanding who God is. We found that out when the followers of Allah attacked us September 11th of last year. Their definition of their "god" is the same.

So what is the difference between Allah and the God of the Bible? Let's let the New Testament speak to us. First John 4:8 and 4:16 simply state "God is love." In 2 Corinthians 13:11, He is the "<u>God of love</u>." We <u>must</u> renew our minds to <u>know</u> that God, our Father, doesn't just have love—He <u>is</u> Love! We are not talking about the love of God. We are really talking about Love, who <u>is</u> God.

Let's go now to 1 John 4:18 and see why this is so important: "There is no fear in love; but perfect love casteth out fear: <u>because fear hath torment.</u> He that feareth is not made perfect in love." *The Amplified*

Bible sheds even more light on this verse:

> 18   There is no fear in love [dread does not exist], but <u>full-grown</u> (complete, perfect) love turns fear out of doors *and* <u>expels every trace of terror!</u> For fear brings with it the thought of punishment, and [so] he who is afraid has not reached the full maturity of love [is not yet grown into love's complete perfection].

Do you see that? Expels every <u>trace</u> of <u>terror!</u> The renewing of our minds to the fact that <u>God is Love</u> is the first step toward perfected, or a full-grown, revelation of Love (<u>who is God</u>) in our lives. As that revelation grows in our spirits, it flushes fear out. There is no fear in Love—who is God. There is no fear in God—who is Love.

With this in mind, let's read John 3:16:

> 16   For Love who <u>so</u> loved the world gave His only begotten Son—the Son of Love—that whosoever believes on Him should not perish but have everlasting life.

Now, let's do the same with Psalm 23:

> 1   Love is my shepherd; I shall not want.
>
> 2   Love makes me lie down in green pastures: Love leadeth me beside the still waters.
>
> 3   Love restoreth my soul (life): Love leadeth me in the paths of righteousness for his name's sake.
>
> 4   Yea, (even) though I walk through the valley of the shadow of death, <u>I will fear no evil!</u> (Why?) Because Love (<u>who is God</u>) is with me. Love's rod (to protect me) and His staff (to guide me) comfort me.
>
> 5   Love prepareth a table before me in the presence of mine enemies: Love anointest my head with oil; My cup runneth over (because He loves me).

6 Surely (Love's) goodness and (Love's) mercy (and unfailing love) shall follow me all the days of my life: and I will dwell in the House of Love (<u>who is God, who is Love</u>) all the days of my life.

See what I mean? What a heart thrill! Now every time we read the word *God*, or *Him*, we <u>know</u> who <u>He</u> is—<u>LOVE.</u> Love is never a taker. Love is always a giver. For Love so loved, He (Love) gave. There is no loving without giving.

We began this by talking about translating and meditating the word *Christ* as "the Anointed One and His Anointing." Let's look at Ephesians 3:17-21:

17 That [the Anointed One and His (Love's) Anointing—burden-removing, yoke-destroying power of Love (God)]—may dwell in your hearts by faith; that ye, being rooted and grounded in <u>Love</u> [<u>who is God</u>],

18 May be able to comprehend with all saints what is the breadth, and length, and depth, and height;

19 And to <u>know</u> the <u>love</u> of [the Anointed One and His (Love's) Anointing (the burden-removing, yoke-destroying power of Love)], which passeth knowledge, that ye might be <u>filled</u> with all the <u>fulness</u> [all He has and all He can give] of [Love].

20 Now unto him that is able to do exceeding abundantly above all that we ask or think, according to the power that worketh in us [<u>casting out fear and terror</u>],

21 Unto [Love Himself] be glory in the Church by [the Anointed One and His (Love's) Anointing] Jesus throughout all ages, world without end. Shout amen [somebody!!].

Think about it. Every act of anointing is an act of Love. Removing burdens and destroying yokes is why Jesus—the Son of Love—came.

Think how easy it was for the devil to lie about God through religious ideas and wrong interpretations of His Word. A supreme being might do some bad thing like bring sickness and disease, poverty, etc., but Love would never do that. Love has no sickness. Love is never behind something that is a curse to people. Love reaches out to break the grip of sickness. Love is filled with kindness, mercy and pity for the downtrodden.

The only sickness Love ever had was when He (not it) bore our sins and carried our sicknesses and diseases away in His (Love's) own body on the Cross. Love became obedient even to death in order to destroy him who had the power of death—that is, the devil—that you and I might be delivered from the fear of death (Hebrews 2:14-15) and be delivered from all bondage.

Love has set us free! He has broken the power of the law of sin and death for us through the law of the spirit of life in Christ Jesus—the Son of Love:

Psalm 27:1:

1 [Love] is my light and my salvation; whom shall I fear? [Love] is the strength of my life; of whom shall I be afraid?

Isaiah 41:10-13:

10 Fear thou not; for I [who am Love] am with thee: be not dismayed; for I [who am Love] am thy God: I will strengthen thee; yea, I [who am Love] will help thee; yea, I [who am Love] will uphold thee with the right hand of my righteousness.

11 Behold, all they that were incensed against thee shall be ashamed and confounded: they shall be as nothing; and they that strive with thee shall perish.

12   Thou shalt seek them, and shalt not find them, even them that contended with thee: they that war against thee shall be as nothing, and as a thing of nought.

13   For I (who am Love and am) the Lord thy God will hold thy right hand, saying unto thee, Fear not; I will help thee.

<u>Receive your victory in every area of your life!</u> <u>Believe the Love!</u> You came to know Love (God) when you received Jesus as your Lord and Savior. At that time God, who is Love, was shed abroad in your heart by the Holy Ghost, the Spirit of Love. You were not given the spirit of fear but of power, Love (who is God) and a sound mind—receive it!

You were given the Spirit of adoption. Love is your Father—cry out right now, "Abba, Father—I have a Daddy—I have a Father who loves me as much as He does Jesus (John 17:23)!" Receive it! Love changes everything!

Now you and I must take this fear-ripping, burden-removing, yoke-destroying Word to this fear-riddled, terror-stricken world! Especially to the Body of Christ! Get in this with me. Pray! Rise up in faith! Give! Commit yourself to be fearless and strong. We have the victory, and we must exercise it on the devil. That is our part in the war effort, and we will get it done!

Gloria and I thank you for being our faithful Partner. We love you and pray for you every day.

Love,

Ken

Fear Tolerated Is Faith Contaminated

Dear Partner

If there has ever been a time for fearless, praying, people of faith to come forth, this is it. And we are that people. We are the people of the Book! Not only that, we are the people of the "back of the Book." We win!

In this letter I want to go back to our discussion of what Jesus commanded Jairus in Luke 8:50. Let's start with verse 49:

> 49 While he yet spake, there cometh one from the ruler of the synagogue's house, saying to him, Thy daughter is dead; trouble not the Master.
>
> 50 But when Jesus heard it, he answered him, saying, Fear not: believe only, and she shall be made whole.

FEAR NOT!...and she <u>shall</u> <u>be</u> made whole. Notice the absolute certainty in what Jesus said. Faith with no fear. Fear tolerated is faith contaminated. Trying to believe God and worrying at the same time just won't work.

Now let's go to 1 John 4:18:

> 18 There is no fear in love; but perfect love casteth out fear: because fear hath torment. He that feareth is not made perfect in love.

It's not just love that casts out fear. It's *perfected* love that casts out fear.

Now couple that verse with 1 John 2:5:

> 5 But whoso keepeth his word, in him verily is the love of God perfected: hereby know we that we are in him.

Jairus obeyed Jesus, or "kept His Word," and the result was exactly what Jesus said it would be. The word *perfected* is also translated "complete, fully grown, matured." So, it is complete, fully grown, matured love that casts out fear.

That then brings up the question how do we mature, or grow up, in Love and have Love grow up in us?

Do you recall what Jesus said about "the sower soweth the Word"? He said if you can understand this parable, you can understand all parables. He also said the kingdom of God is compared to planting a seed and it <u>growing</u>. When His staff members said, "Increase our faith," He said, "Plant it and it will increase."

Well, if the entire kingdom of God is compared to that, then Love, who is God Himself, is certainly no exception. We "<u>grow</u>" love by using it. The more we love, the bigger it gets. The bigger it becomes, the less room there is for fear.

Now let's get the Word on it. First John 4:12 tells us if we love one another, God, who is Love, dwelleth in us and His love is perfected—<u>or grown,</u> or matured—in us. Now verses 16-18 again.

> 16 And we have known and believed the love that God hath to us. <u>God is love;</u> and he that dwelleth in love dwelleth in God, and God in him.
>
> 17 Herein is our love made perfect, that we may have boldness in the day of judgment: because as he is, so are we in this world.
>
> 18 There is no fear in love; but perfect love casteth out fear: because fear hath torment. He that feareth is not made perfect in love.

There it is. Love, who is God, grows when it is used or planted.

Faith works by Love—Galatians 5:6. Trying to live by faith and walking in strife at the same time just won't work. The Word says where there is strife there is confusion and <u>every</u> evil work. Not a little evil work, but every evil work. Now we can better understand why the devil has had such great success when all the time the Word says Jesus totally defeated him. Love defeated him, and Love keeps him in his place—under our feet.

Now 2 Timothy 2:24-26 becomes abundantly clear:

24   And the servant of the Lord must not strive; but be gentle unto all men, apt to teach, patient,

25   In meekness instructing those that oppose themselves; if God peradventure will give them repentance to the acknowledging of the truth;

26   And that they may recover themselves out of the snare of the devil, who are taken captive by him at his will.

Strife is deadly, especially during times of war. Notice how Jesus included it and warned against it in His teaching on faith in Mark 11:22-26:

22   And Jesus answering saith unto them, Have faith in God.

23   For verily I say unto you, That whosoever shall say unto this mountain, Be thou removed, and be thou cast into the sea; and shall not doubt in his heart, but shall believe that those things which he saith shall come to pass; he shall have whatsoever he saith.

24   Therefore I say unto you, What things soever ye desire, when ye pray, believe that ye receive them, and ye shall have them.

25   And when ye stand praying, forgive, if ye have aught against any: that your Father also which is in heaven may forgive you your trespasses.

26   But if ye do not forgive, neither will your Father which is in heaven forgive your trespasses.

If we ignore verses 25-26, we can forget about verses 22-24. The reason is without the Love—who is God—fear is still present, faith is contaminated, and satan is not resisted so he does not flee. That's where all the struggling to believe comes from.

Faith rests, it doesn't struggle. Faith comes easy to the born-again believer because the faith of Jesus, who is the author of our faith, lives within us. Faith comes by hearing, and hearing by the Word of Love. Love doesn't bring struggle. It brings peace. Fear brings torment. It never brings peace. Faith which works by Love—who is God—brings peace even when we can't understand it.

Love always does His work. He is always there and always does His part. Our part is to focus on Him. It's to focus on His love, which is Him, and to keep our minds, every thought, on what He has done for us. Then transfer those thoughts into action by living His love—loving.

Loving one another is not a strong suggestion. It is a commandment. Think about that. In His love for us, He commanded us to be free from fear—Victory in Jesus! In every area of life, spirit, soul, body, financially and socially—Victory.

The Word, the Name, the Blood, the whole armor of God—who is Love—working at full power in our lives! Fullness. Fullness of calling. Fullness of the gifts of the Spirit. Fullness of Love's desire to manifest Himself among us. This is the fullness of times the Word talks about. We are in it, now! It's yours. Go for it.

This is the message you and I must take to this fear-filled world. Together we can do it!

Gloria and I want to thank you, and all our Partners, for being so faithful to pray and to give. The past six months have been like having all of you around us all the time. It's hard to explain in words, but the peace and courage that comes from it is awesome.

As you sow your financial seed this month, pray over it like you were personally handing it to Jesus. Then "see" Jesus bless it, and then turn and hand it to Gloria and me. Hold that image. "See" Gloria and me receive it and take the "bread" to the nations! Teaching, preaching, healing in Jesus' Name—in the Name of the Son of Love.

We love you and pray for you every day.

Love,

Ken

Fear-Based Praying Is Disastrous!

Dear Partner

This is a victory letter! We win! Jesus, our champion, is on the throne. It matters not what the news media reports or what anyone else thinks or says, the battle is His and victory is ours.

Since we launched our war on fear in October 2001, the Lord has revealed many things about it. He is still opening new insights and concepts into living totally free from fear and its running buddy, doubt. God, our Father, does not want <u>any</u> fear in us or any of us in fear— Ever—<u>NONE,</u> because fear has torment (1 John 4:18). The idea of being completely fear free is almost unheard of, the reason being we live in a fear-filled world and are surrounded by a fear-based society.

Most Christians pray fear-based, instead of faith-based, prayers. Fear-based praying is disastrous.

In order to rise above that kind of thinking, we must look at fear the way God looks at it, or through the eyes of the Word rather than the eyes of the world. First of all let's see where the Word places fear. Revelation 21:7-8 says:

7   He that overcometh shall inherit all things; and I will be his God, and he shall be my son.

8   But the fearful, and unbelieving, and the abominable, and murderers, and whoremongers, and sorcerers, and idolaters, and all liars, shall have their part in the lake which burneth with fire and brimstone: which is the second death.

Look at the company fear keeps. Now that answers those who say, "Everybody is afraid of something. Besides that, what does it matter if there's some fear in your life? It may even be a healthy thing to have a little fear about some things." Well, is it a healthy thing to have a little unbelief? Does it matter to have abominations in your life? Is a little murder OK? Or idols? Or lying? Absolutely not. God sees fear as an enemy to your soul and a work of the devil.

Jesus came to destroy the works of the devil on the cross. Let's look at Hebrews 2:14-15:

14   Forasmuch then as the children are partakers of flesh and blood, he also himself likewise took part of the same; that through death he might destroy him that had the power of death, that is, the devil;

15   And deliver them who through fear of death were all their lifetime subject to bondage.

His flesh and blood on the cross delivered us from fear. Look at Romans 8:15:

15   For ye have not received the spirit of bondage again to fear; but ye have received the Spirit of adoption, whereby we cry, Abba, Father.

Now look at these two passages together. We were delivered from the spirit of bondage, being subject to bondage through fear, at the Cross. We then received the Spirit of freedom from bondage and fear. Does the Spirit of God have a little healthy fear in Him? No! No more than He steals, kills or destroys.

First John 4:16 declares that God is Love. He doesn't have love. He is Love! It also states that he that dwelleth in Love dwelleth in God and God (who is Love) dwells in him. Verse 18 of that same chapter says there is no fear in Love. There is no fear in God. He is in us and we are in Him!

Romans 5:5 tells us God (who is Love) is shed abroad in our hearts by the Spirit of Love. As Love (God) is growing and maturing in us, its expansion flushes out fear. All of it.

And finally 2 Timothy 1:6-7 says:

6   Wherefore I put thee in remembrance that thou stir up the gift of God, which is in thee by the putting on of my hands.

7   For God hath not given us the spirit of fear; but of power, and of love, and of a sound mind.

We have a habit of quoting verse 7 alone. Take a closer look at them together—stir up the gift of Love (who is God) which is in you. There could not possibly be any trace of fear in that gift because it came from Love, and there's no fear in Love. <u>Now</u> read verse 7. When you stir up the Spirit, God (who is Love) has given you, you stir up power and Love who casts out fear and produces a sound mind which is a fear-free mind. That's the reason Jesus told Jairus, "Stop the fear! Believe <u>only</u>." Fear tolerated is faith contaminated.

Faith is of God who is Love. It doesn't take very much of it to defeat sickness, sin, bondage or any other works of darkness. Faith is of Light. It is never difficult for Light to dispel darkness, nor does it take much of it.

<u>We have faith.</u> It came into us when we were born again. Faith is fed and strengthened by hearing, and hearing by the Word of Love. The struggling to have more faith to overcome the works of sickness and poverty, etc., comes from having our priorities out of place.

Increasing faith without dealing with fear is an uphill battle. Stop the fear and believe only. With fear removed, faith works. Galatians 5:6 puts it straight for us: "<u>Faith worketh</u> by love." Faith works. There's no such thing as faith, or anything else from God, that doesn't work—but it works by <u>Love.</u>

Jesus said to Peter, "I pray that your faith fail not." But 1 Corinthians 13:8 says Love <u>NEVER</u> fails. When fear is in the mix, more faith isn't the answer. "Stop the fear! Believe only! <u>AND</u> <u>SHE</u> [or you] <u>WILL BE MADE WHOLE!</u>" Shout amen, somebody!

Do it NOW! Stop the fear.

How? Read the 23rd Psalm, <u>but instead of saying *Lord,* say *Love*</u>

is my shepherd. Love makes me lie down in green pastures, etc. Then read Isaiah 41:10-14 the same way: "Fear thou not for I—Love—am with you." Read it that way each time "I" or "Lord" or "God" appears in those four verses. Read John 3:16: "For Love so loved the World that He [Love] gave His only begotten Son, the Son of Love, so that whosoever believes on Him should not perish but have LIFE forever." Love could not rest until death was defeated.

Then after reading and meditating and rejoicing on those and other promises Love has made, begin applying those Love Words to your situation. Begin doing what Romans 8:15 says. Shout, "I have a Father! I have a Daddy who loves me! I have a Father and He's God! He's Number 1, the Most High! And He Loves Me. He's mine and I'm His! I have a Father! I have a Daddy! And He's Rich! Rich! Rich! He's my Healer! He's my Deliverer! I refuse to fear!"

Don't be quiet about it. Shout and stomp and praise your way to total victory.

Be fearless about your tithing and sowing offerings—it will release your faith to open the floodgates of abundance. Think about it. All of us together, fearlessly storming the very gates of hell and darkness with the message of Jesus' Love. Together we can do it. Let's get it done.

Gloria and I love you and pray for you every day.

Love,

Ken

Rest Is the Key to Victory—Victory Is the Key to Rest

Dear Partner

I want to begin this letter by giving God (who is Love) all the praise for all the wonderful, marvelous things that are happening through the Body of Christ—especially in this ministry. He is moving, saving, healing, baptizing with the Holy Ghost and delivering His people. He is doing the miraculous everywhere someone will believe. Glory be to God! And you and I are right in the middle of it all.

Our last audit shows more than 57 million people have come into the kingdom through this ministry. Think about that! All you and I had to do was be willing and obedient and He, blessed be God forever, did the rest. Then He gave us credit and reward and heavenly blessing as though we had done it all. But, then, that's the way Love is. He just keeps on giving and giving.

There is a Bible truth I have spoken and written about before that I want to look into a bit deeper in this letter. Faith-based prayers bring victory. Fear-based prayers bring disaster. We know for a fact that faith has rest.

Let's look at Hebrews 4:2b-3a:

> 2b ...But the word preached did not profit them, not being mixed with faith in them that heard it.

> 3a For we which have believed do enter into rest, as he said, As I have sworn in my wrath, if they shall enter into my rest....

Faith enters into God's divine rest. Now let's look at 1 John 4:18a:

> 18a There is no fear in love; but perfect love casteth out fear: because fear hath torment....

Fear has torment. So you could say it like this: Prayers that rest on God's Word and the faith it produces bring victory. And: Prayers based on fear and torment bring disaster. Remember 1 John 5:4:

> 4   For whatsoever is born of God overcometh the
>   world: and this is the victory that overcometh
>   the world, even our faith.

That's only seven verses down from "fear hath torment." Faith brings victory that overcomes the world. Fear brings the world and all its torment to camp on the doorstep of your life. Not only that, but it's there to stay until Love, faith and victory run it off and keep it off.

The rest and peace from God is already yours and it's already there. It does not have to come from anywhere except from within your born-again spirit. Jesus said in John 14:27:

> 27   Peace I leave with you, my peace I give unto
>   you: not as the world giveth, give I unto you.
>   Let not your heart be troubled, neither let it
>   be afraid.

He said not as the world gives...how is that?

The world gives only what is earned. The world always demands return—"You owe me" for every little favor.

How does Jesus give?

Matthew 10:7-8:

> 7   And as ye go, preach, saying, The kingdom of
>   heaven is at hand.
> 8   Heal the sick, cleanse the lepers, raise the
>   dead, cast out devils: freely ye have received,
>   freely give.

Romans 8:32:

32   He that spared not his own Son, but delivered
        him up for us all, how shall he not with him
        also <u>freely</u> give us all things?

1 Corinthians 2:12:

12   Now we have received, not the spirit of the
        world, but the spirit which is of God; that we
        might know the things that are <u>freely</u> given to
        us of God.

Revelation 21:6:

6   And he said unto me, It is done. I am Alpha
        and Omega, the beginning and the end. I will
        give unto him that is athirst of the fountain of
        the water of life <u>freely.</u>

Then Revelation 22:17:

17   And the Spirit and the bride say, Come. And
        let him that heareth say, Come. And let him
        that is athirst come. And whosoever will, let
        him take the water of life <u>freely.</u>

Jesus gives <u>FREELY!</u> He bought it! He paid for it! Now He has given to us His peace—shalom—nothing missing, nothing broken. His resting place in the Father who is Love!

Nowhere in the Word does it say to labor to enter into salvation. In no place does it say to labor to enter into healing or to enter into financial blessing. The Word does not say to labor to enter into a new car or home. Nowhere does it say, "Pastor, labor to enter into a bigger church."

What does it say? Look at Hebrews 3:18 through 4:16. We labor to <u>enter into rest.</u> His rest. His peace. He has already given it. It is already ours.

Verses 12-16 describe in detail the process. First, the living Word. Second, Jesus our great High Priest is standing ready (Hebrews 3:1-2) to bring to pass our words of faith or prayers of resting on His Word and Love.

Finally, notice the two key <u>rest</u> words in verse16. They are *obtain* and *find*. Not *maybe* and *hope so*. God is Love. Love loves. That's what He does.

Love does not steal, kill or destroy. Love does not find fault (Isaiah 54:8-10). Love loves. He has always loved you even when you thought He didn't. He loves you now, in spite of what you think or how you feel. He will always love you regardless of what anyone or anything might say. You can <u>rest assured</u> on that. On Him.

Begin right now ministering His Word and Love to <u>your</u> faith. Meditate on these <u>true</u> promises until you enter into <u>His</u> rest.

Jesus is not upset. He is not afraid. He is not in financial stress. He is at rest at Love's right hand. Well, SO ARE WE! He has raised us up together and made us sit together with Him in heavenly places.

Turn your faith up to high setting and believe, because as 1 John 4:17 says, "as he <u>is</u> so are we...."

After we die and go to heaven?

No! As He is <u>so are we in this world</u>! It's yours. Love has said so! Grab it like a bulldog and run off with it. You're a prayer and faith champion! An overcomer!

Enter into His rest. He will take care of everything else. This is the message you and I are called to take to this fear-filled world. We are doing it now and will continue to do even more—together—<u>Hallelujah!</u>

Sow every seed in faith and rest. Sow in joy. Increase your praise, and you'll increase your harvest. Sow the seed, water with praise and take your rest, knowing that the peace of your Father is at work in all of your life.

Well, that's enough for one letter. Be blessed. Gloria and I love you very much, and we pray for you every day.

Love,

Ken

God <u>Is</u> Love!

Dear Partner

God <u>is</u> love. He doesn't have love. He <u>is</u> love.

He (Love) is a giver—not a taker. Love gives when times are good. Love gives when times are not good. Love gives when it has it to give. Love gives when it does not have it to give. Love's lifestyle is to prosper every person with whom it comes into contact.

On the other hand, satan is a taker. He's never a giver. A taker takes when times are good. He takes when times are bad. He takes when he has. He takes when he has not. The taker's lifestyle is to take and keep from every person with whom he comes into contact.

Selfishness is the king of all fear, doubt, unbelief and misery. It is the great thief of peace and quietness. It is the robber of assurance. Self protection is the beginning of disobedience to God. Jesus said in five different places in the gospels, "Whoever tries to preserve, or save, his own life will lose it, but whoever loses his life will save it."

Fear is the spirit connector to destruction. Remember what we learned in Isaiah 54:14?

> 14   In righteousness shalt thou be established: thou shalt be far from oppression; for thou shalt not fear: and from terror; for it shall not come near thee.

Therefore <u>the fear of death connects one to the death he fears.</u> On the other hand, one who puts his <u>faith</u> in Love, who is God, and turns his life over to Love, is connected by the connector to life. Faith in life connects one to the safety he desires. Selfishness always tries to be its own god.

Think about the Ten Commandments. "Thou shalt have no other

gods before Me." God, who is Love, said that to a people with whom He already had made covenant to meet their every need. "Thou shalt not steal." Why? "Because you have a covenant with Me. I'll meet your needs."

However, selfishness says, "Yeah, but I need it by Friday. There's no way God or anybody else could get that much to me by then." Selfishness gave birth to fear. Fear gave birth to sin. Thou shalt not steal is not the only commandment broken here. The command to not have any other God has also been broken. Trying to be your own provider is trying to be your own god.

Fear connects to sin. Fear connects to the disaster. But that's not all. There is another problem here. When God, who is Love, commanded to fear not, it was and is just as much a commandment as steal not. Stealing is not OK. Fear is not OK.

Both stealing and fearing have the same answer. Perfected Love. Love developed and full grown. The very highest kind of Love has been born into our spirits when we were born again.

Romans 5:5 boldly states that the Love of God, or Love Himself, has been shed abroad in our hearts (spirits) by the Holy Ghost which has been given to us. What Love is that? It is the Love that answered the prayer of Jesus in John 17:26:

> 26 And I have declared unto them thy name, and will declare it: that the love wherewith thou hast loved me may be in them, and I in them.

Look at that again—that the love that God, who is Love, loves Jesus with may be in us! Not just that He would love us with the same love, which would be far-out enough. In fact, He prayed that also in the 23rd verse:

> 23 I in them, and thou in me, that they may be made perfect in one; and that the world may know that thou hast sent me, and hast loved them, as thou hast loved me.

But He went the whole way and said, "The Love that You love me with be in them and that I (Jesus) may be in them!" He said it. God, who is Love, heard it and the Holy Ghost, the Spirit of Love, did it.

Galatians 5:22-23 says that He's in us with all His wonderful, lovely attributes and ways. These have been born into us just waiting to be released as a witness to the world that Jesus is alive and is the same yesterday, today and forever.

Love is the greatest witness under heaven. Selfishness has reigned until the world has become love-starved.

Love is the answer to the problems in every home. The Word says that a soft answer turns away wrath. Just a soft, "Sweetheart, I'm so sorry. The whole thing is my fault. I love you," would have stopped the downhill slide toward divorce.

When we develop our faith in God, who is in us, we become aware that when we say, "I love you," we are speaking about and releasing more than human love. Human love is spiritually bankrupt. We are going deeper than that. Faith reaches down into our reborn spirit and taps in to the anointing to Love. Ephesians 3:19 calls it the Love of Christ. The Love of the Anointed One and His Anointing is in there. That's what Jesus' prayer was all about.

First John 2:5 says:

> 5   But whoso keepeth his word, in him verily is the love of God perfected: hereby know we that we are in him.

The word He is referring to here is the word of His commandment to us. That commandment is to have faith in the Name of Jesus and love one another as He gave commandment.

That's 1 John 3:23. Now look at 1 John 4:12:

> 12   No man hath seen God at any time. If we love one another, God dwelleth in us, and his love is perfected in us.

Practicing that love commandment by faith in the promise that it (Love) never fails is what develops or perfects its presence in our lives.

Now go on to 4:16-18:

16   And we have known and believed the love that God hath to us. God is love; and he that dwelleth in love dwelleth in God, and God in him.

17   Herein is our love made perfect, that we may have boldness in the day of judgment: because as he is, so are we in this world.

18   There is no fear in love; but <u>perfect love</u> casteth out fear: because fear hath torment. He that feareth is not made perfect in love.

Now connect all the dots! He has commanded us to love. Keeping that commandment perfects or develops His love in us. That developed love casts out fear! It gets completely rid of selfishness.

You begin to realize with great joy: "I no longer have my self on my hands. I'm forever in the hands of Love. I keep His Word. He keeps His Word. He loves me. I love Him. I'm taking His love for me to this sick and dying world.

"I have no fear! I have a job to do. A Love job. A faith job. I cannot fail. I cannot stay sick. Sickness cannot abide in this Love-filled house. Love so loved the world that He, Love, sent His only Son, the Son of Love, so that whosoever would believe on Him should not perish but have everlasting life."

Love is life. Life without Love is not life. It's death. <u>The person who has missed Love has missed the highest kind of life.</u> Life in the heavenlies right here on earth. Right in the midst of this crooked and perverse generation. Selfishness has been dethroned. Jesus has brought Life—the God-kind of Life, the Love-kind of Life—to us in Himself.

You and I are commissioned to take this marvelous Word to the whole world. Together we can and will do it! The results are manifestations of the glory—God Himself in His fullness, setting people free from every bondage hell has bound them with.

Let's get it done!

As you sow your seed-faith offerings this month, be especially aware that they are seeds of Love. Sow them in Love. Love for Jesus. Love for the lost. Love for your family who need God to manifest Himself to them as Savior and Healer. I know you get the picture. God is Love and so are you.

Pray for Gloria and me and all of us here at KCM and EMIC. We have received orders from heaven to double—everything! In the natural we could never do that. But we're not in the natural. Love said it's time to double, so we're going for it.

That also means He has to double our—yours and my—harvest. All that means double results. Twice the number of souls won. Twice the healings. Twice the miracles. Twice the money with which to get it done. Twice the praise. Twice the joy.

So here we go! We're going to hit satan and his crew with such a blast of the Word of faith and Love that he will never recover from it. Shout amen, somebody!

Gloria and I love you and pray for you every day.

Love,

Ken

Married in April 1962, the anointing of Love has been working in the marriage of Kenneth and Gloria for more than 40 years.

Double the Love!

Dear Partner

Double anointing
  power from above.
Double good,
Double good,
Double the Love!

We're on the go for the double.

Elisha asked for and received double the anointing of his teacher and mentor, Elijah. That amounted to twice anything he had ever heard of or seen. So he refused to allow his reasoning to take over. Instead, he stepped out in faith and "went for the double."

Reason is just another word for fear and unbelief. Reason might say, "Double <u>everything</u> is just too much to ask. How could God ever do that for me?" The answer is because He loves you <u>at least</u> twice as much as you believe He does. Besides that, He's the One calling us to increase. We <u>must</u> do it and do it <u>NOW.</u>

This world and all the people in it are in deep trouble, and Jesus and His Lordship are the answer to <u>all</u> their needs. You and I are a vital part of that answer. God (who is Love) wants this job done. Jesus wants this job done. The Holy Spirit wants this job done. That's more than enough reason for you and me to stir ourselves up and get it done—at any cost!

When you and I begin to grasp how very much Love (who is God) loves, we begin to understand His heart-willingness to save and deliver. It's not His will that any be lost.

The issue here is not whether or not He's willing to manifest Himself in His glory. He's been willing all the time. The problem has been with us—not that we didn't want Him to move, but fear to act, fear to be willing to pay the price and do our part, has always been the holdup. Fear is the reason for struggle. Faith contaminated by fear creates what the Holy Ghost said through the Apostle James in James 1:5-8:

> 5   If any of you lack wisdom, let him ask of God, that giveth to all men liberally, and upbraideth not; and it shall be given him.
> 6   But let him ask in faith, nothing wavering. For he that wavereth is like a wave of the sea driven with the wind and tossed.
> 7   For let not that man think that he shall receive any thing of the Lord.
> 8   A double minded man is unstable in all his ways.

In verse 7 he says that the wavering, unstable person will not receive anything from the Lord. Asking in faith, nothing wavering, is a solid stand on the promises of Love—knowing He loves you and wants you completely free from every sin, sickness, demon, fear, grief or sorrow. Jesus has already borne all that along with every pain and every disease. The great God (Love) laid them on Him. However, it would not have accomplished anything if He, the Son of Love, had not taken or received them into Himself and borne them away. He took them in to hell and dumped them there forever. That's what Love did for you.

When we begin to think about that more than we think about anything else, His love which has been shed abroad in our hearts begins to rise like the tide. It pushes and rises until it overflows, leaving nothing in your spirit but Himself and those things born of Him.

"Whatsoever is born of [Love] overcometh the world. And this is the victory that overcometh the world, even our faith" (1 John 5:4). "There is no fear in Love [God]" (1 John 4:18). Developed, full-grown Love flushes out fear. Faith is the spirit-connector to Love (who is God), and fear is the connector to death.

THE FEAR OF DEATH CONNECTS YOU TO THE DEATH YOU FEAR!

Faith has no struggle to receive. (Now that's different from fighting the good fight of faith. Fighting the fight of faith is to stand firm on Love's promises and resist the devil and he will flee.) Struggling to receive has torment—nagging unbelief that hangs around in our thoughts and in our words. Faith enters into rest knowing that our heavenly Father loves us just as much as He does Jesus (John 17:23). Faith always makes its stand and fights its fight in a place of peace and rest in Him.

In closing let's read Hebrews 4:9-16:

9   There remaineth therefore a rest to the people of God.

10   For he that is entered into his rest, he also hath ceased from his own works, as God did from his.

11   Let us labour therefore to enter into that rest, lest any man fall after the same example of unbelief.

12   For the word of God is quick, and powerful, and sharper than any twoedged sword, piercing even to the dividing asunder of soul and spirit, and of the joints and marrow, and is a discerner of the thoughts and intents of the heart.

13   Neither is there any creature that is not manifest in his sight: but all things are naked and opened unto the eyes of him with whom we have to do.

14   Seeing then that we have a great high priest, that is passed into the heavens, Jesus the Son of God, let us hold fast our profession.

15   For we have not an high priest which cannot be touched with the feeling of our infirmities; but was in all points tempted like as we are, yet without sin.

16   Let us therefore come boldly unto the throne of grace, that we may obtain mercy, and find grace to help in time of need.

Notice the Word did <u>not</u> say labor to enter into healing. Nor did it say labor to enter into a debt-free lifestyle, or a new house, or a bigger church building. It did not say labor to get the double. It said to labor to enter into <u>rest</u>—the peace that the Son of Love bought and paid for at Calvary's tree.

That rest is in His Love. The sense of insecurity and impending failure flows away under Love's rising tide when we fix our minds on the promises upon which we are standing, and stay focused on how much the One who gave those promises loves us.

Faith rests. Fear struggles. Love <u>NEVER</u> fails.

Hold Gloria and me up in prayer. We are in the middle of the most intensive schedule of ministry we've had in 25 years. We are stronger both spiritually and in our physical bodies than ever, thanks to the life of Love in us and to His Word and power.

As you sow your financial seed of faith and love this month, say out loud over it: "This is a seed of faith and love. It came from Love Himself, and now it's going back to Him through His work in the earth. I sow it in love and I receive my harvest in love. His love. I enter into His arms of abundance of peace and rest. He loves me as much as He does Jesus, and this seed will help others to know He loves them the same way. Today I sow for the double."

Double anointing
  power from above.
Double good,
Double good,
Double the Love!

Gloria and I love you and pray for you every day.

Love,

The Moment of Faith Is <u>NOW!</u>

Dear Partner

Gloria and I went into the summer of 2002 standing on a word we received from the Lord. It was a word of promise of great spiritual strides of growth and manifestations of His glory. We have certainly not been disappointed. Every meeting during the entire summer in some way took us to a higher level. <u>At the beginning, the Lord gave us direction to double this ministry</u>—everything! TWICE! At that time it looked totally impossible. But in only four months our faith has leaped upward and forward to a place of victory.

That's the way it's been all summer long. The Anaheim meeting in July was the best we've ever had in the 24 years of the West Coast Believers' Convention. It went to a higher place. Then came the Southwest Believers' Convention in Fort Worth. This was our 22nd year of that convention, and it, too, took off and didn't look back. I don't think any of us will ever be the same after those meetings. If you were not there, get the tapes of both conventions and listen to every one at least twice.

Then there were other meetings and TV broadcasts, and without exception a higher anointing was manifest. Believing and receiving from the Lord Jesus and His Word and Spirit seemed so easy. This is definitely a new day of miracles, healing and joy from heaven.

If there ever were a time to get every need met it is NOW. This is the time to turn loose of everything else and jump in to the things of God totally and completely. In fact, I want to talk to you about the <u>NOW.</u>

Yesterday is gone. <u>Turn it loose!</u> Tomorrow doesn't exist yet. There is only <u>NOW.</u> In fact <u>tomorrow is waiting to see what you do with NOW.</u> Jesus said in Matthew 6:34:

> 34   Take therefore no thought for the morrow: for
>   the morrow shall take thought for the things

of itself. Sufficient unto the day is the evil thereof.

Now let's look at the same verse in *The Amplified Bible:*

34   So do not worry or be anxious about tomor-
        row, for tomorrow will have worries and
        anxieties of its own. Sufficient for each day is
        its own trouble.

I want you to notice the words *worry* and *anxious.* These two things exist where fear is present. Worry, anxiety and fear are present only if you allow them to be. That's the bottom line. We have been commanded to "fear not."

Let's look at the dictionary definition of anxiety:

Concern or solicitude respecting some event, future or uncertain, which disturbs the mind, and keeps it in a state of painful uneasiness. It expresses more than uneasiness or disturbance, and even more than trouble or solicitude. It usually springs from fear or serious apprehension of evil, and involves a suspense respecting an event, and often, a perplexity of mind, to know how to shape our conduct. *(American Dictionary of the English Language,* Noah Webster 1828 edition)

All that because of fear. Fear is there because of not being developed in Love. Now look at 1 John 4:18:

18   There is no fear in love; but perfect love
        casteth out fear: because fear hath torment.
        He that feareth is not made perfect in love.

Now faith is. Right NOW. Stop whatever you are doing and believe on purpose that God loves you. Forget about whether you feel like it or not. Go deeper than that. Go beyond the surface of your mind and believe. Right NOW.

Now take another small step and believe He can totally handle whatever your situation is. If you have to go back through those decision steps again, ignore your feelings about whether He can or not. Go deeper. You know He can. NOW believe it.

Now take the next step. Believe He will. Believe it RIGHT NOW. Don't look back at yesterday. Forget about tomorrow. NOW is the moment of faith. One more step. Believe He can and that He will for one reason—He loves you. Don't struggle with it. Turn loose and rest on it. In the face of every thought that tries to crowd in, answer it with "Yes, but He loves me this moment." "There is therefore NOW no condemnation to them which are in Christ Jesus" (Romans 8:1). That's you. That's me. That's us—right NOW.

One of the great secrets of living the life of faith is to stop for a faith moment every so often during your day: "I love You, heavenly Father, and I know You love me right NOW." Practice the presence of God until you live by faith from moment to moment. You don't have to imagine He's there. He is there. Not only *with* you but *in* you.

Remember, tomorrow is waiting to see what you do with your faith today—Right NOW! Psalm 46:10 says, "Be still, and know that I am God (who is Love)"—Be still and know that I am Love.

I am believing for your double.

Double anointing
  power from above.
Double good,
Double good,
Double the Love!

Lay your hands on your seed and declare the double. Zechariah 9:11-12, *The Amplified Bible:*

> 11   As for you also, because of and for the sake
>   of the [covenant of the Lord with His people,
>   which was sealed with sprinkled] covenant
>   blood, I have released and sent forth your
>   imprisoned people out of the waterless pit.
>   (The Drought is over.)

12   Return to the stronghold [of security and prosperity], you prisoners of hope; even today do I declare that <u>I will restore double</u> your former prosperity to you.

That's shoutin' ground!!

Gloria and I love you and pray for you every day.

Love,

Ken

P.S. <u>Don't forget to vote! Pray and obey.</u>

Love <u>Never</u> Fails

Yes! You can! You can do it, whatever it is. Whatever you're up against is not enough to overcome an overcomer. Let's look at 1 John 5:1, 4:

> 1   Whosoever believeth that Jesus is the Christ is born of God: and every one that loveth him that begat loveth him also that is begotten of him.
>
> 4   For whatsoever is born of God overcometh the world: and this is the victory that overcometh the world, *even* our faith.

In verse 1 you can find yourself. You are a "whosoever" and you do believe that Jesus is the Christ. In verse 4, you are a "whatsoever" and you are born of God. Therefore you are a world overcomer. You may not be overcoming right now, but you <u>are</u> an overcomer. An overcomer is what you <u>are.</u> Overcoming is what you do.

"But Brother Copeland, you don't understand. I can't do it."

That's right. <u>You</u> can't. But you're not in this by yourself. You are in Christ Jesus and He is in you. All of heaven is on your side—including Gloria and me, all this ministry and all our other Partners. However, as long as you continue to declare "I can't," you have isolated and separated yourself from the victory that's already yours. The Almighty God has authorized you to shout "<u>Yes, I can!</u> I can do all things through Christ, the Anointed One and His Anointing which strengthens me."

Let's go back to 1 John. We were reading from the fifth chapter, but the overcoming victory begins in chapter 4, verse 4:

> 4   Ye are of God, little children, and have overcome them: because greater is he that is in you, than he that is in the world.

The overcoming factor is "ye are of God."

Now look at verses 7-8:

> 7   Beloved, let us love one another: for love is of God; and every one that loveth is born of God, and knoweth God.
>
> 8   He that loveth not knoweth not God; for God is love.

And verse 12:

> 12   No man hath seen God at any time. If we love one another, God dwelleth in us, and his love is perfected in us.

Tie those verses together with verse 18:

> 18   There is no fear in love; but perfect love casteth out fear: because fear hath torment. He that feareth is not made perfect in love.

Look at the word *perfected*. It means developed, or growing or full grown. It's God Himself having full charge of your life. It's as simple as this: When we use the love of God that has been shed abroad in our hearts, it develops the Love—who is God—until all fear is gone. "I can't" is a fear-based statement. "I can" is a faith-based statement, and faith is the victory.

In order to walk in all this, you must change your focus. "I can't" is focused entirely on yourself. Love is never zeroed in on itself. It is always fixed on meeting someone else's needs.

This is where faith comes in. You are not the Savior, but you do represent Him. You have His Spirit, His Name and His Word. You start by believing what Jesus said in John 16:23: <u>God loves you as much as He does Jesus.</u> Then, on purpose, believe what He said in John 17:26: the love wherewith He, the Father, loves Jesus is in you <u>right now!</u> It's in there. And you have been given the divine privilege of using it to meet the needs of others and to set them free.

Focus on that. I know you don't know much about it, but that's the whole point—using it develops it. It's the Holy Spirit's job, to lead and guide and teach. That's what He's been sent to do.

The problem has been that we've been so centered on our own problems and have developed such an awareness of our own failures and weakness, He hasn't had much to work with in our lives. However, when we get our eyes on Jesus—the Son of Love—and what He wants to do, we become aware of His strength and victory—not for Himself but for us. That's what the Cross was all about.

Start by <u>writing down</u> John 17:20, 23 and 26. Then pray those verses and believe the love that God, who is Love, has for you. Don't get off that step until it's settled in your heart.

Next, fix your mind on someone who needs God's love—someone you need to forgive or a person who needs God's peace. To begin with, it will be better if it's someone outside your immediate family, especially if there are problems there. After a while you can come back to your family situation, but right now that's too close to focusing on yourself, especially if that's the problem that started it all.

Now that you "see" the person in your mind's eye, pray this: "Father in heaven, show me this person the way You, in Your mercy and compassion, see them." Then hold the picture of that person in your mind and in your heart. See them raising their hands, worshiping and praising God. See them totally engulfed in Jesus' arms. Forgive them, all the time reminding yourself that Love <u>never</u> fails.

The next step is to ask the Father to show you ways to bless someone else without them knowing who blessed them. Your reward is seeing someone blessed. It doesn't have to be big. Just love. Remember all the while, the love of God in you is growing, developing, perfecting and, best of all, casting out <u>all</u> fear. Deuteronomy 10:19 says we should love strangers.

Now begin to bring it home. Don't try to preach it yet. Just do it.

Watch it work. It may take awhile but Love never fails. Even if someone else is able to resist it, it's still working in you. It will heal, provide, direct, protect and raise you up until you are victorious in every area of life.

Now comes 1 John 5:18:

> 18   We know that whosoever is born of (Love) sinneth not; but he that is begotten of (Love) keepeth himself, and that wicked one toucheth him not.

Victory! Jesus! His cross, His resurrection, His blood, His Name and His Word are our Victory.

Don't wait. Start now. It's yours. Go for it!

As you sow your financial seed this month, see it going out to deliver a sick and dying, terrified world. Hold Gloria and me, and all of us here at KCM, in your love. Our schedule is tight and there's no place to quit. Together we can do it! We love you and pray for you every day.

Love,

Ken

P.S. Don't forget to vote! Pray and obey. This is very important to the Lord Jesus right now.

MERRY Christmas!
Joy FiLLeD   The ANoinateD
HAppy   ONE AND His
FiLLeD with BurDeN Removing
Laughter   Power
            celebrate

Dear Partner

Jesus said in Matthew 16:19, "I will give unto thee the keys of the kingdom of heaven." Then in Luke 11:52, He rebuked lawyers for taking away the key of knowledge. In that verse He was referring to the written Word of God. Hebrews 4:12-13 says:

> 12   For the word of God is quick, and powerful, and sharper than any two-edged sword, piercing even to the dividing asunder of soul and spirit, and of the joints and marrow, and is a discerner of the thoughts and intents of the heart.
>
> 13   Neither is there any creature that is not manifest in his sight: but all things are naked and opened unto the eyes of him with whom we have to do.

There is no thing or situation in this earth that can hide from or outsmart the written Word of the Living God. It is THE KEY to all things, because all the key issues to every situation are covered in its pages.

Every problem situation has a key issue. Satan tries to hide those keys in order to keep his work in place. That's the reason his doings are called works of darkness. And as long as people try to solve problems by figuring them out in the natural or carnal realm, they are stumbling around in darkness. Following this process will bring disaster.

On the other hand, Psalm 119:130 says:

> 130   The entrance of thy words giveth light; it giveth understanding unto the simple.

Not only does the light of the Word reveal the real problems, but it also has within itself the power to change everything. One Word from

God can change your life forever.

Walking in the Word is the master key to successful living. Look at 1 John 2:5: "But whoso keepeth his word, in him verily is the love of God perfected: hereby know we that we are in him." And then verses 10-11:

10   He that loveth his brother abideth in the light, and there is none occasion of stumbling in him.

11   But he that hateth his brother is in darkness, and walketh in darkness, and knoweth not whither he goeth, because that darkness hath blinded his eyes.

Fear, the destroying force of evil, thrives in darkness. The thief does his work in the dark. Turn on the light and he's caught. Finished! Turn the light off and the thief comes right back in to steal, kill and destroy. "Faith cometh by hearing, and hearing by the word of God" (Romans 10:17). Choke the Word and faith becomes feeble and weak. Fear comes by hearing and hearing by the lies of satan, the thief. Let's shine the light of the Word on his operation and find the <u>key issues to the sources of fear.</u>

Of course, satan is the spirit of fear, so he is the true source of it all. But remember, he is a thief and works in the dark. He uses people, situations and things. Things that look complicated and dangerous. Incurable, unchangeable messes of destruction. However, they boil down to five basic things—all of which Jesus has defeated by the Word, by His Name and by His blood. Let's go to Mark 4:14-20:

14   The sower soweth the word.

15   And these are they by the way side, where the word is sown; but when they have heard, Satan cometh immediately, and taketh away the word that was sown in their hearts.

16   And these are they likewise which are sown on stony ground; who, when they have heard the word, immediately receive it with gladness;

17   And have no root in themselves, and so endure

but for a time: afterward, when affliction or persecution ariseth for the word's sake, immediately they are offended.

18 And these are they which are sown among thorns; such as hear the word,

19 And the cares of this world, and the deceitfulness of riches, and the lusts of other things entering in, choke the word, and it becometh unfruitful.

20 And these are they which are sown on good ground; such as hear the word, and receive it, and bring forth fruit, some thirtyfold, some sixty, and some an hundred.

Here they are:

1. Affliction = pressure
2. Persecution = to pursue—to stalk
3. Cares of this world = distraction to cause anxiety
4. Deceitfulness of riches = faith in money
5. Lusts of other things = pressure from desire of the flesh and mind

That's all satan has to work with. He works them in a lot of different, tangled-up ways, but they're still all the same. Nothing new; just the same old, same old.

All these things generate fear. But in order for them to choke the Word, a person has to make room for them. All five of these weapons of darkness came on every believer in Mark 4:14-20. However, in verse 20 we see people who stayed rooted and grounded. The seed of the Word grew in them to a place where the sources of fear could not enter in and tear down the stronghold of faith.

It comes down to this: Where is your attention? Your focus?

Faith comes by hearing. But so does fear. The choice is yours. No one else can make that choice but you. No one can have faith for you. No one can choose for you.

You have the faith. You have the hope. You have the Love. All three are abiding in you this very moment if Jesus is your Lord and Savior. He has given you His Word, His blood and His Name. Therefore, fear not! Rise up and shout, "All things are possible unto me. I'm a believer. I have the keys of the kingdom. Jesus is Lord and He loves me!" First John 4:15-16 says,

15   Whosoever shall confess that Jesus is the Son of God, God dwelleth in him, and he in God.

16   And we have known and believed the love that God hath to us. God is love; and he that dwelleth in love dwelleth in God, and God in him.

Shout it, confess it, sing it until all fear is gone. Then continue confessing it until boldness comes in to every area of your life. Strive to enter that solid state of mind brought on by faith and peace, knowing the Love of Christ that passes all human understanding.

Rest! Lie down beside still waters in green pastures, while outside the storm rages on. A fear-free, love-filled life belongs to you. Grab hold of it and don't let go. It will come to pass much sooner than you think.

Gloria and I and all of us here at KCM are on our way to the doubling of everything. We must! The kingdom of God is at hand and the time is NOW to take this glorious gospel to this fear-crazed world satan is doing his best to destroy. His best is not good enough. Jesus is Lord, and together with all of you, we will get it done. We love you and pray for you every day.

Love,

Ken

P.S. Gloria and I and all of us at KCM are joining our faith with yours for the greatest Christmas EVER—DOUBLE GOOD!

Have a Happy, Blessed and Prosperous New Year

Dear Partner

There's never been a time like this time. Reports of entire cities coming to know Jesus have come in. In one place the jail has been closed for several years.

That's what happens when Love takes over. In a very short time it will go from cities to whole nations. We're not seeing it on the TV news yet—except on Christian stations—but it's coming. The year 2003 is marked by God as a very special year. Unusual miracles in strange places will take place to the glory of God. You and I are part of the greatest thing heaven has done on the earth since the coming of the Holy Spirit on the day of Pentecost.

In this letter I want to talk to you about believing when you don't feel like it. Believing in the times when you are just too tired to even think, or when there's pain in your body and all your attention is going toward where it hurts.

These, and situations like them, are what satan looks for as he seeks whom he may devour. Have you ever watched on one of the nature channels as a big cat circles a big herd of animals? That big cat will hang around the outer perimeter of the herd looking for weakness. He knows he doesn't have a chance against that whole herd. He also knows the danger of attacking a strong, healthy animal. He's looking for a loner—one he can attack with little to no resistance. That's a picture of the devil and the way he operates.

Believing is not an act of your feelings. Faith doesn't come from your mind or your body. It doesn't come from, or because of, your emotions. It comes out of your spirit. You can release a powerful flow of faith even when you <u>feel</u> like it was a dud.

Let's look again at 1 John 4:16:

16   And we have known and believed the love that God hath to us. God is love; and he that dwelleth in love dwelleth in God, and God in him.

You <u>know</u> God loves you! He <u>is</u> love. Now <u>believe</u> the Love.

1.   Believe it's in you <u>NOW.</u>

"And now abideth faith, hope, charity, these three; but the greatest of these is charity" (1 Corinthians 13:13, *New King James Version*).

Stop and believe that right now.

2.   Believe it <u>never</u> fails.

"<u>Love never fails.</u> But whether there are prophecies, they will fail; whether there are tongues, they will cease; whether there is knowledge, it will vanish away" (1 Corinthians 13:8, *NKJV*).

Stop and believe that now. Don't argue with it. Believe it.

3.   Believe it is God.

"And Jesus answering saith unto them, <u>Have faith in God</u> [who is Love]. For verily I say unto you, That whosoever shall say unto this mountain, Be thou removed, and be thou cast into the sea; and shall not doubt in his heart, but shall believe that those things which he saith shall come to pass; he shall have whatsoever he saith" (Mark 11:22-23).

Stop and believe *God is Love and He is in me at this very moment.* <u>Say out loud, "I believe that."</u>

<u>Now turn against satan.</u> Read to him those verses you just believed. Stir yourself up. Shout them at him. He'll try to make you <u>feel</u> ashamed for shouting. That's fear—he's afraid of you. Shout it.

Stop <u>feeling</u> sorry for yourself. You're part of the most powerful body of people the world has ever seen. You're the child of the King. You're a blood covenant warrior. <u>Blood warriors never quit.</u> You are more than a conqueror through Him who loves you. He gave Himself for you and He's still giving Himself for you. He has not forsaken you and never will. You are a soldier in the army of the Lord attached by Jesus, Commander in Chief, to this ministry of faith, power and victory.

We have a whole new year of wonderful opportunities ahead of us. Opportunities to bring multitudes to a new life in Jesus. Opportunities to preach the Word to dying, sick, hurting people and see them rise up in glorious victory in Jesus.

We <u>will</u> do our job. We'll strip the fear from the Body of Christ and watch while Jesus slaps the spirit of terror flat on his face. This is our year! Victory has come!

Say it with me: "2003 belongs to me. It's my Year of Victory."

As you sow your financial seeds into the work of the ministry this month, "see" it going into the things I've just said. We're Partners. We're soldiers together, and the victory belongs to us.

Gloria and I love you and we pray for you every day.

Love,

Ken

Preaching the Word to dying, sick, hurting people and seeing them rise up in glorious victory in Jesus is made possible because of our Partners!

2003 Belongs to Me!
It's the Year of My Victory!

Dear Partner

The new year is up and running. It's here, and so is a marked increase in the anointing of the Body of Christ.

It's like the Father just turned the volume knob up—way up. There's never been a time like this before. People everywhere are ready to hear the gospel. People who a short time ago didn't have time for us are eager to listen and receive Jesus.

At the same time, some who have been around a long time are falling into sin traps satan has laid for them. His pitfalls are all around us, so it's of vital importance to stay in the Word.

It's the Word of God that lights the way. Look at Psalm 119:105: "Thy word is a lamp unto my feet, and a light unto my path."

No one would even think about driving at night without their headlights on: "Well, you see I just was so busy I didn't have time to turn them on. Besides, I figured the Lord would watch over me." If you heard someone say that after they wrecked their car while driving around in the dark, you'd think surely they had completely lost their mind. Well, it's not any more crazy to do that than to try to get by without your spiritual lights on and burning as bright as you can get them.

Let's talk about the Word of God being alive. Let's read Hebrews 4:12-13 very carefully. I know you're familiar with it, but let's go over it slowly and notice some very important things:

> 12 For the word of God is quick, and powerful, and sharper than any twoedged sword, piercing even to the dividing asunder of soul and spirit, and of the joints and marrow, and is a discerner of the thoughts and intents of the heart.

13   Neither is there any creature that is not manifest in his [the Word's] sight: but all things are naked and opened unto the eyes of him with whom we have to do.

A great number of people are battling the flu and different kinds of infections in their bodies. A viral infection is caused by a virus, which is a living thing. A bacterial infection is caused by bacteria, which are living things. Look at verse 13. Neither is there any <u>creature</u> that is so small it can hide from the living Word. However, words have to be heard and spoken in order to do what they are designed to do.

Think about it like this: What if you were sitting in your own home, and you looked up and saw a stranger come into the room? If you just sit there and say nothing and do nothing, the stranger can go about your home doing whatever he wants.

That stranger is a virus of some kind with only one thing in mind—and that's to steal, kill and destroy <u>YOU</u>! The best thing to do is to keep the Word going at all times and keep your house so well-protected that the flu and all the other "bugs" just can't get in. If they do get in though, the worst thing you could do is to try to defeat them by using medicine, etc., while completely ignoring your most powerful weapon—the living Word of God.

The Word must be first on your priority list—not somewhere down the line after you've tried everything else. "But, Brother Copeland, I was so sick I couldn't pray or do anything else." I know. That's what satan and his bug army set out to do—to shut you and your prayer life down.

Get your tape player and keep it going. Play a preaching tape on healing or the New Testament on tape. Go to sleep with it on. Keep it on all day. Turn everything else off.

I don't care how badly your body feels, talk healed. Praise God for your healing constantly. Don't praise the devil by telling everyone you talk to how sick you are. Keep praising and thanking God.

See yourself rising up against that stranger who has come into your house. Talk to that virus: "No you don't come in here. This house belongs to Jesus and me, and you cannot come in here! Now get out. NOW!" Quote the Word to him. Let the Living Word fight its own fight. Don't let up. Stay with it. Proverbs 4:20-27 is the step-by-step process:

20   My son, attend to my words; incline thine ear unto my sayings.

21   Let them not depart from thine eyes; keep them in the midst of thine heart.

22   For they *are* life unto those that find them, and health to all their flesh.

23   Keep thy heart with all diligence; for out of it *are* the issues of life.

24   Put away from thee a froward mouth, and perverse lips put far from thee.

25   Let thine eyes look right on, and let thine eyelids look straight before thee.

26   Ponder the path of thy feet, and let all thy ways be established.

27   Turn not to the right hand nor to the left: remove thy foot from evil.

It works. It is the Living Word. It is God Himself. However, it only works when it is put to work. It's never too late. Start right NOW. You are a world overcomer—so start overcoming.

Don't forget the power of sowing in a time of distress. As you sow your financial seed this month, lay your hands on it and declare it the seed for your perfect health. It never ceases to amaze me how powerful this is. I've heard Brother Oral Roberts say it so many times: "Don't ever attempt to receive anything from God without first planting a seed."

All of us here at KCM are believing with you for your greatest victories ever. Shout it: "2003 belongs to me! It's the year of my victory!" I really believe that.

Hold Gloria and me up in prayer. We're launching out in areas and ways we've never seen before. We are in the process of doubling everything. Especially the TV broadcast. Pray, Pray, Pray. Together we can do it!

We love you and pray for you every day.

Love,

Ken

"2003 Is The Year of Harvest—Everything Planted Will Come Up"

Dear Partner

What a time to be alive and serving God! There's never been a time like this before. Not in all of man's time on the earth. We have never been this close to the catching away of the Church. This is the season of the greatest harvest of souls ever, and thanks be to God, you and I are right in the middle of it all.

During the first week of January of this year, Gloria heard the Spirit of God say, "2003 is the year of harvest—everything planted will come up." She and I just shouted, and we've been shouting ever since. Now here we are finishing the first quarter of the year, and it's already very obvious that it is happening.

Let's look at some verses from the New Testament that very plainly confirm that Word. Let's read Galatians 6:6-9:

6   Let him that is taught in the word communi-
     cate unto him that teacheth in all good things.
7   Be not deceived; God is not mocked: for what-
     soever a man soweth, that shall he also reap.
8   For he that soweth to his flesh shall of the flesh
     reap corruption; but he that soweth to the
     Spirit shall of the Spirit reap life everlasting.
9   And let us not be weary in well doing: for in
     due season we shall reap, if we faint not.

In verse 6 the word *communicate* in the *King James Version* translates the Greek word meaning "to use what is common" or "to share." So it is referring to an offering, which would mean money or goods, etc. However, verse 7 broadens it to mean any kind of seed. "Whatsoever" covers anything. Good or bad. Godly or ungodly.

Later the same day Gloria heard, "I said every thing will come up in 2003." Meaning everything. Whatsoever.

Did you ever notice the weeds in a garden mature about the same time as the flowers? The junk seeds harvest at the same time as the main crop. In Matthew 13:26, Jesus said, "When the blade was sprung up, and brought forth fruit [harvest time], then appeared the tares also." Tares are darnel—a weed that looks like corn. It's no good. The no-good seed and the good seed will grow in the same soil right alongside each other. However, the bad steals moisture, light, nutrients, etc., away from the good seed. Even to the point of choking the good completely out.

The way to keep that from happening, of course, is to not sow anything but the good. Then even when you do let sin seed slip through, REPENT! Clean it out right now. It's much easier to kill it while it's a seed than to wait until it has put down roots.

The primary seeds are words. In Mark 4 Jesus taught that the Word of God is seed and it is ours to sow. However, all words are seeds and, if allowed to, they will harvest. When we sow the seed of God's Word into our lives, satan comes to steal it. When we sow the seeds of fear, doubt, unforgiveness, etc., we are the ones who must dig them up and kill them with the Word, the blood of Jesus and the Name of Jesus.

First John 1:9 says, "If we confess our sins, He [Jesus] is faithful and righteous to forgive us our sins, and to cleanse us from all unrighteousness" (New American Standard). All unrighteousness would include all bad seed sown. The problem most people have with bad word seeds is not realizing they are sin and should be destroyed.

This is particularly true in the area of love and forgiveness. To love one another is not just a good suggestion to keep when you can. It is the commandment. It's a sin to break it.

Hard, unlovely words are dangerous. They carry sickness and poverty. Not only to the people to whom they are spoken, but even more so to the one who speaks them and doesn't immediately repent and kill that seed. If allowed to go unchecked they will grow and come to harvest. This is harvest time. It's harvest time like never before. All these seeds are coming up. NOW!

Get busy! Kill those bad seeds NOW. Start watering the good seed of God's Word in your life immediately. Spend some time every day sowing the promises of the Word into your life by reading them, then speaking them. Sow seeds of love—God's love—to everyone you meet. You'll be shocked at how fast they'll mature.

As you sow your financial seed this month make sure you do so without any fear. Hold it in your hand and declare, "I am fearless in my giving. God is my source. Whom shall I fear?"

Together we are reaping the fields of God's harvest. We are glorifying the Name of the Lord of the harvest, Jesus of Nazareth, the Son of the living God.

Gloria and I love you and pray for you every day.

Love,

Ken

Fear Torments
Faith Rests

Dear Partner

It is amazing to me what our heavenly Father has done for us to protect us. Especially at times like these, when so many are trying so hard to bring pain and death through the use of fear as a weapon of terrorism. Remember, now, the definition of *terrorism*—"the planned, organized use of fear as a weapon." First John 4:18 defines fear as torment. Satan is the spirit of fear, or spirit of torment, and Jesus called evil spirits tormentors.

Torment is a place where there is <u>no</u> rest. God has given a place of rest to us. Not just after we die and go to heaven, but right here, right now.

Hebrews 4:9 says, "There remaineth therefore a rest to the people of God." This is really good news. However, just as everything else that comes from heaven, it must be received by faith. It belongs to us through Jesus and what He did for us at Calvary. The process is very simple and, as always with anything of faith, it comes through the Word of God.

The Word is separate from the world and is not affected by it in any way. Neither the world, nor our enemy satan, nor demons, nor anything of the world order can change or keep the Word from working. <u>The only thing that stops the Word is unbelief.</u> Unbelief is always fear-based. Jesus taught that in Mark 4:14-20. He taught that once the Word is sown as a seed in one's heart, only unbelief of that Word can keep it from producing a hundredfold.

Let's go to Hebrews 4:1-2 and get the rest of the story.

1   Let us therefore fear [be aware], lest, a promise being left us of entering into his rest, any of you should seem to come short of it.

2   For unto us was the gospel preached, as well as unto them: but the word preached did not

profit them, not being mixed with faith in
them that heard it.

The Word not mixed with faith brings no results. Now read verse 6:
"Seeing therefore it remaineth that some must enter therein, and they
to whom it was first preached entered not in because of unbelief." This
verse is, of course, referring to the nation of Israel in the wilderness. God
preached through Moses His Word concerning the land of promise.
When the spies or witnesses reported what they saw, only two, Joshua
and Caleb, mixed faith with the promise. The rest did not. Why? It was
not because the land was not as God said it would be. It was everything
He promised—it flowed with milk and honey. What kept them from
entering in was their fear of the giants.

Mixing faith with the Word brings rest followed by confession
and action. Mixing fear with the Word brings torment followed by
confession and action.

Rest, then confession, then action = victory.

Torment, then confession, then action = complete disaster.

Verse 11 says it all again: "Let us labour therefore to enter into that
rest, lest any man fall after the same example of unbelief." Our job is to
see to it, or labor, to enter into that rest. It is not our job to buck and run
at the first bad news or sudden danger. It is our calling to immediately
draw upon the promises of the Word of God and meditate in them until
that rest comes to stay.

I know this is easier said than done, but that's why Jesus has provided
the Holy Spirit, His Name and His blood to help. He's always right there,
whether you feel like He is or not. Anyone can do this. The sad thing is
most people won't—not that they can't, but that they just won't. That's
not you and me, however. We are people of faith and action.

The rest of Hebrews 4 tells exactly how we enter into the rest:

12   For the word of God is quick, and powerful, and
        sharper than any twoedged sword, piercing

> even to the dividing asunder of soul and spirit, and of the joints and marrow, and is a discerner of the thoughts and intents of the heart.
>
> 13 Neither is there any creature that is not manifest in his sight: but all things are naked and opened unto the eyes of him with whom we have to do.
>
> 14 Seeing then that we have a great high priest, that is passed into the heavens, Jesus the Son of God, let us hold fast our profession.
>
> 15 For we have not an high priest which cannot be touched with the feeling of our infirmities; but was in all points tempted like as we are, yet without sin.
>
> 16 Let us therefore come boldly unto the throne of grace, that we may obtain mercy, and find grace to help in time of need.

Oh, with what power and magnificent simplicity Jesus could say things! He laid all of this out to Jairus in Luke 8:49-50 when the terrible news came that his little daughter was already dead. He put it all in a four-word command: "Fear not! Believe only!" The results? "And she shall be made whole!"

Obviously Jairus did that. He didn't say a word. He had already spoken his faith when he said, "Come and lay your hand on her and she will live" (Matthew 9:18, *New King James Version*). When the bad news came, he just rested in Jesus and did exactly what Jesus said. We know what happened. That's what always happens.

God has done His part as He promised. Jesus has done His part—He ratified those promises with His own blood, then authorized you and me to use His Name and all His authority to stop satan, fear, demons, sickness and disease. Sin cannot lord it over us.

Jesus has declared us free! It is, therefore, our duty to be free. To take our stand and having done all to stand, stand therefore, fully clad with the full armor of God. Stand until the rest and peace of God comes. It will come. You have His Word on it.

My, what a message of hope this is for a terrorized, war-torn world. It's <u>our</u> message. Together we are taking it to the top of this world and to the bottom and all the way around the middle.

We're doing it! It's happening! We are doubling our outreach on TV and some awesome things are taking place because of it. I'll bring you a report on it all soon.

This is our time. Victory 2003 belongs to us!

Gloria and I love you very much and pray for you every day.

Love,

Ken

Protection in the Marketplace

Dear Partner

There have always been dangers in the marketplace, the mall, or any place where large crowds of people gather. They bring their contagious diseases and all kinds of strange, demonic behavior with them. Just by their very nature, crowds have always presented certain opportunities for satan's work, which is to steal, kill and destroy. However, now more than ever the marketplace is a dangerous place.

Have you noticed lately the "new" strains of dangerous diseases? Old-timers like the flu and pneumonia have put on new, medically untouchable faces. New kinds of infections and etc. are looming up to threaten our lives. All of this plus terrorism, too? No. All of this is terrorism. Satan is the terrorist. That is what stealing, killing and destroying adds up to—fear and terror.

For those who don't know how to take advantage of what Jesus has provided for the believer, it is a terrible, fear-filled way to live. War news every morning. Fear all day. War news every evening. Fear all night. Since 1 John 4:18 says "fear hath torment," that amounts to a life of torment which brings disaster.

Remember this:

Mixing faith with the Word brings rest, followed by confession then action = total victory.

Mixing fear with the Word brings torment, followed by confession of worry then action = total disaster.

Jesus' word of command to Jairus in Luke 8:50 is totally complete. "Fear not: believe only, and she shall be made whole!" There is no "yeah, but" or "what if" in that statement.

Let's talk about establishing our hedge of protection around ourselves and our families. The 91st Psalm is our standing promise from our heavenly Father. It depends, however, on our establishing our stand in that place of faith. Ephesians 6:11-18 <u>must</u> be acted on before what belongs to us can be manifest around us:

11   Put on the whole armour of God, that ye may be able to stand against the wiles of the devil.

12   For we wrestle not against flesh and blood, but against principalities, against powers, against the rulers of the darkness of this world, against spiritual wickedness in high places.

13   Wherefore take unto you the whole armour of God, that ye may be able to withstand in the evil day, and having done all, to stand.

14   Stand therefore, having your loins girt about with truth, and having on the breastplate of righteousness;

15   And your feet shod with the preparation of the gospel of peace;

16   Above all, taking the shield of faith, wherewith ye shall be able to quench all the fiery darts of the wicked.

17   And take the helmet of salvation, and the sword of the Spirit, which is the word of God:

18   Praying always with all prayer and supplication in the Spirit, and watching thereunto with all perseverance and supplication for all saints.

Notice that just putting on the armor is not enough. Then must come "having done all to stand, stand therefore." In verse 18, praying in one's supernatural prayer language is part of the armor and part of the standing.

Now let's look at some more verses that apply here. Let's read 1 John 4:18:

18   There is no fear in love; but perfect love casteth out fear: because fear hath torment. He that feareth is not made perfect in love.

Now Jude 20-21:

20   But ye, beloved, building up yourselves on your
        most holy faith, praying in the Holy Ghost,
21   Keep yourselves in the love of God, looking
        for the mercy of our Lord Jesus Christ unto
        eternal life.

Now 1 John 5:18:

18   We know that whosoever is born of God
        sinneth not; but he that is begotten of God
        keepeth himself [in Love], and that wicked
        one toucheth him not.

Read them all now, one after the other—together as one. Glory to God! Do you see that? Read them again and again. Now do it. Take the armor. Make the stand. Fear not, believe only. And you will be made whole. If that weren't enough, read Isaiah 54:14-15:

14   In righteousness shalt thou be established:
        thou shalt be far from oppression; for thou
        shalt not fear: and [far] from terror; for it shall
        not come near thee.
15   Behold, they shall surely gather together, but
        not by me: whosoever shall gather together
        against thee shall fall for thy sake.

There it is again.

Now close the deal with the Blood. Take Communion. Read all these scriptures out loud, then drink the whole cupful: Romans 3:24, 5:9; Ephesians 1:7; Hebrews 10:19-20, 13:12, 20-21; Revelation 1:5 and 12:11. See yourself seated at the table with Jesus and His disciples: "And he took the cup, and gave thanks, and gave it to them, saying, Drink ye all of it; for this is my blood of the new testament, which is shed for many for the remission of sins" (Matthew 26:27-28).

Read these words of the new covenant in His Blood out loud again, only this time hear Jesus' voice in your voice speaking to you:

You have been made righteous freely by My grace through the redemption that is in Me (Romans 3:24). *Being now righteous by My Blood, you shall be saved from wrath through Me* (Romans 5:9). *Through My Blood, you have redemption, the forgiveness of sins, according to the riches of My grace* (Ephesians 1:7).

Therefore boldly enter into the holiest by My Blood, by this new and living way, which I have consecrated for you, through the veil, that is to say, My flesh (Hebrews 10:19-20). *It was in order to sanctify you with My own Blood that I suffered outside the gate* (Hebrews 13:12).

Now the God of peace, who brought Me—the Great Shepherd of the Sheep—again from the dead through the Blood of the everlasting covenant, make you perfect in every good work to do His will, working in you that which is well-pleasing in His sight, through Me and My Anointing (Hebrews 13:20-21).

I—the faithful witness, and the first begotten of the dead, and the Prince of the kings of the earth—love you and have washed you from your sins in My own Blood (Revelation 1:5). *Therefore, do not love your life unto the death, but overcome the devil—the accuser of the brethren—by My Blood, and by the word of your testimony* (Revelation 12:11).

Take your time. You're settling something.

In the future when you declare, "I plead the Blood of Jesus," you will <u>know</u> what you're talking about. So will the devil. "Faith cometh by hearing and hearing by the Word of God." Your faith in the Blood brings faith in the Name of Jesus. It also builds faith in the Word, which builds faith in the Blood, which builds faith in the Name, which builds faith in the Blood, which builds faith in the Word and so on and so on and so on and...

Instead of beginning the day on fear news, start off on the Blood. Instead of going to bed at night on fear, let the Blood promises be the last thing on your mind. Stay inside the hedge of protection. Do this as a family. Talk about it together. <u>A lot!!</u>

Read Psalm 91 and declare your place in the secret place of the <u>Most</u> <u>High</u> God, who is also your Father. Cry out, "I have a Father. I have a Daddy! I'm <u>supposed</u> to be protected. I'm <u>supposed</u> to prosper. I'm <u>supposed</u> to be well. I'm a believer. I'm not a doubter."

All of this is wonderful, but it won't accomplish a thing if you don't take the time and effort to establish yourself in it. Do it. <u>Do it now.</u> We are in this together. The victory is ours!

There is no way to express to you in a letter how much Gloria and I love and appreciate you. There is a bond in the Spirit that gets sweeter day by day. The Blood, the Name and the Word do that. Not only do she and I feel that way, but our whole family and our ministry family do also. We love you and pray for you every day.

Love,

Ken

Partner, you are one in a million! Together we are preaching this gospel from the top of the world to the bottom and all the way around the middle!

Let Not Your Heart Be Troubled

Dear Partner

Let's begin by reading Matthew 24:1-7. Don't just skim through these verses. Read them slowly and carefully, and think about what Jesus is saying:

1 And Jesus went out, and departed from the temple: and his disciples came to him for to show him the buildings of the temple.

2 And Jesus said unto them, See ye not all these things? verily I say unto you, There shall not be left here one stone upon another, that shall not be thrown down.

3 And as he sat upon the mount of Olives, the disciples came unto him privately, saying, Tell us, when shall these things be? and what shall be the sign of thy coming, and of the end of the world?

4 And Jesus answered and said unto them, Take heed that no man deceive you.

5 For many shall come in my name, saying, I am Christ; and shall deceive many.

6 And ye shall hear of wars and rumours of wars: see [to it] that ye be not troubled: for all these things must come to pass, but the end is not yet.

7 For nation shall rise against nation, and kingdom against kingdom: and there shall be famines, and pestilences, and earthquakes, in divers places.

Notice what He said in verse 6: <u>See to it</u> that you do not allow wars and rumors of wars to trouble you. Don't let the bad news get to you. If He said see to it, then it's our responsibility. However, He did not leave us to have to attempt to see to it on our own strength. Jesus also said in John 14:1, "Let not your heart be troubled: ye believe in God, believe also in me." In this verse He makes it plain that He has provided the way to keep our hearts from being troubled.

Let's go back to the root of trouble. Trouble is a form of torment. That's one of the meanings of the word *trouble*. "Let not your heart be tormented" means the same thing.

First John 4:18 always jerks the cover off trouble, worry and torment of any kind. Fear! Fear must be present for trouble to be present. That verse solves the problem. Let's read it: "There is no fear in love; but perfect love casteth out fear: because fear hath torment. He that feareth is not made perfect in love." Perfected, or growing, developing love casts fear out. The trouble, the worry, the pressure all leaves with the fear.

Let's go back to Matthew 24 and look at verse 14: "And this gospel of the kingdom shall be preached in all the world for a witness unto all nations; and then shall the end come." Someone is going to fearlessly preach the gospel of the kingdom right in the middle of all this trouble. That's us. You and me!

But where does the strength to do all this come from? Verse 35 is the key that gives anyone the super strength, super peace, super joy and super whatever else it takes in the midst of all this hell on earth you and I are witnessing: "Heaven and earth shall pass away, but my words shall not pass away."

We choose the Word. In every situation, large or small, the Word of our God must be final authority. All of this is going to turn out exactly like our heavenly Father has already said—WE WIN!

Psalm 119:89-90: "For ever, O Lord, thy word is settled in heaven. Thy faithfulness is unto all generations: thou hast established the earth, and it abideth." His Word is settled in heaven. It's going to be that way. Therefore His Word is settled in my heart. It's that way and none other. I don't care how things look. It doesn't matter how things sound. I know how things are.

When bad news comes, it's time to stand and declare: "My Father loves me. His Word says in Psalm 37:18-19: 'The Lord knoweth the days of the upright: and their inheritance shall be for ever. They shall not be ashamed in the evil time: and in the days of famine they shall be satisfied.'"

Put those words in your mouth and keep them there. Don't let the deceivers (newscasters, etc.) or anyone else lead you off your faith. You stay with Jesus. Keep your heart in agreement with what is already settled in heaven.

Look at 2 Thessalonians 2:1-3: "Now we beseech you, brethren, by the coming of our Lord Jesus Christ, and by our gathering together unto him, That ye be not soon shaken in mind, or be troubled, neither by spirit, nor by word, nor by letter as from us, as that the day of Christ is at hand. Let no man deceive you by any means."

And Philippians 1:27-28: "...that whether I come and see you, or else be absent, I may hear of your affairs, that ye stand...in nothing terrified by your adversaries: which is to them an evident token of perdition, but to you of salvation, and that of God."

We have a choice to make. Fix our minds on Jesus or trouble, the Word or circumstances, what God has said or what "they" say.

There are two things that <u>must</u> come to pass according to Jesus. One is all these things—the wars and all the other sorrows we are witnessing—and the other is the preaching of the gospel until the end. It's the gospel of Jesus and His Love and anointing that will end it, not the trouble!

Get even more involved with the gospel. Preach it, teach it, support it, love it, think it, live it night and day. Romans 1:16 says it is the power of God. Ephesians 6:15 says our feet must be shod with it—walking in that power. In 2 Corinthians 4:4 it's called the <u>glorious</u> gospel. <u>Walking</u> in power <u>and</u> glory. Living like this leaves no room or time for trouble. Trouble begins to back away as fear flees from the power of His glory. That's who you are—a glory child of God, joint heir with Jesus.

Take your stand and don't let your heart be troubled, neither let it be afraid.

Now's a good time to shout, "I'm one in a million. I'm a Partner with Kenneth and Gloria. We're preaching this gospel from the top of the world to the bottom and all the way around the middle!"

Gloria and I love you and pray for you every day.

Love,

Ken

We Are <u>MORE</u> Than Conquerors!

Dear Partner

Never before, in my lifetime at least, has there been such worldwide terror and unrest. Even during World War II, the enemy wore a uniform and came from a certain place. For the most part, he was easily identified and it was obvious when he was defeated.

Now it seems as though the terrorists have the upper hand. Don't you believe it! Not for one second! I know it seems that way when you watch the news on TV, but they know so little. Our leaders, both military and civilian, know far more than the media, and they are not telling what they know. Thank God for that.

The thing that is <u>so</u> <u>important</u> for us to remember is that God knows every one of our enemies. No matter where, or how deep, they go in an attempt to hide, they cannot hide from God. We <u>must</u> keep our faith active and strong in this truth. Our faith is God's connection in the earth. It's when we take our stand as the people of faith that God's knowledge and wisdom is released. That's our advantage.

God is in the middle of this war. It's His battle and our victory. The <u>nation</u> of Islam has attacked Jesus. Christians and Jews are the object of their hatred which is inspired by the devil himself. He hates Jesus! That means he hates us. However that also means he's the loser—defeated forever.

Every time he has ever attacked Jesus personally, he has lost big time. In his first attack he was kicked out of heaven along with all the angels that followed him. The next time in the wilderness he was defeated by the written Word. The third time was at Calvary. When Jesus was resurrected from death and hell, satan lost it all. Jesus said only moments after He was raised up, "<u>All</u> <u>authority</u> has been given to me both in heaven and in earth."

Now satan is trying to make a comeback by openly attacking the

Body of Christ and Israel at the same time. His defeat this time is to our credit and will overflow into an even greater move of God than what is happening now.

Victory in Iraq is far more important to Jesus and the Body of Christ than anyone really knows. It had to come to pass, and He's not through there yet. The end-time arrangement of the nations is taking place and it's all in our favor.

Don't turn loose in the spirit of that victory. Military victory was only the first step. The next step is to be won in the spirit realm. That victory is by the Word of God—not only praying according to the Word but also by the preaching of the Word. There are already spiritual troops in there and God is sending more. People who know Jesus. Spirit-filled, faith-empowered believers who are not afraid to preach the Word in power. Fearless operators in the Holy Ghost.

We are listening for our orders and instructions. TV, books and everything else we can send—including ourselves—are being prepared. It's time to pray. It's time to listen. It's time to obey. It is <u>not</u> time to fear.

Doors are already open and even more are beginning to open all over that part of the world. The victories that are won in the spirit realm are the only ones that last. Especially in the Middle East. That's the heart of the war. That's the real battleground. Win there and the rest of the so-called "hard spots" will fall in line.

Pray for Gloria and me and all of this ministry. Hold all of our other Partners up before the throne of Grace. <u>We are all in this together as a team.</u> If we pray as a team, believe as a team, then obey as a team, we are unstoppable. Failure is not an option. Losing is unacceptable. Jesus is Lord. His Word will <u>NEVER</u> pass away.

Remember what we learned last month from Psalm 119:89: "For ever, O Lord, thy word is settled in heaven." Get on the Word. Line your heart and mouth up with what is already settled in heaven.

Make up your heart and mind that Jesus is the champion and His victory belongs to you and me. Together we can do anything He needs us to do. We are <u>more</u> than conquerors through Him who loved us and loves us now. That love casts out all fear of defeat.

Rise up and shout. Your breakthrough is <u>NOW.</u>

Gloria and I love you and pray for you every day.

Love,

Ken

P.S. I am enclosing a copy of the 8th chapter of Romans. Carry it with you. Read it at least twice a day. Notice the last verse. No one can separate you from the <u>LOVE</u> of <u>GOD.</u> Read this chapter out loud until it gets down deep inside your spirit and overflows into your mind. You have nothing to fear! Let me know in a few days the results from reading this chapter twice a day, every day. —Ken

I Am MORE Than a Conqueror Through Him Who Loves Me! Romans 8

1   There is therefore now no condemnation to them which are in Christ Jesus, who walk not after the flesh, but after the Spirit.

2   For the law of the Spirit of life in Christ Jesus hath made me free from the law of sin and death.

3   For what the law could not do, in that it was weak through the flesh, God sending his own Son in the likeness of sinful flesh, and for sin, condemned sin in the flesh:

4   That the righteousness of the law might be fulfilled in us, who walk not after the flesh, but after the Spirit.

5   For they that are after the flesh do mind the things of the flesh; but they that are after the Spirit the things of the Spirit.

6   For to be carnally minded is death; but to be spiritually minded is life and peace.

7   Because the carnal mind is enmity against God: for it is not subject to the law of God, neither indeed can be.

8   So then they that are in the flesh cannot please God.

9   But ye are not in the flesh, but in the Spirit, if so be that the Spirit of God dwell in you. Now if any man have not the Spirit of Christ, he is none of his.

10   And if Christ be in you, the body is dead because of sin; but the Spirit is life because of righteousness.

11   But if the Spirit of him that raised up Jesus from the dead dwell in you, he that raised up Christ from the dead shall also quicken your mortal bodies by his Spirit that dwelleth in you.

12   Therefore, brethren, we are debtors, not to the flesh, to live after the flesh.

13 For if ye live after the flesh, ye shall die: but if ye through the Spirit do mortify the deeds of the body, ye shall live.

14 For as many as are led by the Spirit of God, they are the sons of God.

15 For ye have not received the spirit of bondage again to fear; but ye have received the Spirit of adoption, whereby we cry, Abba, Father.

16 The Spirit itself beareth witness with our spirit, that we are the children of God:

17 And if children, then heirs; heirs of God, and joint-heirs with Christ; if so be that we suffer with him, that we may be also glorified together.

18 For I reckon that the sufferings of this present time are not worthy to be compared with the glory which shall be revealed in us.

19 For the earnest expectation of the creature waiteth for the manifestation of the sons of God.

20 For the creature was made subject to vanity, not willingly, but by reason of him who hath subjected the same in hope,

21 Because the creature itself also shall be delivered from the bondage of corruption into the glorious liberty of the children of God.

22 For we know that the whole creation groaneth and travaileth in pain together until now.

23 And not only they, but ourselves also, which have the firstfruits of the Spirit, even we ourselves groan within ourselves, waiting for the adoption, to wit, the redemption of our body.

24 For we are saved by hope: but hope that is seen is not hope: for what a man seeth, why doth he yet hope for?

25 But if we hope for that we see not, then do we with patience wait for it.

26 Likewise the Spirit also helpeth our infirmities: for we know not what we should pray for as we ought: but the Spirit itself maketh

intercession for us with groanings which cannot be uttered.

27 And he that searcheth the hearts knoweth what is the mind of the Spirit, because he maketh intercession for the saints according to the will of God.

28 And we know that all things work together for good to them that love God, to them who are the called according to his purpose.

29 For whom he did foreknow, he also did predestinate to be conformed to the image of his Son, that he might be the firstborn among many brethren.

30 Moreover whom he did predestinate, them he also called: and whom he called, them he also justified: and whom he justified, them he also glorified.

31 What shall we then say to these things? If God be for us, who can be against us?

32 He that spared not his own Son, but delivered him up for us all, how shall he not with him also freely give us all things?

33 Who shall lay any thing to the charge of God's elect? It is God that justifieth.

34 Who is he that condemneth? It is Christ that died, yea rather, that is risen again, who is even at the right hand of God, who also maketh intercession for us.

35 Who shall separate us from the love of Christ? shall tribulation, or distress, or persecution, or famine, or nakedness, or peril, or sword?

36 As it is written, For thy sake we are killed all the day long; we are accounted as sheep for the slaughter.

37 Nay, in all these things we are more than conquerors through him that loved us.

38 For I am persuaded, that neither death, nor life, nor angels, nor principalities, nor powers, nor things present, nor things to come,

39 Nor height, nor depth, nor any other creature, shall be able to separate us from the love of God, which is in Christ Jesus our Lord.

Pay Attention! Shut Up! And Fear Not!

Dear Partner

A few days ago while reading the Word in Isaiah I came across something in chapter 7 that really caught my attention. The armies of Syria and Ephraim were joining together to come against Judah. When word of this new alliance came, verse 2 says the hearts of King Ahaz and of his people were moved as the trees of the wood are moved with the wind. Things were not looking good at all.

Now verses 3-4:

> 3   Then said the Lord unto Isaiah, Go forth now to meet Ahaz, thou, and Shear-jashub thy son, at the end of the conduit of the upper pool in the highway of the fuller's field;
>
> 4   And say unto him, Take heed, and be quiet; fear not, neither be fainthearted....

He said <u>take heed,</u> or <u>pay attention.</u> <u>Be quiet,</u> <u>or shut up.</u> And then <u>fear not.</u> I suddenly realized that this is the way of victory.

First of all, pay attention. There's more to paying attention than just listening. The word *pay* is a good explanation of take heed. To *take heed* is to be serious about giving your attention. To *pay out* means to expect something in return.

Casual, halfhearted listening does not produce faith. Faith cometh by <u>hearing</u> and hearing by the Word of God. To pay something out expecting something in return is an on-purpose transaction. When I pay I <u>expect</u> to receive what I paid for. In this context I am exchanging my determined attention, expecting faith to be the result of what I hear.

I learned many years ago that, if I made a quality decision <u>before</u> going into a service, nothing by any means could distract me from hearing what the Spirit of God had to say to me. It amazed me how much greater the depth of my understanding was when I purposely "paid" my attention to hear.

I began to realize that my attention was my seed and I was harvesting or gleaning faith and direction for my life. I began to do this every time I listened to a tape or read my Bible. My attention mixed with my faith brought greater understanding. Faith cometh! That's when acting on the Word becomes so much easier.

The next thing He said to Ahaz was "be quiet." Hush. Shut up. No one can learn and talk at the same time. When you talk you are saying what you already know. To learn more, close your mouth and open your ears. This is true with anyone, but it is especially true with God.

Rufus Moseley, a powerful man of God, wrote that he realized while praying one day he wasn't receiving a thing. Then it dawned on him: *Here lies a fool doing all the talking to Someone who knows everything.* He wasn't paying attention. He was talking.

I remember when that same thing happened to me in December 1966. Gloria and I had just moved kids and all to Tulsa, Oklahoma, to go to Oral Roberts University. No money. Nothing. Just questions. *What do I do now? How long will I be here?* I was so frustrated that I finally locked myself in the bedroom and fell on my face and began crying all the questions out to God: "Why did You send me here? What? Why? Where? When? Oh me!" In the middle of all that, fear just became worse and the problems seemed to grow like giant thunderstorms on a spring afternoon. Then the dark clouds began to loom overhead. "Oh, woe is me...."

Then, suddenly, the thought came into my mind, *I'm not learning a thing. I wonder what would happen if I just got real quiet and just listened. Do you suppose the Lord would speak to me?* Without realizing it I began to pay attention. Then I heard plainly in my spirit, *Well, it's about time. I haven't been able to get a word in edgewise. Get up on your feet.* I stood to attention and heard, *I sent you here and I'll take care of you here.*

From that day until now I have never doubted whether or not I was called to do what He sent me to do. I wish I had known Isaiah

7:4, but thank God for His patience. He got this powerful process over to me anyway. Most parents know that a child's attention is the most important part of raising a child up in the way that he should go. Without it, it's a losing game.

The next thing He said to Ahaz was "fear not." In verse 9 He said, "If you believe not you will not be established." In other words you can't win.

That's exactly what Jesus said to Jairus in Luke 8:50: "Fear not: believe only, and she <u>shall</u> be made whole." Did you ever notice that once Jairus spoke his faith to Jesus, he never said another word. He paid attention to every word Jesus said and kept his eyes on what He did. He paid attention. He shut up. And he refused to fear. Victory was his.

Think about all the "yeah-buts" and "what-ifs" he could have come up with when he heard those devastating words: "Your daughter is dead." He could have burst out in grief crying, "My baby's dead. Oh Jesus, why did You take so much time with that issue of blood woman. Couldn't she have waited until You finished ministering to my little girl?"

"Jairus, fear not! Believe only! She shall be made whole!" But what if he hadn't heard that? What if he had been crying and "praying" and shouting his fear and grief? "Oh, I'll never see my baby again. Oh, what will I do now? My life is ruined. Over." And walked way from Jesus never hearing heaven's life-giving command?

Pay attention.

Shut up.

Fear not.

Then finally, in Isaiah 7:4, "Neither be fainthearted."

Quit being a chicken. Act like a believer. Second Peter 1:5 says, "And besides all this giving all diligence, add to your faith virtue." One translation says to add *moral energy*. The most revealing translation of this verse says do what a hero would do. Not because you're trying to look good, but because faith demands action. You're not a chicken.

You're an eagle. You are not a barnyard cackler that can't get off the ground. You are a mighty <u>bird of prey.</u> You are the joint heir of Jesus, <u>the Lion of the tribe of Judah!</u> Now act like it.

Together we are going into dangerous and dark places and taking the light of the gospel to frightened, hurting people. We are tearing down fear and bringing faith through the gospel. What a team we are. Jesus, you, Gloria, me, and all of this great KCM team of eagles.

As you sow your financial seeds this month, do so in this process to victory. Take your seed in your hands and go before the Lord Jesus and bless Him with it. Sow it. Then pay attention. Be quiet. Fear not. He will not only bless you, but He will also direct you. Then fly like an eagle. Do what He says.

Fear not, believe only, and you shall be whole.

Gloria and I love you very much. We pray for you every day.

Love,

Ken

Faith Is Connected to Righteousness
Fear Is Connected to Sin

Dear Partner

Have you ever wondered how Jesus kept from sinning?

Have you ever thought: *If faith works, and I know it does, why doesn't more happen when I pray?*

These questions and many more like them need to be answered. Faith does work. The Word works. Everything Jesus did for us on the cross worked. Everything He bought and paid for with His precious blood works. Healing always comes. Salvation always comes. We <u>are</u> the righteousness of God. <u>NOW!</u> Not later on sometime in heaven. <u>NOW!</u>

So where is the problem?

Let's go back to the beginning of the problem. Romans 5:12 shows us the order in which things happened:

> 12   Wherefore, as by one man sin entered into the world, and death by sin; and so death passed upon all men, for that all have sinned.

Sin came into the world, and death by sin, so death passed upon all men. Now let's go to Hebrews 2:14-15:

> 14   Forasmuch then as the children are partakers of flesh and blood, he also himself likewise took part of the same; that through death he might destroy him that had the power of death, that is, the devil;
> 15   And deliver them who through <u>fear of death</u> were all their lifetime subject to bondage.

There's the problem in a nutshell. Sin came into the world. Death followed sin. Fear followed death. Sin, death and fear are always connected. One activates the other. Now let's look at Romans 8:2:

> 2   For the law of the Spirit of life in Christ Jesus hath
> made me free from the law of sin and death.

THANK GOD! The Blood, the Name, the Word of Jesus has delivered us from that awful process—sin, death, fear and all the bondages associated with it. Romans 6:18 shouts at us from the empty tomb:

> 18   BEING THEN MADE FREE FROM SIN, YE BE-
> CAME THE SERVANTS OF RIGHTEOUSNESS.

We are free from sin. That means free from death and its threat, therefore free from fear.

The key word in all this for you and me as born-again believers is "fear." We stand firm against sin in all of its forms. We rebuke death with everything in us.

For the most part, however, fear has been treated lightly as though it didn't matter one way or another. It does matter. God has not given us the spirit of fear. That's easy to understand. God did not give us sin. Therefore He did not give us death. Therefore He did not give us fear. Second Timothy 1:7 backs that up:

> 7   For God hath not given us the spirit of fear;
> but of power, and of love, and of a sound mind.

First John 4:16 says that God is Love and verse 18 that there is no fear in Love (God). God has no fear in Him because there's no death in Him because there's no sin in Him.

Now back to our questions: "How did Jesus keep from sinning and why are there not more results when I pray?" Jesus answered these questions in John 15:7-12:

> 7   If ye abide in me, and my words abide in you,
> ye shall ask what ye will, and it shall be done
> unto you.

8   Herein is my Father glorified, that ye bear much fruit; so shall ye be my disciples.

9   As the Father hath loved me, so have I loved you: continue ye in my love.

10   If ye keep my commandments, ye shall abide in my love; even as I have kept my Father's commandments, and abide in his love.

11   These things have I spoken unto you, that my joy might remain in you, and that your joy might be full.

12   This is my commandment, That ye love one another, as I have loved you.

Look at verse 10. He stayed in the center of Love, where there is no sin, death or fear. He has made a way for us to do the very same thing by keeping the <u>commandment</u> of Love. In doing so, we develop spiritually into strong people of faith. That developing or "perfecting love" casts out fear. The result of that process is "ask what you will and it <u>shall</u> be done unto you."

In closing I'll make this statement. Every thing Jesus did for us on the cross and everything He is doing for us NOW as Head of the Church works if fear is not there to stop it.

When fear is present, it works all the time to bring sin and death. <u>Don't confuse fear with fright.</u> Many people have the idea that fear is not present unless they are frightened. No. Fright is the result of fear, just as worry is the result of fear, torment is the result of fear, jealousy is the result of fear, unforgiveness is the result of fear, sickness is the result of fear and doubt is the result of fear.

All sin is selfish and all selfishness is fear dependent. Fear will not just go away. It has to be removed. Once it is removed, it has to be kept out and away through the Word.

Faith is connected to righteousness.

Fear is connected to sin.

Righteousness is connected to life.

Sin is connected to death.

All of this is the reason Jesus issued a commandment, not a suggestion. John 15:12 and 1 John 3:23 state this commandment very clearly: Believe on the Name of Jesus the Anointed and love one another even as He has loved us. That is a standing order to the Church and a direct order to every individual. To disobey a direct order is insubordination—SIN! Keeping that order at all times keeps the divine process alive. Loving develops, or perfects, love. Fear is cast out and kept out. Faith is not contaminated. And the joy of the Lord is present. The joy of the Lord is our strength. No wonder 1 John 5:18 says boldly that keeping ourselves in love stops sin and the wicked one touches us not.

Our commandment is a freedom order. It's an order that produces a fear-free lifestyle. The results of that are absolutely stunning—heaven having its way completely in our lives. It is the work of the Lord, and it's marvelous in our eyes.

Stand up and shout, "I'm free!" Free from the law of sin and death. Take your stand for keeping and obeying orders and standing against fear, sin and death.

These are the greatest days of God's glory on earth in the history of this planet. Throw yourself into it. Pray. Act on the Word. Develop the passion to love people. Together we are taking this fear-free message to a weak but eager Body of Christ throughout the world. Fear not! Believe only! And you shall be made whole.

Gloria and I love you and pray for you every day.

Love,

Ken

In His Presence Is Fullness of Joy

Dear Partner

The key word in this letter is "fullness."

We could be called the "fullness generation."

If time were a cup, its days would be full. Things are being <u>ful</u>filled on every hand. Galatians 4:4 says that God sent Jesus to the earth when the fullness of time was come.

Well, the fullness of time has come for Him to be sent again. It is also time for the Holy Spirit to manifest Jesus through His Body to this world in fullness.

We've never seen the ministry anointings of the apostle, prophet, evangelist, pastor and teacher in their full manifestation. Not even in Jesus when He was on the earth. He said that a time was coming when His Body on the earth would do even greater works because He was going to the Father.

We've never seen the gifts of the Spirit, listed in 1 Corinthians 12: 1-11, in fullness. Full manifestation would be <u>ALL</u> He is able to do! That's Ephesians 3:20:

> 20   Now unto him that is able to do exceeding abundantly above all that we ask or think, <u>according to the power that worketh in us.</u>

We haven't yet seen Jesus do beyond what we can ask or <u>think</u>—but we are about to. We are, however, in the beginning of it now. It's <u>time!</u>

Let's read some eye-opening verses of Scripture.

John 1:16:

16   And of his fulness have all we received, and grace for grace.

Ephesians 1:10:

10   That in the dispensation of the fulness of times he might gather together in one all things in Christ, both which are in heaven, and which are on earth; even in him.

Ephesians 1:23:

23   [The Church] which is his body, the fulness of him that filleth all in all.

Colossians 2:9-10:

9   For in him dwelleth all the fulness of the Godhead bodily.

10   And ye are complete in him [and in His Anointing], which is the head of all principality and power.

We, the Body of Jesus, are the fullness of Him in this earth!

Why haven't there been more full manifestations among us before now? Is God just now finally ready to bring these things to pass? No. A hundred times no! He's been ready since the day Jesus was raised from the dead. He has been waiting on us. We're not waiting on Him. He has been willing all the time.

Let's go to 1 Corinthians 12 and look at the nine ways the Holy Spirit manifests Himself in the earth:

7   But the manifestation of the Spirit is given to each one for the profit of all:

8   for to one is given the word of wisdom through the Spirit, to another the word of knowledge through the same Spirit,

9   to another faith by the same Spirit, to another
        gifts of healings by the same Spirit,
10   to another the working of miracles, to another
        prophecy, to another discerning of spirits, to
        another different kinds of tongues, to another
        the interpretation of tongues.
11   But one and the same Spirit works all these
        things, distributing to each one individually as
        He wills *(New King James Version).*

Now let's look at chapter 13:1-3:

1   Though I speak with the tongues of men and
        of angels, but have not love, I have become
        sounding brass or a clanging cymbal.
2   And though I have the gift of prophecy, and
        understand all mysteries and all knowledge, and
        though I have all faith, so that I could remove
        mountains, but have not love, I am nothing.
3   And though I bestow all my goods to feed the
        poor, and though I give my body to be burned,
        but have not love, it profits me nothing *(New
        King James Version).*

Remember, now, 1 John 4:16: "God is Love." The Holy Spirit is God.
Without Love, who is God, these are not manifestations of the Holy
Spirit. They are manifestations of men. Powerless.

Now remember 1 John 4:18:

18   There is no fear in love; but perfect love
        casteth out fear: because fear hath torment.
        He that feareth is not made perfect in love.

Without Love (God) there is nothing to cast out fear. Fear is
connected to death. Death is connected to sin. Sin is the blocker
of blessings—it's anti-Christ, or anti-anointing. All of the gifts or
manifestations of the Holy Spirit are anointings. They all remove
burdens and destroy yokes. That explains Ephesians 3:17-19:

17   That Christ may dwell in your hearts by faith;
     that ye, being rooted and grounded in love,
18   May be able to comprehend with all saints
     what is the breadth, and length, and depth,
     and height;
19   And to know the love of Christ, which passeth
     knowledge, that ye might be filled with all the
     fulness of God.

No one can comprehend the anointings and manifestations of the Holy Spirit, who is Love, without being rooted and grounded in Love. Now let's go back to 1 Corinthians 13 and read verse 8:

8   Love never fails. But whether there are
    prophecies, [without love] they will fail;
    whether there are tongues, [without love]
    they will cease; whether there is knowledge,
    [without love] it will vanish away *(New Kings
    James Version)*.

Now verse 11:

11   When I was a child, I spake as a child, I under-
     stood as a child, I thought as a child: but when I
     became a man, I put away childish things.

He's talking about still thinking selfishly as children do. But after being rooted and grounded in Love, I put away selfishness. I earnestly desire Love to manifest Himself in fullness of glory, totally destroying the yokes the devil has used to steal, kill and destroy. Jesus in full manifestation! Doing exceeding abundantly beyond all we can ask or think!

Where do we go from here? What's the next step for us, the Body? <u>Repent for not keeping the commandment Jesus issued to the Church.</u> It is a direct order.

1 John 3:23-24:

23 And this is his commandment, That we should believe on the name of his Son Jesus Christ, and love one another, as he gave us commandment.

24 And he that keepeth his commandments dwelleth in him, and he in him. And hereby we know that he abideth in us, by the Spirit which he hath given us.

Then repent for allowing fear to remain part of our lives. Fear is not OK. It is sin.

Then commit to 1 John 2:5-6: "Whoso keepeth his [commandment] in him verily is the love of God perfected: hereby know we that we are in him. He that saith he abideth in him ought himself also so to walk [in His commandment], <u>even</u> as he walked [in His Father's commandment]." Receive it as a direct order. That's what it is. To disobey it is insubordination, or willful disobedience to higher authority. IT IS SIN.

I cannot stress strongly enough how very important and how serious this is. People are dying because of it. The time to get it straightened out is NOW.

The next step is glorious! We're on our way to the fullness of God. Fullness of Love. Fullness of miracles. Fullness of healing power. Fullness of soul-winning anointings. Fullness of abundance of finances to take to this hurting, dying world.

God is ready now. He will have a people who will obey. Why? So the whole earth can be <u>filled</u> with His Glory so His house will be <u>filled</u> with His children so Jesus can call us to Himself!

You and I are Partners in this. We are that PEOPLE. We are Love people, faith people, miracle people, healing people, prosperity abundance people. We are the Body of Jesus in this earth going to <u>all</u> the world with the Word of His Love. <u>Together we will get it done!</u>

We have had the greatest meetings and conventions this year we've ever had. Fullness is happening all around us.

Come get in it with us. The best is yet to come. Gloria and I love you and we pray for you every day.

Love,

"What a life this man lived before us! He lived by faith. He lived it in such a stable and steady manner that there was no mistaking what he was doing. Whatever the question asked, the answer was, 'Walk by faith. What does the Word say? Then that's the answer.'

And make no mistake about it, we are answering every question the same way: If God said it, then believe it and walk by faith."

—*Kenneth Copeland*

The Day of Salvation
The Time of the Double

Dear Partner

This is the day of salvation. In fact, it's the greatest day of salvation in the history of the human race. To be called by God to assist Him in such a great time is just awesome.

The day I am writing this letter is the day of the home-going of Kenneth E. Hagin—one of God's greatest prophets. His ministry spanned almost 70 years. There is no nation on earth that has not been touched in some way by the revelation of Jesus and His Holy Word that Brother Hagin brought to the Body of Christ.

In November 1966, Oral Roberts laid hands on Gloria and me during a meeting on the ORU campus. At that moment, the original anointing for this ministry came on us. I immediately enrolled as an ORU student and began classes in January of 1967. I know that you and all our Partners know the story of how I came to be part of the Oral Roberts Evangelistic Association team and how this ministry grew out of that experience.

Just a few days after we moved to Tulsa, my mother gave us our first tape by Brother Hagin. On one side was "You Can Have What You Say," and on the other, "Paul's Revelation." That tape absolutely revolutionized our lives.

Suddenly the integrity of the written Word became totally real to me. If the Book said it, it was true. It hit me like a freight train—this Book is God's <u>Word,</u> His <u>bond.</u> He's behind every word of it.

Over the next five months we were caught up by the Holy Spirit into the most awesome time of training one can imagine. Because of my job with OREA I was in every meeting Brother Roberts preached. I was also his driver. I was assigned to assist him as he laid hands on people in what was called the invalid room—the place where he ministered to the sick and infirm who were so far gone they could not manage the prayer line.

I saw miracles and healings take place that were absolutely awesome. Marvelous things happened, and I was there to witness them firsthand.

Every moment—and I mean every moment—I was not in the meetings or sleeping, I was listening to Brother Hagin on tape. Then as soon as the meetings were over, it was back to school for me. I was studying Bible courses by day and listening to tapes by night. No TV. No newspapers. Just the Word. The anointings on these two ministries began to merge into one glorious image of Jesus. Jesus the Healer. Jesus the Redeemer. Jesus the Lord, head of the Body of Christ. The hope of my calling and the vision of this ministry was born and exploded in Gloria and me during those intense, wonderful days.

The greatest thing that took such a fast hold of my spirit can be expressed in one word: reality. "These things are real," I remember saying over and over. We really are redeemed. The Word really is God speaking. This is not just religion. It's reality. I remember the titles of Brother Hagin's taped messages were "The Reality of Redemption." "The Reality of the Integrity of the Word." "The Reality of Righteousness." "Fellowship With the Father." "The Authority of the Believer"—oh my, how that one changed everything forever!

What a life this man lived before us! He lived by faith. He lived it in such a stable and steady manner that there was no mistaking what he was doing. Whatever the question asked, the answer was, "Walk by faith. What does the Word say? Then that's the answer. If God said it, then believe it and walk by faith."

He taught it line on line. He lived it out day by day. He never changed. He never altered the message one way or another. To him there was only one way—the Word way, the faith way.

He preached that same message day in and day out until it went all over the world. It went behind the Iron Curtain and helped tear down the Berlin Wall. It opened prison doors for no telling how many inmates all over the world. It gave birth to countless ministries and thousands of churches. Millions of people have been saved, and heaven only knows how many have received their bodies made well.

Thank God that entire body of Word preached did not leave with him. It's still here. Millions of books, tapes, videos and preachers all over the world are still doing the work—including Gloria, me and our KCM family. And make no mistake about it, we are answering every question the same way: Walk by faith. What does the Word say? Then that's the answer. If God said it, believe it and walk by faith. We love Brother Hagin dearly and we're looking forward to seeing him soon.

Gloria and I love you, Partner. We're standing with you in faith and we pray for you every day. These are days of salvation. You and I are taking the Word of that salvation and its reality to hurting people all over the world. In fact, the double is a reality. It's happening NOW. Grab hold of it. Zechariah 9:11-12 is just as real as John 3:16. It's the Word. Believe it! Sow the seed and walk by faith.

We love you and God loves you.

Jesus is Lord.

Love,

The Time to Preach, Teach and Heal Like Jesus Is NOW

Dear Partner

Here it is December already. My what a year we have had!

We have seen more souls come into the kingdom than ever before in our history. We are still working on the final count, and I'll let you know what it is as soon as I get it. Everything is up. Every department of the ministry is growing.

If there ever were a time to preach, teach and heal like Jesus did, it's now. <u>Anointing, Anointing, Anointing!</u> We are right in the middle of wars and rumors of wars, just like Jesus said in Matthew 24, along with every kind of hell on earth one can think of, and the anointing to preach the Word of faith is <u>far</u> greater than ever before.

Let's go to the book of Isaiah, chapters 10 and 11, and get a fresh look at the Bible's definition of the Anointing of Jesus.

Isaiah 10:27:

> 27 And it shall come to pass in that day, that his burden shall be taken away from off thy shoulder, and his yoke from off thy neck, and the yoke shall be destroyed because of the anointing.

Then 11:1-3:

> 1 And there shall come forth a rod out of the stem of Jesse, and a Branch shall grow out of his roots:
> 2 And the spirit of the Lord shall rest upon him, the spirit of wisdom and understanding, the spirit of counsel and might, the spirit of knowledge and of the reverence [Hebrew word *yirah*] of the Lord;

3 And shall make him of quick understanding in
the reverence [Hebrew word *yirah*] of the Lord....

Hallelujah! Look at that. The Anointing placed on Jesus to bring
to all mankind is the burden-removing, yoke-destroying Spirit of
wisdom and understanding, counsel, might, knowledge and quick
understanding in the reverence of the Lord.

Now let's shine the light of these verses on what Jesus said in Luke
4:18-19:

18 The Spirit of the Lord is upon me, because
he hath anointed me to preach the gospel
to the poor; he hath sent me to heal the
brokenhearted, to preach deliverance to the
captives, and recovering of sight to the blind,
to set at liberty them that are bruised,
19 To preach the acceptable year of the Lord.

He actually said the burden-removing, yoke-destroying Spirit of
wisdom and understanding, counsel, might, knowledge and quick
understanding in the reverence of the Lord is upon me to deal with
poor, brokenhearted captives and blind, bruised people who need
deliverance not only from all of the above, but also from debt and
slavery (the acceptable year of the Lord).

The Anointing! The presence of the Almighty Himself released
into this earth to love, heal and forgive. No wonder the angels were
exploding with excitement at the birth of Jesus. Luke 2:10-11—There is
born TO YOU! A SAVIOR the Lord Anointed-Christ-MESSIAH.

We've never really tapped into the almost uncontrollable excitement
throughout the New Testament about God the Father granting us this
fabulous gift of life the way heaven knows life. Not only in and on Jesus
Himself, but also for us.

Let's look at 1 John 2:20: "But ye have an anointing [Greek word
chrisma] from the Holy One, and ye know all things." No wonder we have
access to all things. We have the anointing of not only burden-removing

and yoke-destroying power, but also of wisdom and understanding, counsel, might, knowledge, and quick understanding of the reverence of the Lord abiding on the inside of us if Jesus has been received as Lord and Savior.

No wonder the Apostle Paul said in Philippians 4:13: "I can do all things through the anointing of Jesus which strengthens me." "Greater is He who is in me than he who is in the world" suddenly explodes with new meaning and revelation. We are talking about the same awesome power in the face of Jesus that lights all of the planet Heaven. They have no need of a sun. They have The Son and His Anointing.

2 Corinthians 4:6-7:

> 6   For God, who commanded the light to shine out of darkness, hath shined in our hearts, to give the light of the knowledge of the glory of God in the face of Jesus [the Anointed].
>
> 7   But we have this treasure in earthen vessels, that the excellency of the power may be of God, and not of us.

Look at Colossians 1:27:

> 27   To whom God would make known what is the riches of the glory of this mystery among the Gentiles; which is [the Anointing] in you, the hope of glory.

Only after much careful study and prayer can we even begin to understand the word "Christmas." We know why Christmas. "Mas" is celebration. It's not just a birthday party for Jesus. It's the celebrating of the birth of the Anointed bringing His glorious Anointing into the earth. Without understanding this gift from the Father, we lose the impact of John 3:16. For God so loved, He gave us Jesus. Not only the man, but also His Anointing, His Spirit, His glory.

Maybe this year's greatest Christmas scripture should be Ephesians 3:16-21:

16   That he would grant you, according to the riches of his glory, to be strengthened with might by his Spirit in the inner man;

17   That [the Anointing] may dwell in your hearts by faith; that ye, being rooted and grounded in love,

18   May be able to comprehend with all saints what is the breadth, and length, and depth, and height;

19   And to know the love of [the Anointing], which passeth knowledge, that ye might be filled with all the fulness of God.

20   Now unto him that is able to do exceeding abundantly above all that we ask or think, according to the power that worketh in us,

21   Unto him be glory in the church by [the Anointed] Jesus throughout all ages, world without end. Amen.

2004 is the Year of Anointing beyond anything the human race has ever seen. Christ-mas, Anointing celebration for a whole year. Expect it in your life, your family, in everything you set out to do this year. It's here now. It will increase at an astounding rate. Get on the Word like never before in your life. We have a job to do, a world to reach with the Word of God's love and faith. Together we can do it.

As you sow your financial seed this month, lay your hands on it AND shout Amen before Jesus, thanking Him for coming and being so good to us. Thank Him for being so faithful. Most of all, thank Him for giving us all of Himself including His Anointing.

Merry Christmas to you and all yours. Gloria and I and all of our family love you very much and are thrilled to serve you by and through the Anointing of Jesus and His Word. We pray for you every day.

Love,

Ken

Precious Seed!

Dear Partner

A few days ago Dr. Leroy Thompson came to Eagle Mountain, and we did two weeks of daily broadcasts together. I always learn so much when such powerful men of God come on the *BVOV* with me.

During his teaching, Brother Leroy referred to the 126th Psalm. While he was ministering from it, I heard the Lord direct me to write to you and share some of the fabulous truths that are just crying out to us from this great psalm.

Let's read it together. Read it to yourself out loud and remember this is God speaking to <u>us:</u>

1   When the Lord turned again the captivity of Zion, we were like them that dream.

2   Then was our mouth filled with laughter, and our tongue with singing: then said they among the heathen, The Lord hath done great things for them.

3   The Lord hath done great things for us; whereof we are glad.

4   Turn again our captivity, Oh Lord, as the streams in the south.

5   They that sow in tears shall reap in joy.

6   He that goeth forth and weepeth, bearing precious seed, shall doubtless come again with rejoicing, bringing his [harvest] with him.

In verse 1 the fact is established that this psalm is, as I said, God speaking to and about us, the Body of Jesus, the Church. Hebrews 12:22-24 declares that the Church is Mount Zion.

Our Father desires our life in Jesus to be so good that it's like a dream. After all, Jesus said that He came that we might have life, and have it abundantly—so much so, that it fills our mouths with laughter and singing.

Notice in verse 2 this laughter and singing is not just in church when someone is leading praise and worship. It must be talking about all day long, out where the sinners are. So much so, <u>they</u> say, "My, what great things the Lord has done for them!"

Take the time every day to read out loud the things the Lord has done for you. Read it. Listen to it until it stirs up the joy of the Lord that lives in your spirit.

"But Brother Copeland, I can't laugh and sing right now. So much is wrong in my life."

If you will begin to major on what Jesus has done, and fill your mouth and mind with what is right instead of what's wrong, the right Jesus has done will change the wrong that the devil has done. I know it's not easy, but all it takes on your part is the decision to do it and <u>start now</u>. The Word, the Spirit, the Blood, the Name of Jesus will take over.

Verse 3:

> 3   The Lord hath done great things for us; where-
> of we are glad.

As you read and say out loud to yourself the great things Jesus has done for you, stop and say: "<u>I'm glad</u> Jesus did that for me. Oh, thank God, I'm <u>so</u> glad!" Then read on, and stop again and say: "That makes me so glad!"

One day, as I was praying over Deuteronomy 28:47, I stopped and began searching deeply inside myself. I found that my heart's desire was to serve God with a glad heart and with joy. So I prayed that right then: "Lord it is my desire to serve You with gladness and a joyful heart."

The moment I prayed that, I "felt" no joy or gladness. In fact I felt just the opposite. But as I began to say "I serve God with gladness and a joyful heart," my feelings began to change. The more I said it, the more gladness and joy came. Now I say it all the time, keeping my mouth filled with it. As long as my mouth is filled, my heart is filled. I was surprised how rapidly my "feelings" changed.

Verses 5-6:

> 5   They that sow in tears shall reap in joy.
> 6   He that goeth forth and weepeth, bearing precious seed, shall doubtless come again with rejoicing, bringing his [harvest] with him.

Here is a great truth! If we learn to sow immediately when trouble comes, we will reap a harvest in joy. I cannot overemphasize the joy. Jesus overcame the death and shame of the cross with the joy of the Lord. We have His joy. We received it when we were born again, when He became the Lord of our lives.

When joy is released, nothing can overcome it. It is part of the fruit of the spirit, and against it there is no law. You must remember, however, it is not a feeling. It is a spiritual force. It can and will change your feelings, but the way you feel is not the way joy is measured. Joy, like faith, comes by hearing and believing the Word.

A seed sown in tears is precious seed. Precious seed! It's precious to Jesus and precious to you. In fact, every seed you sow should be precious to you. It's the source of your harvest. The precious seed of the Word is the source of your life.

I've had Partners come to me with tears in their eyes saying, "Brother Copeland, this is the seed for my healing," or "this is the seed for my son's salvation," or other things too private and precious to write in this letter. I'll tell you, that seed was so precious to me. It was holy in my eyes—I can only imagine how precious it was to Jesus. Look at verse 6:

> 6   He that goeth forth and weepeth, bearing precious seed, shall doubtless come again with rejoicing, bringing his [harvest] with him.

He <u>shall</u>—not could, not maybe—He will <u>DOUBTLESS</u>!! Do you see that? <u>DOUBTLESS</u>!! He shall doubtless come again with rejoicing, <u>bringing his harvest</u> with him.

We must never, I mean never get so caught up in the harvest when it comes that we forget to bring it to the Lord immediately and laugh with Him over it. He gave it to us. It did not come because you or I were so smart, or so talented, or whatever. It came because He is the Lord of the Harvest, and our seed is so precious to Him.

Isn't this a marvelous psalm? This is a wonderful Word from heaven to you. Take it. Put it into action. Make it a priority to keep the 126th Psalm in your heart and mouth throughout this new year.

Gloria just walked into the room and said, "Tell them to put abundance in their mouths." Yes! Do it! Start NOW. The harvest is ready. Put your precious seed before the Lord with tears before Him. He has done great things for you. You will come again with singing, bringing your harvest with you.

Thank you so much for being our Partner. I mention you to God in every prayer I pray. Helping you get your needs met by helping you become strong in faith is the priority of this ministry. 2004 is the greatest year ever.

Gloria and I love you and pray for you every day.

Love,

Ken

Have a Happy and Blessed New Year!

Fullness = Faith-Filled Love!

Dear Partner

Just a few weeks before the close of 2003, the Lord began talking to me about 2004 being the year of fullness. Then on the 27th day of November 2003, He spoke a short, but extremely powerful, word to me about His will and plan for this year. He said, "All callings will come into fullness by the end of 2004, including all forms of prosperity."

God's will and plan for the Body of Christ to come into its <u>full</u> stature did not begin last year. It has always been His heart's desire for His people to be in His image, complete and full in every way. That's obvious from the way He created Adam and the garden He placed him in. That garden was a place of fullness. Everything was in the image of God.

Of course, we know Adam and satan brought sin into the world, and death by sin, and fear by death. The result was <u>emptiness,</u> lack, heartache, sickness and disease. <u>The curse.</u> Think about it. Everything about the curse empties instead of fulfills. Sickness takes away from good health. Poverty takes away from life. Death is a thief. Sin is a destroyer.

Jesus was heaven's answer to the emptiness that sin and death brought into the human family. Until He came, heaven and earth were at odds with each other to the point of, in some cases, all-out war. Satan and his stealing, killing and destroying ways looked as though he could never be stopped.

Then on that fateful night 2,000 years ago, heaven shouted its announcement just outside Bethlehem: "PEACE ON EARTH. <u>GOOD</u> WILL <u>TOWARD</u> MEN!" A man had just been born into the earth—the fullness of God! This man later said, "I am come that they might have life and that they might have it <u>more</u> <u>abundantly.</u>" Not empty. Full. He said things like, "Seek ye first the kingdom of God, and His righteousness; and <u>all</u> these things shall be <u>added</u> unto you." *Added* means to fill—not to empty.

Ever since Jesus came and demonstrated fullness of ministry, He has been developing His Body of ministry to come to that same awesome place of preaching, teaching, and healing that He walked in. That's what the whole 20th century was about—restoring and filling, restoring and filling the Body of Christ with revelation from heaven. Each generation a step higher and closer to fulfilling His redemption dream in the earth. Remember, Jesus said in John 14:12:

> 12   [I most solemnly assure you,] He that believeth on me, the works that I do shall he do also; and greater works than these shall he do; because I go unto my Father.

That's fullness of calling. That's fullness of the gifts of the Spirit in manifestation. Thank God, we are there!

Something else the Lord pointed out to me about all this really opened my eyes. He said, "The recent outbreaks of terror [from the bombings in Israel, 9-11, etc., till now] are not political. They are manifestations of satan using his captives in an attempt to regain the ground he has lost in the last 100 years through the restoration of revelation to the Body of Christ." He's fighting a losing battle and he knows it.

The weapons of our warfare are not carnal, natural weapons. They are mighty through the Holy Ghost—the Spirit of the fullness of God. We are right now—in 2004—in position to see the Apostle Paul's prayer in Ephesians 3:14-20 come to pass and be fully manifest in the earth:

> 14   For this cause I bow my knees unto the Father of our Lord Jesus Christ,
> 15   Of whom the whole family in heaven and earth is named,
> 16   That he would grant you, according to the riches of his glory, to be strengthened with might by his Spirit in the inner man;
> 17   That Christ may dwell in your hearts by faith; that ye, being rooted and grounded in love,
> 18   May be able to comprehend with all saints

> what is the breadth, and length, and depth,
> and height;
>
> 19 And to know the love of Christ, which passeth
> knowledge, that ye might be <u>filled with all the
> fulness of God.</u>
>
> 20 Now unto him that is able to do exceeding
> abundantly above all that we ask or think,
> according to the power that worketh in us....

Nobody in the earth has ever seen the fullness of God! Even Jesus said there was more than what He did. Greater works than these, He said. How can that be? What would that be? I don't know, but we're about to find out!

After praying that prayer in Ephesians 3:14-20, the Apostle Paul continued to outline the concept of being filled with the fullness of God. The definition is laid out in Ephesians 4:11-13:

> 11 And he gave some, apostles; and some,
> prophets; and some, evangelists; and some,
> pastors and teachers;
>
> 12 For the perfecting of the saints, for the work of
> the ministry, for the edifying of the body of Christ:
>
> 13 <u>Till we all come</u> in the unity of the faith, and
> of the knowledge of the Son of God, unto a
> [full grown] man, unto the measure of the
> stature of the <u>fulness</u> of [the Anointed One
> and His Anointing].

Then verse 15 reveals the key:

> 15 But speaking the truth in love, may grow up
> into him in all things, which is the head, even
> Christ.

That's where we are right now. That's the key issue. <u>Growing up</u> into Him.

How?

By speaking nothing but Love. Think Love. Act Love. Keep the commandment of Love above all else. After all, every manifestation of the Holy Spirit is a manifestation of Love. God is Love. Faith works by Love.

There is no fear in Love. Developed, growing Love casts out fear. Love leaves no room for fear. When fear is gone, faith fills the room with power until it is <u>full.</u> Sickness is no match for faith-filled Love. Poverty can't hang around faith-filled Love. Death is a defeated foe, and it's faith-filled Love that brought it down from its place of authority.

<u>Get the strife and disobedience out of your life.</u> Don't wait. Do it now. Begin to read and confess every day John 17:23: "God loves me just as much as He loves Jesus. Therefore what shall I fear?" Fix your mind on that and don't let it go.

Then look at every person you meet through the eyes of that confession. "God loves that person just as much as He loves Jesus and me." I mean really work at this. You'll be shocked at how fast it will begin changing everything around you. Your faith will leap into action with fearless, bold expectations of Holy Ghost miracles.

Growing up into Him in all things! Praise God! Our time has come! Let's get it done!

As you sow your financial seed this month, lay your hands on it and <u>read John 17:23 aloud over it.</u> Sow it without fear. Sow it in love. Sow it in faith.

Then hold fast to that confession all month long: "I am a fearless, faith-filled sower of Love. Therefore I am a reaper of Love's full abundance. This is my year of the fullness of God. I will walk in it by the end of 2004. To God be all the glory!"

Gloria and I love you and we pray for you every day.

Love,

Greater is He that is in you, than he that is in the world!

Dear Partner

A number of years ago the Lord said to me while I was in prayer, "Become God-inside minded."

I instantly knew exactly what He meant. In my normal, everyday way of thinking and without realizing it, the God to whom I was praying was in heaven. I pictured Him somewhere away from me. Maybe He was aware of what was happening to me and around me and maybe not.

Until that day in 1967, it had not occurred to me that my mind needed to be renewed in this. I realized a powerful leap of faith immediately when the reality of that statement hit me. God is in me NOW. How could He not know what I was going through? He was going through it too!

Take a look at the rest of the verse in 1 John 4:4 that I quoted at the top of the letter:

> 4   Ye are of God, little children, and have over-come them: because greater is he that is in you, than he that is in the world.

Let's look at two more mind-awakening, heart-stirring words from God.

1 Corinthians 6:19-20:

> 19   What? know ye not that your body is the temple of the Holy Ghost which is in you, which ye have of God, and ye are not your own?
> 20   For ye are bought with a price: therefore glorify God in your body, and in your spirit, which are God's.

Now 2 Corinthians 6:16-18:

16   And what agreement hath the temple of God
      with idols? for ye are the temple of the living
      God; as God hath said, I will dwell in them,
      and walk in them; and I will be their God, and
      they shall be my people.

17   Wherefore come out from among them, and
      be ye separate, saith the Lord, and touch not
      the unclean thing; and I will receive you,

18   And will be a Father unto you, and ye shall be my
      sons and daughters, saith the Lord Almighty.

In verse 18 notice that God is not an absentee Father. He's right there, <u>always</u> doing His part—leading, guiding, strengthening, healing, coaching, encouraging, warning, protecting and, most importantly, loving with all His great heart. Jesus promised that He would not leave us orphans. God promised that He would do all these things, and He does—<u>all the time.</u>

What's the problem, then? Why is it so many Christians have the idea that God never does any of these things for them? Instead of <u>believing</u> He <u>is</u> doing all these things, most Christians <u>believe</u> He <u>isn't.</u>

<u>Faith is the connection</u> to His leading, guiding, strengthening, healing, coaching, encouraging, warning, protecting and loving voice. You hear His prompting in your spirit to do one thing, but your fear-trained mind says, *That can't work.* And almost without thinking about it any further, you follow the fear instead of faith.

It wasn't that the Father didn't lead. You didn't listen. Those of you who are parents know exactly what that's like. It's never a matter of God not doing. It's a matter of our not receiving and walking in what He has already done in Jesus on the cross, and what He is doing <u>now</u> in us through His Word and the Holy Spirit.

Before the end of 2004, those who believe and will obey His Word will be walking fully in His leadings and directions in life. Think about what that means! <u>He</u> <u>knows</u> <u>everything.</u>

"Brother Copeland do you mean He will tell us everything He knows? Do we have the spiritual capacity to know all He knows? After all, we're only human."

First of all you are not just human. You are a born-again, re-created in Christ Jesus, human.

First question: Is He telling us all He knows? The answer: Yes. Look with me at John 16:13-15:

> 13 Howbeit when he, the Spirit of truth, is come, he will guide you into all truth: for he shall not speak of himself; but whatsoever he shall hear, that shall he speak: and he will show you things to come.
> 14 He shall glorify me: for he shall receive of mine, and shall show it unto you.
> 15 All things that the Father hath are mine: therefore said I, that he shall take of mine, and shall show it unto you.

Second question: Do we have the spiritual capacity to know all He knows? The answer, again: Yes. The re-created human spirit has the same capacity to know as Jesus does.

Let's take Him at His Word and renew our minds by becoming God-inside minded. Remember first of all, that 1 Corinthians 2:16 says we have the mind of Christ. We have the anointing that's on the mind of Jesus available to us. Confess that aloud right now by faith. Also, remember GOD IS LOVE.

Now let's look at Ephesians 3:16-20:

> 16 That he would grant you, according to the riches of his glory, to be strengthened with might by his Spirit in the inner man;
> 17 That Christ may dwell in your hearts by faith; that ye, being rooted and grounded in love,
> 18 May be able to comprehend with all saints

what is the breadth, and length, and depth, and height;

19   And to know the love of Christ, which passeth knowledge, that ye might be filled with <u>all the fulness of God.</u>

20   Now unto him that is able to do exceeding abundantly above all that we ask or think, according to the power that worketh in us.

In verse 16 we see that God, the Holy Spirit of Truth, is ready to fulfill what Jesus promised by expanding our re-created inner man to the place of receiving ALL THE FULLNESS OF GOD!!

Verse 18 declares that He's here to do this for ALL the saints—everyone who knows Jesus as Lord and Savior. Thank God, He's no respecter of persons. Verse 20 says exactly what we're talking about in this letter. He's working in you NOW.

The two key elements that come from us into the working of all this are in verse 17: Faith and Love. Faith worketh by Love and Love is released by faith. The gifts of the Spirit work by faith, not by fear. Fear works against the anointing. Faith works with the anointing.

The spirit of fear and the spirit of antichrist are the same spirit. God (Love) has not given us the spirit of fear. Love has given us the spirit of power, Love and a sound (renewed) mind.

Verse 17 also gives us the place to start, which is <u>faith in Love.</u> When the Word says Love <u>never</u> fails, BELIEVE IT! When Jesus said the Father loves you just as much as He loves Him, BELIEVE IT!

When Jesus said I command you to love one another <u>JUST</u> <u>AS</u> <u>I</u> <u>HAVE</u> <u>LOVED</u> <u>YOU,</u> first believe that God (Love) in you has the capacity to love as He loves and then <u>do</u> <u>it</u>! Obey. Commit to it. There are no excuses for disobeying the direct order left us by our Commander in Chief, Jesus the Anointed Son of the Living God.

"If I do that, won't people just run over me?"

That's fear speaking. Faith in Love (God) says, "I may look to the world like a lamb to the slaughter, but I know I am more than a conqueror! Greater is Love (He) that is in me than he (fear) that is in the world. Love (God) has been shed <u>abroad</u> in my re-created human spirit.

"I throw myself completely over on Him. His Word is first place in my life. His desire and plan for me is my life. In Him (in Love) I have my life and my being. Victory is, therefore, assured. I can do all things through Christ (through Love, God in me) which strengthens me. Before the end of this year, I will be walking in the fullness of God for my life!"

Shout amen! Read it again and shout amen until it becomes reality and not just religious.

<u>This year fullness. Next year overflow.</u> Gloria and I love you and pray for you every day.

Love,

Ken

We believe you are receiving the fullness of God promised for this year—the fullness of His life, His love and His burden-removing, yoke-destroying power in you. The Lord has instructed us throughout the year that His fullness does not come from the outside but from the inside and is determined by our life being led by the Spirit. His fullness comes from the revelation and activation of His love within us!

Become God-Inside Minded

Dear Partner

"The year of 2004 will be known as the year of fullness."

That, you remember, is what the Lord said to me New Year's Eve 2003.

Let's look again at one of our scripture prayers—Ephesians 1:16-23:

16   [I] Cease not to give thanks for you, making mention of you in my prayers;

17   That the God of our Lord Jesus Christ, the Father of glory, may give unto you the spirit of wisdom and revelation in the knowledge of him:

18   The eyes of your understanding being enlightened; that ye may know what is the hope of his calling, and what the riches of the glory of his inheritance in the saints,

19   And what is the exceeding greatness of his power to us-ward who believe, according to the working of his mighty power,

20   Which he wrought in Christ, when he raised him from the dead, and set him at his own right hand in the heavenly places,

21   Far above all principality, and power, and might, and dominion, and every name that is named, not only in this world, but also in that which is to come:

22   And hath put all things under his feet, and gave him to be the head over all things to the church,

23   Which is his body, <u>the fulness of him that filleth all</u> in all.

Look at verses 22-23. The Lord Jesus, when He was raised up, was appointed by the Father to be the head over all things to the Church, which is His Body. <u>Then it boldly states that we—you and I—are the</u>

<u>fullness of Him.</u> If it just stopped there we wouldn't know what to do next. How could we ever be His fullness? The very next sentence tells us how. <u>He is the One who does the filling.</u> <u>He is the fullness of us,</u> both as individuals and as a Body. He is the One who filleth.

Fullness is not a "thing." Fullness is a person. Fullness is somebody. Fullness is not some sort of feeling. Fullness of physical healing would be to be <u>completely</u> whole in your body. Absolutely, totally whole—whatever miracles and healings it takes to get there. Nothing in your body missing or broken. Everything done just one step short of receiving your glorified, resurrected body. <u>That's fullness!</u>

We are the Body of Jesus and His Body should have no sickness or disease whatsoever. NONE! Jesus is the "filler" of the fullness. He is our health, and we should not be satisfied with just getting by on pills and pain. No! In Jesus' Name, No! We are His fullness and He is ours. <u>Let's rise up in the Word and faith and receive</u> what belongs to us. Let's do it not just so we feel better. That's great and it's a part of it, but we are also to <u>do it to bring honor and glory</u> to the One who suffered so in order to bring us our freedom from sickness, weakness and pain.

What about our finances? What would be fullness of financial prosperity to you? Just enough to pay your bills? Just enough to make it a little easier on you? Financial lack and the spirit of poverty caused just as much of the suffering of Jesus as sickness and disease. I know most Christian people don't realize that, but it's true nevertheless. Third John verse 2 is as much a fullness scripture as Ephesians 1:16-23:

> 2   Beloved, I [pray] above all things that thou mayest prosper and be in health, even as thy soul prospereth.

That's a very familiar verse of scripture, but the next verse is not as well known or quoted:

> 3   For I rejoiced greatly, when the brethren came and testified of the truth [Word] that is in thee, even as thou walkest in the truth [Word].

Jesus' sacrifice and suffering (Passion) was not more for one thing, like sickness, than another, like poverty. <u>Adam's sin caused it all.</u> All sickness, disease, weakness, pain, poverty, suffering, danger, bondage and yokes of all types are manifestations of death coming into the world. Romans 5:12 gives the order in which it came:

> 12 Wherefore, as by one man sin entered into the world, and death by sin; and so death passed upon all men, for that all have sinned.

Now add to that Hebrews 2:14-15, and the picture becomes very clear:

> 14 Forasmuch then as the children are partakers of flesh and blood, he also himself likewise took part of the same; that through death he might destroy him that had the power of death, that is, the devil;
> 15 And deliver them who through fear of death were all their lifetime subject to bondage.

So then by one man, Adam the 1st, sin came into the world, and death by sin, and fear by death, and bondage (sickness, disease, pain, poverty and etc.) by fear. Then by one man, Jesus, Adam the 2nd, deliverance came. How? It's right there in verse 14, by His great suffering on <u>THE CROSS!</u>

<u>But don't stop there. The tomb is empty! He's alive!</u> Resurrected in great glory! His resurrection is as much ours as His suffering. The same Spirit that raised Him up and set Him totally free from all our sin and death dwells in you right now. Stop this very moment and tell Him how grateful you are and how much you love Him for loving you so.

<u>Become "God-INSIDE minded."</u> Call to your attention every morning when you wake up that the God to whom you pray is not off somewhere in a faraway place. What? Know ye not that your body is the temple, or dwelling place, of the Holy Ghost? He's not busy doing other things. He is right there. He's not just with you, He is dwelling inside you. Does He know what you're going through? Absolutely! He's going through it, too. Then why hasn't He done something about it?

He has. Jesus said when the Spirit of truth comes, He <u>WILL</u> lead, guide, protect, warn, strengthen, heal, prosper and be a Father to you. Read 2 Corinthians 6:17-18:

> 17   Wherefore come out from among them, and
>   be ye separate, saith the Lord, and touch not
>   the unclean thing; and I will receive you,
> 18   And will be a Father unto you, and ye shall be
>   my sons and daughters, saith the Lord Almighty.

<u>He is not an absentee Father.</u> He is doing all these things—and much more—<u>all the time.</u> He's not the problem. If there are problems, they are in our hearing and receiving. He's doing everything He was sent to do. I say again: Become God-inside minded. Spend quality time with Him in His Word. Tell Him a hundred times a day how grateful you are to have Him live and bring His fullness into your life.

Jesus said in Matthew 22:37-39:

> 37   Thou shalt love the Lord thy God with all thy
>   heart, and with all thy soul, and with all thy mind.
> 38   This is the first and great commandment.
> 39   And the second is like unto it, Thou shalt love
>   thy neighbor as thyself.

<u>In that order.</u> If you'll tell the Lord thy God you love Him first thing in the morning and the last thing before you sleep and every time you wake up during the night, you'll have no trouble loving your neighbor as yourself. The One who knows the answer to everything is right there in your spirit. Stop. Be quiet. Listen. You'll hear Him say "I love you too."

Just a quick report on the Elite CX team. We are growing day by day. We are sooooo close to taking delivery on the Citation X. What a get-together we're going to have when we do. I'll let you know.

Pray for Gloria and me. We're the busiest we've ever been. Also stand with us in the healing anointing. The Lord is increasing it daily on us both. Look for it to increase in your life and ministry also.

We love you and pray for you every day. I am so grateful for the privilege of being your Partner.

Love,

Ken

Love is <u>THE</u> Comforter

Dear Partner

My, what a world we live in!

A better way to say it is: "What a time to be alive." One side headed for glory, the other bound for hell, and both doing it with the "gusto of a hound dog." Wide open.

That's because heaven has declared this to be the year of fullness. Not only is the Body of Christ coming into the fullness of God, but sin is coming into its fullness also. That's the way it works. Stealing, killing, destroying and all the works of hell and darkness coming into their fullness.

That's the reason it's so important to preach the word of faith, healing and deliverance. Never in the history of the human race has there been such a great time to preach this gospel. Everywhere our TV broadcast is being aired, people are coming to Jesus. We've always had good results because God's Word works—but never like this!

I see now why the Lord was so adamant two years ago that we believe for the double. It's time to "double up" on everything. Especially when it comes to His Word. More Word in, more faith out. Less Word in, more fear out. There's more fear and terror available today than ever before. But there's also more faith which works by Love available, thanks to Jesus and what He did for us on the cross.

In this letter let's look at something from the Word that will leave the devil and his demons standing totally helpless in our lives.

Let's go once again to 1 John 4:18:

> 18 There is no fear in love; but perfect love casteth out fear: because fear hath torment. He that feareth is not made perfect in love.

Notice it says <u>fear *has* torment</u>—not fear *and* torment. Fear is not one thing and torment another. The torment is in the fear.

Look at the definition of *torment:* "To put to extreme pain or anguish and misery; that which gives vexation; to tease, harass or annoy; to put into great agitation." A tormentor is one who inflicts anguish and, or, torture.

<u>PRESSURE.</u>

In Luke 16:22-23 Jesus described the stingy, rich man who died and was in hell as "<u>being in torments</u>...." Hell is a fear-filled place of torments and tormentors. However, all the tormentors are not in hell. They are active right here on earth. <u>Wherever there is fear, there's torment.</u> Wherever there is torment there are tormentors. That's what the devil does. That's the way he controls people.

Torment is physical and mental pressure. <u>Pain</u> pure and simple. Pain always seeks relief. That's the method of control. Change to a healthy diet and pressure, torment—unusually strong desire—comes on your mind to eat fat! And do it NOW! Fix this! Get up and go to the kitchen NOW! Cookies NOW!

The same process is at work whether it's in regard to food, drugs, alcohol, adultery or any other sin. Torment is the watch dog that has been sent by satan to keep you in line with the world: "Get back in your cage." How can he do that to a born-again believer? <u>He cannot if fear is not present.</u> The torment is in the fear.

When Jesus went to the cross, He stripped the devil of the power of death. Hebrews 2:14-15:

14   Forasmuch then as the children are partakers of flesh and blood, he also himself likewise took part of the same; that through death he might destroy him that had the power of death, that is, the devil;

15   And deliver them who through fear of death were all their lifetime subject to bondage.

Without the power of death, satan lost the threat of death. He can't just torment someone just because he wants to. That someone must have fear present in his or her life for him to have something to work with. Without it he's helpless. Jesus has seen to that.

Not only has He removed the devil's power, but He also opened the door for the Holy Ghost to come and shed abroad in our hearts the thing that casts out all fear along with its torment—the Love of God. There is no fear in Love. Of course not! Love is God. There is no fear in God. Therefore, there is no torment in God. Love is not a tormentor. Love is a <u>comforter.</u> Love is THE Comforter.

Fear works 24 hours a day, 7 days a week, attempting to shape every thought to the world's way of thinking: *That won't work. You can't do that. What if it doesn't work this time? What about so-and-so, they didn't get it?* <u>Then the surrounding world confirms the thoughts fear has created.</u> That's when one's feelings and seeings produce the pressure.

At times like this, only the Word can be trusted. Cut off the "feelings and seeings" that support the fear. Separate yourself from the people who reinforce the fear. That's the reason a strong, Love-filled, faith-filled pastor and church are so important. That, along with your tapes and books—and most importantly your every day time in your Bible and prayer—will keep the gifts of God stirred up and the fear flushed out of your life. <u>Work at it.</u> Fear is like a thin layer of "scum" on top of otherwise clear pure water. In your spirit is love, joy, peace, goodness, meekness, longsuffering, gentleness, temperance and faith.

Stir it up. Tell your heavenly Father how grateful you are for all He's given you. Tell Him over and over that you love Him with all your heart, soul, mind and strength. Every time you do, He—Love—responds. Every time, Love increases.

As that continues, there's less and less room for the "scum" layer. It gets flushed out. <u>GONE.</u> Not "coped with." <u>Gone!</u> Where there's no fear, there's no torment. The tormentors have nothing to work with in your life. That's 1 John 5:18:

18   We know that whosoever is born of [Love]

sinneth not; but he that is begotten of [Love] keepeth himself [in Love], and that wicked one toucheth him not.

Get out of the cage! You're free!

You and I are taking this great freedom message into a terror-filled, terrified world. As you sow your financial seed this month, <u>pray over it, and for Gloria and me.</u> We are going into some fear-controlled parts of the world. What good news we have for them! When you pray, it's like having you there with us.

We love you and pray for you every day.

Love,

Ken

The Job Is Great...
The Harvest Is Ripe...
The Field Is Ready Like Never Before

Dear Partner

I'm writing this letter from my hotel room in St. Petersburg, Russia. We just finished four outstanding days of meetings in Moscow.

My, I wish you could have been there. One thing is for sure—the Lord was there with us. The people in this part of the world are so hungry for the Word. They shout. They dance. They praise at the top of their voices. Their faith is so quick to take hold of the Word, it's amazing. It made preaching to them a real joy. Miracles abound in an atmosphere like that. If the Word says it, they see no reason not to believe it.

In every service I asked, "How many have your Bibles?" Just about every person shouted and held up his or her Bible. Think about that. Only a few years ago that was a prison offense. To see 4000 people waving Bibles at you in downtown Moscow shouting at the tops of their voices is enough to make you cry. It did me.

Our Partners, Rick and Denise Renner, who pastor the Good News Church in Moscow, have done an absolutely marvelous job taking the word of faith to Eastern Europe. I preached in their church in Moscow last Sunday morning and it was a fabulous service.

Imagine coming to Moscow and starting a church from scratch. That's what they did. Not only that, they started it across the street from the Kremlin! How's that for faith? They outgrew that building, outgrew another building and have now outgrown the one they're currently in. God is definitely on the move in Russia.

We asked how many watched the *Believer's Voice of Victory* broadcast. As far as I could tell, every hand in the place went up. I can't tell you, Partner, what a thrill that is. In fact, there were people who traveled from as far away as four days by train to get to these meetings. They found out about them by watching *BVOV*. We are on the air now literally from one end of Eastern Europe to the other—all the way to China!

We also spoke in four services for ministers. Gloria and I spoke in two services each, and they couldn't get enough of the Word. This whole part of the world is changing right before our eyes. It will never be the same again. God is filling His house with His family.

It is amazing how powerful the Word of God really is. It is sweeping through this whole world, reaching into every nook and cranny—into places thought by most people to be impossible to penetrate.

I spoke to a TV correspondent who was in Iraq last week. He was in the home of a government official who showed him his big screen TV in his bedroom and said, "I watch the God Channel every night." That just happens to be when the *BVOV* is on the God Channel!

You won't hear that on CNN, at least not yet, but people all over Iraq have satellite dishes. Their favorite programs are Christian. It's happening right under the devil's nose, and he can't stop it. The Word brought communism down and it's bringing down Islam and all the other traps satan has people caught up in. It's falling fast. The devil knows it. That's what all the fighting is about.

As I write this letter, we are on our way to Kiev, Ukraine, where we will have five services before heading home. The same kind of outpouring that we saw in Russia is going on in the Ukraine. And word is coming out of China that it's happening there too—big time. This is the year of fullness.

It's time. Time to pray like never before. Not just for ourselves but for ministries all over the world. They need everything and more of it.

It's time to believe. God is doing just exactly what He said He was going to do. There has never been a greater time to completely commit everything to Him.

It's time to receive. This is the year of fullness. Receive it. Fullness of everything. Spirit, soul and body. What's His is yours. It's yours NOW. Receive it.

It's time to give. In the word the Lord blessed me with about this being the year of fullness, He said, "2005 will be known as the year of overflow. How much overflow you receive depends on how much you sow toward it in 2004." We are experiencing increase on every hand in this ministry. Sowing into increase produces increase.

In closing, let's look at Galatians 6:7:

> 7 Be not deceived; God is not mocked: for what-
> soever a man soweth, that shall he also reap.

While here, I learned something from Rick Renner about this verse that's really powerful. In fact, he wrote it in his book *Sparkling Gems From the Greek.*

The word *soweth* in this verse is the Greek word *speiro,* which refers to any seed sown. This points out that this law pertains not only to finances but to *anything* in life.

<u>Everything is a seed.</u> Love, time, effort, kindness, forgiveness. But also bitterness, unkindness, stinginess and all the other things no one wants to receive. Everything is a seed. Whatever one sows, that is what he will reap in return—in abundance!

The Greek tense of this word does not indicate a one-time sowing. It pictures someone who is a sower. One who habitually sows. Someone who lives a sowing lifestyle. (There are those who seem to live to sow strife and bitterness.) The word for *reap* is in the same tense.

So this verse literally says, "Whatsoever a man sows, sows, sows, and sows and keeps on habitually sowing, and sowing, and sowing and sowing, he shall also reap, and reap, and reap, and keep on reaping with ever-increasing abundance."

This is exceeding, abundantly above all we can ask or think time. It's not the time to sit on the sidelines and watch. It's time to get into the flow holding nothing back but rather going for the very best our God has.

It's out there and it's yours. Fullness!

Gloria and I need your prayers more than ever before. The job is great. The harvest is ripe. The field is ready like never before. She and I are rejoicing like never before. We know that with your prayers and the supply of the Holy Ghost we can do all things.

We love you and pray for you every day.

Love,

Ken

Partners, all of KCM is praying and believing God on your behalf. Together we can do anything!

Becoming God-Inside Minded!

Dear Partner

Gloria and I just finished two weeks of TV broadcast taping at our prayer cabin in Arkansas. We have made programs here every spring for the past 16 years, and they have all been blessed. But this year was extra special.

The anointing was so rich, and the healing power of Jesus went to a new level for TV broadcasts. It's been that way all this year everywhere we've ministered the Word. I don't mean a little bit—<u>I mean a level we have never even been close to before.</u> This is certainly the fullest year of our lives, and it's just now late spring. The best is still to come.

The anointing on those broadcasts yesterday is still on me today as I write this letter. It <u>will</u> come on you as you read and receive.

Over the 37 years we've been in this ministry, I've heard all kinds of strange statements from Christians who have no awareness of the <u>fact</u> that God, the Creator of all things, is actually living on the inside of them. Statements like, "I just can't seem to touch God with my problem," "Oh, God, please be with me" or "I'm bombarding the gates of heaven in prayer." <u>In their consciousness, the God they are "praying" to is somewhere else. He's in heaven, paying little or no attention to them or anything about them.</u>

Religious ideas and forms of worship that deny the power of God have created this kind of thinking. They paint a picture of a cold, detached, disinterested God who is hard or even impossible to involve in our little, unimportant lives.

Nothing could be further from the truth. The Cross of Calvary is proof of that. God's greatest desire is to have a very close and personal relationship with <u>you,</u> not just a hit-and-miss, every-now-and-then kind of thing.

No! We are a family. God never planned on being an absentee father. He planned on being there for you every minute of every day. He's the One who said, "My sheep know my voice."

I remember many years ago when I heard in my spirit, <u>You need to become God-inside minded.</u> Greater is He that is in <u>ME</u> than he that is in the world.

God doesn't have to be summoned from some great distance, have the problem explained and be caught up on what's going on and why you need what you need in your situation. He was there when it started. He's been there every minute of every day while it's been going on. He's been ready to do something about it the whole time.

In fact, if we had been listening like we should He would have led us in a way that probably would have avoided the whole mess. If it was something unavoidable, He would have prepared us so well that the victory would have been won before the fight was ever started. Jesus said, "Be of good cheer I have overcome the world."

That victory is ours!

Look at 1 John 5:4-5:

> 4 For whatsoever is born of God overcometh the world: and this is the victory that overcometh the world, even our faith.
> 5 Who is he that overcometh the world, but he that believeth that Jesus is the Son of God?

You are a world overcomer. However, your Father never planned for you to have to overcome anything by yourself. Let's see what He said about it in 1 Corinthians 6:19-20:

> 19 What? know ye not that your body is the temple of the Holy Ghost which is in you, which ye have of God, and ye are not your own?
> 20 For ye are bought with a price: therefore

glorify God in your body, and in your spirit, which are God's.

Now look at 2 Corinthians 6:14-18:

14 Be ye not unequally yoked together with unbelievers: for what fellowship hath righteousness with unrighteousness? and what communion hath light with darkness?

15 And what concord hath Christ with Belial? or what part hath he that believeth with an infidel?

16 And what agreement hath the temple of God with idols? for ye are the temple of the living God; as God hath said, I will dwell in them, and walk in them; and I will be their God, and they shall be my people.

17 Wherefore come out from among them, and be ye separate, saith the Lord, and touch not the unclean thing; and I will receive you,

18 And will be a Father unto you, and ye shall be my sons and daughters, saith the Lord Almighty.

Now look what Jesus promised in John 14:16-18:

16 And I will pray the Father, and he shall give you another Comforter, that he may abide with you for ever;

17 Even the Spirit of truth; whom the world cannot receive, because it seeth him not, neither knoweth him: but ye know him; for he dwelleth with you, and shall be in you.

18 I will not leave you [orphans]: I will come to you.

God planned it this way from the very beginning. Even before the foundation of the world. He's right there. He's always doing His part.

As I said He is not an absentee father. He's always leading, guiding, strengthening, healing, coaching, encouraging, warning, protecting and, most importantly, loving with all His great heart. He promised He would do all these things, and He does ALL THE TIME!

So what's the problem? Why do most people believe He isn't? That's it—they believe He isn't. So, they never hear and have no awareness of His presence.

Faith is the connection. Faith not only believes He is listening but also believes He is answering. Faith believes He is going through this with me. Faith tells the Father how much it loves Him a hundred times a day. Faith visits with the Father on a constant basis.

Your Father will wake you up every morning and put you to bed every night. In fact, He'll wake you at a specific time, if you'll ask Him to. You don't need an alarm clock. Ask Him to wake you up at a certain time, tell Him you love Him, and go on to sleep IN PEACE knowing He loves you just as much as He loves Jesus (John 17:23).

In closing, let's pray this prayer for one another.

Ephesians 3:14-20:

14   For this cause I bow my knees unto the Father of our Lord Jesus Christ,

15   Of whom the whole family in heaven and earth is named,

16   That he would grant [my Partner], according to the riches of his glory, to be strengthened with might by his Spirit in the inner man;

17   That Christ may dwell in [my Partners'] hearts by faith; that [my Partner], being rooted and grounded in love,

18   May be able to comprehend with all saints what is the breadth, and length, and depth, and height;

19   And to know the love of Christ, which passeth knowledge, that [my Partner] might be filled with all the fulness of God.

20   Now unto him that is able to do exceeding

abundantly above all that we ask or think, according to the power that worketh in us.

I am praying this for you every day. The word *know* in verse 19 is the Greek word for intimate or intercourse: "That you have an intimate relationship with the Anointed One and His Anointing. Filled with all the fullness of God. His power is working in you this very moment to bring this to pass."

As you sow your financial seed this month, hold it in your hands knowing He is right there. He's believing with you. He's looking at that seed with you. He's going through everything you're going through. Release your faith. Shout the victory.

Together, you, your Savior, Gloria, me, all of KCM and all our Partners are believing God. Together we can do anything.

Send us your victory reports. We love hearing them.

Gloria and I love you and pray for you every day.

Love,

Ken

Have the Faith of God!

Dear Partner

In the afternoon of April 29 while Gloria and I were in Detroit for the 2004 Detroit Victory Campaign, the word of the Lord came to me saying, "There is coming this summer an unprecedented move of God." I heard that word while preparing for my evening service at Word of Faith International Christian Center, Bishop Keith and Deborah Butler's church. The Lord spoke it to me two more times before the service. Since then, I have heard it a number of times more.

The word *unprecedented* means "having no precedent or example; not preceded by a like case." Simply put: "It's never been like this before."

Glory be to God! I'm writing this letter on the 19th of June, less than a week before the first day of summer, and it's already started. I'm telling you, it's here—the outpouring of the Holy Spirit we have all been believing for and have known was coming for so long.

This move of God is not confined to only one area. It's not just a salvation move. It's not just a healing and miracle revival. It is all of that, but it's also an invasion of the political and financial world. It is not just a move in the United States. It is worldwide. In fact there is no one on earth—NO ONE—whose life will not be impacted in some way by this miraculous, marvelous move of Jesus!

Look around you. It's happening. Get in it. Make yourself available to Him for service in any way He needs you. There's no way to know yet what all this is going to turn out to be. He did say "unprecedented." I can promise you this, there's more than enough for all of us to do. After all, this is what we've been training in the Word and in faith for all this time.

What is the most important thing God our Father has ever done for you? Give you the new birth? Fill you with the Holy Spirit? What? He gave you your faith. Without it you could not have been born again or filled with the Spirit or anything else from heaven.

Let's go to the Word in 1 John 5:1-5:

1   Whosoever believeth that Jesus is the Christ is born of God: and every one that loveth him that begat loveth him also that is begotten of him.

2   By this we know that we love the children of God, when we love God, and keep his commandments.

3   For this is the love of God, that we keep his commandments: and his commandments are not grievous.

4   For whatsoever is born of God overcometh the world: and this is the victory that overcometh the world, even our faith.

5   Who is he that overcometh the world, but he that believeth that Jesus is the Son of God?

Look again at verse 4: "Whatsoever is born of God overcometh the world...." Isn't the Word born of God? Yes. Won't the Word of God overcome the world? Yes it will, but only if it's mixed with faith.

Hebrews 3 and 4 talks about the Holy Spirit being grieved with those who fell in the wilderness and could never enter into the Promised Land. They fell, or were overcome, in that desert. Hebrews 4:2 explains why:

2   ...the word preached did not profit them, not being mixed with faith in them that heard it.

Joshua and Caleb faced the same wilderness and hardships and heard the same word preached the rest of them heard...with one difference—faith. They believed what God said and were willing to stake their lives on it. They, by faith, overcame.

Everything born of God depends on faith. There is nothing—nothing, in this world order that faith won't overcome. NO-THING!

Let's look again at 1 John 5:4-5. What is it that overcomes the world? OUR faith. Who has that faith? Who is included in the word

OUR? He that believes that Jesus is the Son of God!

Do you believe that? Of course you do. Then world-overcoming faith is in your spirit right now. It does not have to come from heaven or anywhere else every time you need it. It came when you made the decision to make Jesus Lord of your life. It was the creative power of God that re-created your human spirit (Ephesians 2:10).

You were born again not of corruptible seed but of incorruptible, by the Word of God. There are no spiritual birth defects. You did not get saved, born of the Word, but left without faith. Nor did you receive an inadequate amount.

No! The seed is the same for everyone. We all receive the same amount. Jesus, the author of our faith, has seen to that. The faith we each received is His faith in the same amount as He had in His ministry when He was on the earth. The difference is in the development of it in our lives. He is not only the author of our faith, but also the finisher, or developer, of it. Faith has to be used, or as Jesus put it in Luke 17:6:

> 6   And the Lord said, If ye had faith as a grain of mustard seed, ye might say unto this sycamine tree, Be thou plucked up by the root, and be thou planted in the sea; and it should obey you.

Like everything else in the kingdom of God—faith is a seed that must be planted to grow.

Let's look at one more New Testament passage about our faith. Mark 11:21-22:

> 21   And Peter calling to remembrance saith unto him, Master, behold, the fig tree which thou cursedst is withered away.
> 22   And Jesus answering saith unto them, Have faith in God.

The cross-reference in my Bible translates the Greek "Have the faith of God." Jesus, referring to His faith, called it the <u>faith of God!</u> Jesus was God manifest in the flesh. So that was God's faith being manifest that <u>overcame</u> that tree. The thrilling thing about this verse is Jesus said <u>you</u> use the <u>faith of God.</u> Then He taught them how it worked.

The Apostle Paul wrote in Romans 4:16-17 that Abraham used faith like God, calling things that be not as though they were. Certainly he did. He was using God's faith. That's the reason he, Jesus, the apostles, you and I must use it exactly as He does. When we do, it will work the same way as when Jesus used it.

I know it sounds too good to be true. It *is* too good to be true. But it is true.

So, fall in love with your faith. God gave it to you so you can live the way He lives—<u>abundantly!</u> The just shall live by faith. With faith, you can do all things—anything. Nothing in this world can overcome you.

Your faith has made you free. The truth of it has empowered you to be victorious in every area of life. Rise up and <u>shout: "I'm a free man!"</u> "<u>I'm a free woman!</u>"

Lay your hands on every troubled spot on your body and declare by faith:

"I'm free of _____. You cannot stay on my body, the temple of the Holy Ghost."

Lay your hands on your bills and mortgages and read John 8:36. Then boldly declare: "I'm free of debt." Say it knowing you are releasing <u>God's</u> faith on those debts when you say it.

Lay hands on pictures of your family members and loved ones and declare by the <u>faith of God</u> they are saved, healed and prosperous in God. Speak out their protection and deliverance—especially if they are in harm's way, such as in the service overseas. If you are in the military, this is the number one weapon that's been issued to you. Use it! Take care of it. It <u>will</u> take care of you.

As you sow your financial seeds this month, release your faith for overflow. Overflow now and overflow in 2005—2005 will be known as the year of overflow. Sow toward it. It's coming <u>big time!</u>

This is the greatest time in the history of this planet. It's our time. It's the back of the Book time. Read it. <u>We win!</u>

Gloria and I love you and pray for you every day.

Love,

This is what happens when fear and
money get together—*Disaster!*

Dear Partner

My heart is full this morning as I write this letter. I am filled with
how awesome the mercy of our heavenly Father is. He is soooo good! I
am grateful to the MAX for how patient He is with all of us.

What a God we serve!

What a time in which to serve! Great things are happening on every
hand. Everywhere we go, in the U.S. and all over the world, people are
hungry for the Word. Not just curious, but truly hungry.

I remember how for many years after Gloria and I first began in
ministry, we searched continuously for people who had a true desire to
grow up spiritually. In many places it was a real struggle. Thank God,
it's not that way anymore.

The real thrill is to know and experience the love and power of this
great spiritual family. We were so few back then, but now we are many
and growing. We're on our way to becoming a million strong. Just think
about that—a million Partners praying together, believing together,
standing together on His Word. That's the work of the Lord, and it's
marvelous in my eyes.

Let's open our Bible today to Mark 10:17-22:

17   And when he was gone forth into the way,
      there came one running, and kneeled to him,
      and asked him, Good Master, what shall I do
      that I may inherit eternal life?
18   And Jesus said unto him, Why callest thou me
      good? there is none good but one, that is, God.
19   Thou knowest the commandments, Do not
      commit adultery, Do not kill, Do not steal, Do
      not bear false witness, Defraud not, Honour
      thy father and mother.

20   And he answered and said unto him, Master, all these have I observed from my youth.

21   Then Jesus beholding him loved him, and said unto him, One thing thou lackest: go thy way, sell whatsoever thou hast, and give to the poor, and thou shalt have treasure in heaven: and come, take up the cross, and follow me.

22   And he was sad at that saying, and went away grieved: for he had great possessions.

Look at what the fear of loss did to this man. It separated him from Jesus. He didn't have to leave. He could have stayed and asked questions. He could have cried, argued, begged—anything but leave. But that's what fear always tries to do. Remember what Adam did the first time he heard God's voice after he fell? He ran away. Separated himself.

That's the difference between fear and faith. Faith cometh by hearing His Word. Fear is just the opposite. It can't <u>make</u> you leave, but it is the source of the pressure that satan uses to cause you to back off the Word—back off your faith: *What if it doesn't work? What will I do? That's just too much.* Don't <u>ever</u> yield to that. Speak directly to it: "No, fear! I am a free person! You don't tell me what to do. I tell you what to do. Leave now!"

Let's go back to Mark 10 and look again at what Jesus said. He pointed out six commandments that this young man had kept from his youth. Then He put a situation before him that brought light on the commandment he was failing to keep. In Matthew 22:37-40 Jesus said,

37   Thou shalt love the Lord thy God with all thy heart, and with all thy soul, and with all thy mind.

38   This is the first and great commandment.

39   And the second is like unto it, Thou shalt love thy neighbour as thyself.

40   On these two commandments hang all the law and the prophets.

Had the man been developed in this, fear would have never been able to produce fear of loss (grief) in him. Why? Because perfected or developing love casts out fear.

Now apply what Jesus said in Matthew 22 to what He said to the young man in Mark 10. First of all, it's obvious what was on Jesus' mind because the scripture says, "beholding [or looking at] him [He] loved him, and said unto him...." So the words He spoke came flowing out of love. What love? The two great commandments. If Jesus had just quoted them to him, he probably would have said, "Oh, I have also kept them from my youth." Instead, Jesus proved to him that he hadn't.

The young man had become his own god and didn't realize it. That's the problem when fear and money get together. The very first commandment, "Love the Lord thy God," is also "Have no other gods before me or in my presence."

When a person becomes his own god, he must have money as power to meet his own needs. That's when money takes over first place in his thinking. Before long it becomes "Love the lord thy money with all thy heart, soul, and strength, and love thy possessions as thyself." However, when you tell the Father a hundred times a day that you love Him with all your heart and you love your neighbor as yourself, something happens in your inner man. Strengthening with might by the Holy Spirit—that's what happens!

John 15:10:

> 10   If ye keep my commandments, ye shall abide in my love; even as I have kept my Father's commandments, and abide in his love.

Had this man been doing this, selling what he had and giving to the poor would have sounded like fun and adventure instead of sounding like disaster. Not only that, but Jesus said, "You'll have treasure in heaven." That's the eternal life the man ran to Jesus about in the first place.

Then, on top of that, he would have heard in his fear-free heart: *Leave the business world and come follow Me!* Apostleship! Judas' replacement?? Probably so. But the most fun and joy of all would have been having Jesus personally direct his giving to the poor. Glory to God! But look what he missed, not to mention the hundredfold harvest on top of all that.

As the love and compassion of Jesus would have developed in him to love his neighbor, he would have learned to lay hands on the sick and then watched them recover—just like when Jesus laid hands on them. He would not have been afraid it might not work for him. By keeping the great commandments, fear wouldn't even have been there.

We could go on and on, deeper and deeper, but you see why Jesus said what He said to him. Do you also see why Jesus has COMMANDED, yes <u>COMMANDED,</u> us to do the same?

Just exactly what is the commandment to the Church? It is spelled out exactly in 1 John 3:23: "And this is his commandment, That we should believe on the name of his Son Jesus Christ, and love one another, as he gave us commandment." We are to (a) believe on the Name of His Son Jesus the Anointed, and (b) love one another <u>as He gave</u> commandment.

But how did He give commandment? Luke 10:27: "Love the Lord thy God with all thy heart, and with all thy soul, and all thy strength, and with all thy mind; and thy neighbor as thyself."

There it is, word for word. Now it is vital to remember that the first thing the Holy Spirit wrote in the book of 1 John was, "If we confess our sins, he is faithful and just to forgive us our sins, and to <u>cleanse</u> us from all unrighteousness" (verse 9).

We now understand that unrighteousness is, first of all, <u>FEAR.</u> The very moment anyone violates the command in any way, <u>fear is there.</u> Repent! Confess it immediately. Look at 1 John 2:1:

> 1   My little children, these things write I unto you, that ye sin not. And if any man sin, we have an advocate with the Father, Jesus Christ the righteous.

The sin He's talking about is violation of the law of love. That's what the whole book of 1 John is about. To what end?

1 John 5:4-5:

>4   For whatsoever is born of [Love] overcometh the world: and this is the victory that over-cometh the world, even our faith.
>
>5   Who is he that overcometh the world, but he that believeth that Jesus is the Son of [Love]?

And 5:18:

>18   We know that whosoever is born of [Love] sinneth not; but he that is begotten of [Love] keepeth himself, and that wicked one toucheth him not.

That's the one thing the devil did not want you to know! Read it again.

And read it again—no, shout it out loud right in the devil's face! Now we know what Romans 8:2 is all about. The law of the Spirit of life in Christ Jesus is the law of love. It has made us free from the law of sin and death. Free from the spiritual force that connects us to sickness, disease, poverty and death—FEAR!

When the Spirit of Love begins speaking to you about giving, any kind of giving—of yourself, of your goods, of your money, don't hesitate or back away. Rebuke fear and repent on the spot. Tell your lovely, heavenly Father how much you love Him and leap forward with great joy.

Fun and adventure with Jesus are at hand. Only fear can separate you from it, and it's totally defeated by the blood and body of Jesus on the cross. Faith is the victory. That's what we do. We're believers. We're overcomers. Champions. Blood warriors. Our time has come. Stand up and shout amen, somebody!

Take a stand with Gloria and me and the KCM victory team—

September through October—as we travel and preach in Sydney, Brisbane, Perth, Australia and Singapore, then to our troops in South Korea, winding up with a Victory Campaign in Honolulu, Hawaii. Together we can do everything Jesus calls us to do.

Gloria and I love you very much and we pray for you every day.

Love,

Ken

Love by Faith by Love Is the Process of Power

Dear Partner

In this month's letter, let's first review the basics of faith—the laws of faith. Everything in the kingdom of God is governed by spiritual laws, just as the material or natural world is governed by natural laws. They are called "laws" because they work when they are put to work regardless of who activates them.

Let's begin by looking at Romans 3:27:

> 27   Where is boasting then? It is excluded. By what law? of works? Nay: but by the law of faith.

Laws are made up of elements or building blocks. So let's start by answering the question where does faith come from?

Romans 10:17:

> 17   So then faith cometh by hearing, and hearing by the word of God.

God's Word is the source. Not tribulation or experience. Faith is a spiritual force.

Next, where does it get its power? Galatians 5:5-6:

> 5   For we through the Spirit wait for the hope of righteousness by faith.
> 6   For in Jesus Christ neither circumcision availeth any thing, nor uncircumcision; but <u>faith which worketh by love.</u>

Again we see faith works through the spirit. <u>It is powered by love.</u> We know from 1 John 4:16 that God is Love. The faith that is imparted into the believer when he or she is born again is God's faith—the very faith by which Jesus conquered sin, sickness, demons and fear. So God's Word is the source. God's love is its power.

How is it released?

Faith is brought to bear on the material world in <u>two primary ways: words and corresponding actions.</u>

Jesus' classic teaching on faith and how it works is in Mark 11, beginning with the 22nd verse. Let's read through verse 24:

22   And Jesus answering saith unto them, Have faith in God.

23   For verily I say unto you, That whosoever shall say unto this mountain, Be thou removed, and be thou cast into the sea; and shall not doubt in his heart, but shall believe that those things which he saith shall come to pass; he shall have whatsoever he saith.

24   Therefore I say unto you, What things soever ye desire, when ye pray, believe that ye receive them, and ye shall have them.

Words are seeds. All life on this earth is governed by seeds sown. Jesus said in Mark 4:26-29 that life in heaven and the laws of heaven are based on seedtime and harvest. Heaven created all matter through that system. How, then, could the earth be governed any other way? It can't. "Whatsoever a man soweth that shall he also reap." That cannot be changed. <u>Only the seed can be changed.</u>

The other part of that law is corresponding action. That's what Mark 11:24 is about. Faith believes when it prays, not when it sees. Faith acts and speaks as though the mountain no longer exists. If God says it's gone, then it's G-O-N-E gone. Well, it's God's faith empowered by God's love. The mountain doesn't know the difference unless fear "takes a look."

How did that get in there? Look at verse 25:

> 25 And when ye stand praying, forgive, if ye have
> aught against any: that your Father also which
> is in heaven may forgive you your trespasses.

Faith is Love-dependent. Break the Love commandment and <u>fear is the instant result.</u> Remember, we are talking about laws. God is the author of laws, both spiritual and physical.

Let's go directly to the foundation upon which all things are laid. Matthew 22:37-40:

> 37 Jesus said unto him, Thou shalt love the Lord
> thy God with all thy heart, and with all thy
> soul, and with all thy mind.
> 38 This is the first and great commandment.
> 39 And the second is like unto it, Thou shalt love
> thy neighbour as thyself.
> 40 <u>On these two commandments hang all the
> law and the prophets.</u>

Notice here Jesus said all the law and the prophets (the New Testament is included in the prophets) hang on these two. All means all—the law of faith included. We've already seen that from Galatians 5:6.

How do we put all this together? We begin with first things first. The commandment is first. Not faith. However, the commandment without faith is legalism. That <u>stinks</u> in the nostrils of God. <u>Love by faith by Love is the process of power.</u>

Let's go to 1 John 4:15-17:

> 15 Whosoever shall confess that Jesus is the Son
> of God, God dwelleth in him, and he in God.
> 16 And we have known and <u>believed the love</u> that
> God hath to us. God is love; and he that dwelleth
> in love dwelleth in God, and God in him.
> 17 Herein is our love made perfect, that we may
> have boldness in the day of judgment: because
> as he is, so are we in this world.

We confess by faith (which works by Love), then we believe the Love by faith. How do we believe the Love? We go through the process "faith cometh by hearing." John 14:21:

> 21 He that hath my commandments, and keepeth them, he it is that loveth me: and he that loveth me shall be loved of my Father, and I will love him, and will manifest myself to him.

In order to <u>develop</u> this in my inner man I must confess it with my mouth: "Jesus, in obedience to Your commandment, I confess it by faith with my mouth: 'I love You, Father, with all my heart, with all my soul and with all my mind. And I love my neighbor as myself.'" I said that by faith. Faith cometh. Love works. Faith is released and fear is removed. Fear will try to bring up unforgiveness. Fight the good fight of faith. Rebuke feelings. Faith which works by <u>Love</u> has already spoken. Believe the Love!

Now we're only halfway through. Look at John 14:21 again. Confessing and keeping the commandment is our part. Jesus said He and the Father would do their part. Does Jesus keep the Father's commandments? Does the Father keep His own commandments? Absolutely!

Now comes the big confession of faith: "My Father in heaven loves <u>me</u> with all of His heart and all of His soul and all of His mind and strength. Jesus loves me as Himself." <u>This is where faith is released.</u> Believe on the Name of His Son Jesus. Believe in the Blood. Believe in the Cross. Believe you are a new creature.

Confess John 14:21 until faith cometh! Say it until your mind is saturated with the commandment. Everything we are called to do depends on it. Fear and terror are being released into the earth as never before in the history of man. Overflow is coming in 2005. Overflow of what? It depends on what seeds we sow in 2004. We can't break the laws and succeed in the process of power and protection.

God is moving in unprecedented ways. We, KCM and our Partners are right in the middle of it all.

Put the process to work over everything. As you sow your financial seeds this month, confess the commandments with all of your strength. Lay your hands on your seed and "hang" the harvest on the law of God. Love by faith, by Love.

Gloria and I pray for you every day. We love you very much.

Love,

Wake Your Faith Up

Dear Partner

Let's begin by reading some <u>very</u> important verses of Scripture. Read each very carefully. Don't just scan through them. Hang on to every word as if Jesus Himself were reading them to you personally. <u>He is!</u>

Acts 11:14:

> 14   Who shall tell thee words, whereby thou and all thy house shall be saved.

Acts 5:20:

> 20   Go, stand and speak in the temple to the people all the words of this life.

Matthew 12:37:

> 37   For by thy words thou shalt be justified, and by thy words thou shalt be condemned.

Proverbs 18:21:

> 21   Death and life are in the power of the tongue: and they that love it shall eat the fruit thereof.

Proverbs 21:23:

> 23   Whoso keepeth his mouth and his tongue keepeth his soul from troubles.

Proverbs 12:18:

> 18   There is that speaketh like the piercings of a sword: but the tongue of the wise is health.

It is an eternal Bible truth that people are saved and healed by hearing and speaking words. That is a fact that will never change. The reason for this is very clear. Receiving anything from God is done with and by faith.

Faith is the connection between God and man. Hebrews 11:6 says it is impossible to please God without faith. Your Father is not pleased when He cannot manifest Himself in your life and meet your needs.

Since faith is the connection by which salvation, healing, financial prosperity, etc. is transferred from heaven to you it's impossible to please Him without it. Jesus went through the horrible death of the cross and suffered in hell so all our needs could be met according to His riches in glory. Then He made available, to whosoever, His faith with which to receive.

Let's remind ourselves just how faith comes to any person.

First, let's look at Romans 10:6-13:

6   But the righteousness which is of faith speaketh on this wise, Say not in thine heart, Who shall ascend into heaven? (that is, to bring Christ down from above:)

7   Or, Who shall descend into the deep? (that is, to bring up Christ again from the dead.)

8   But what saith it? The word is nigh thee, even in thy mouth, and in thy heart: that is, the word of faith, which we preach;

9   That if thou shalt confess with thy mouth the Lord Jesus, and shalt believe in thine heart that God hath raised him from the dead, thou shalt be saved.

10   For with the heart man believeth unto righteousness; and with the mouth confession is made unto salvation.

11   For the scripture saith, Whosoever believeth on him shall not be ashamed.

12   For there is no difference between the Jew and

> the Greek: for the same Lord over all is rich
> unto all that call upon him.
>
> 13   For whosoever shall call upon the name of the
> Lord shall be saved.

Faith is available, as I said, for "whosoever." Whosoever, that is, who will obey the laws that govern it. Now Romans 10:17:

> 17   So then faith cometh by hearing, and hearing
> by the word of God.

God's Word is the source of God's faith.

Everything God has, <u>His very best,</u> is always available to the claim of faith. No one has to sit and wait for some kind of special move of God, or for some special anointing to fall, in order to receive their healing or breakthrough. God is ready now. He's always on. He's always saving. He's always healing. His abundance is always at hand. It is nigh thee, even in thy mouth. There's a miracle in your mouth just waiting to be released.

Words alone are not enough. They must be filled with faith.

Here's the problem. Low-level, feeble faith (either through no Word intake or faith contaminated from being mixed with fear) will allow the enemy into your life. Remember, Ephesians 6:16, talking about the <u>full</u> armor of God, says "Above all, taking the shield of faith, wherewith ye shall be able to quench <u>all</u> the fiery darts [or weapons] of the wicked." The rest of the armor depends on faith to work. The helmet of salvation, breastplate of righteousness, etc., work by faith.

Without the shield of faith, you're uncovered. You're especially vulnerable where your physical body is concerned. Then when pain strikes it becomes very difficult to hold strongly onto right words. Even when you do say the right things, they bring little result because they're mental, empty words. Then you begin to question God: *Why doesn't He help me with this? I wonder what's wrong here.* That's when things get worse instead of better.

It's time—or really past time—to get under the word of faith and

<u>stay there</u> night and day. Put everything else aside.

There's nothing more important.

NOTHING.

After all, what's more important than the authority of life and death being in the power or authority of your own tongue?

When faith is feeble you'll want to do anything but hear and speak words of faith. Sometimes it will even make you mad when someone tries to give you what the Bible says about your situation: "I know it says that, but you don't understand!"

That happens because faith is the product of your spirit. It's not a mental force, therefore it does not come from your mind. The mind will always dominate a weak spirit.

If you continue to talk about your trials and difficulties, your faith will continue to shrivel up until you have no shield at all. Continuing to go on about what all the devil is doing strengthens his place around you until fear and doubt become stronger and stronger and develop into a stronghold—a prison of misery that no child of God should ever be in.

It's time to wake up your faith. It's time to wake up the strong man, the giant that's asleep inside your innermost being. Look pain and failure right in the eye and shout. Listen, now. <u>It's very, very important to shout</u> with <u>every fiber of your being</u>. I mean it, now—you'll have to do it.

In fact, check this out right now. Just say in a normal but firm tone, "Greater is He that is in me than he that is in the world." Now check out your level of faith. Notice your inner condition.

Next, take a deep breath and <u>shout with everything you've got. I mean everything!</u> 1-2-3-SHOUT!

"GREATER IS HE THAT IS IN ME THAN HE THAT IS IN THE WORLD!"

Check yourself out again. Wow! The giant's awake! Let him roar. Let faith talk. "I'M A FREE MAN! I'M COMING OUT OF THIS CAGE! JESUS HAS SET ME FREE. I'M SUPPOSED TO PROSPER! I'M SUPPOSED TO BE HEALED! I'M SUPPOSED TO BE HAPPY AND FILLED WITH JOY! I REFUSE TO GO BACK INTO THAT CAGE OF DOUBT AND UNBELIEF!"

Now that your faith is awake, talk right now about how wonderful your heavenly Father is. Praise Him. Tell Him how grateful you are that you're free: "Thank God, I'm not going to hell!" Don't talk about the devil anymore. Start talking to him. Give him no place.

To keep faith alive and strong, two things must happen:

1.   "Faith cometh by hearing and hearing by the Word of God." No Word in, no faith out.
2.   "Faith worketh by love." No love, no power.

Romans 3:27 says faith works by spiritual law. The law of faith. Jesus said in Matthew 22:37:

37   Jesus said unto him, Thou shalt love the Lord thy God with all thy heart, and with all thy soul, and with all thy mind.

Galatians 5:6 says faith works by love. The law of faith hangs on the commandment of love just like all the rest of the law and the prophets. Nothing that's of God works without love. Of course not. God is love. Nothing of God works without God.

Faith cometh = that's God's part.

By hearing = that's our part.

Faith worketh = that's God's part.

By love = that's our part.

Make the decision of quality that must be made so you'll never be in that weakened position ever again: "I will keep the commandment of love. I will stay in the Word and live by faith." Jesus is the Savior. You are the receiver. He is the Healer. You are the receiver. Now enter into His rest and peace.

Isaiah 26:3:

> 3 Thou wilt keep him in perfect peace, whose mind is stayed on thee: because he trusteth in thee.

And John 14:21:

> 21 He that hath my commandments, and keepeth them, he it is that loveth me: and he that loveth me shall be loved of my Father, and I will love him, and will manifest myself to him.

Jesus is coming! He's coming very soon. Sooner than any of us think. We have a job to do that must be done now. Together we can do it. We can do all things through His anointing which strengthens us.

Lay your hands on your seed-<u>faith</u> offering and <u>shout</u> again. Stir your faith up over that seed. Break out and break free!

Gloria and I love you very much and we pray for you every day.

Jesus is Lord.

Love,

Ken

Back in the Saddle Again!

Dear Partner

When I was just a kid one of my favorite songs was "Back in the Saddle Again" by Gene Autry. I could just see myself "Ridin' the range once more, Totin' my old .44." Being a cowboy at heart and living in west Texas, it wasn't hard to believe that song was written just for me.

And, I still do. I'm healed and strong, and getting stronger every day. I don't have adequate words to express my gratitude to Jesus for being my Savior and to my Partners for standing with me through this whole thing. The prayers of my Partners and my family put me over the top. I will be eternally grateful.

Here we are once again at the most exciting time of the year— Christmas! And what a Christmas this one is going to be. Christmas of 2004, The Year of Fullness. All it takes to have the greatest, fullest year of your life is faith and praise. All it takes to have a fabulous year is for it to end right.

Take the Lord Jesus at His Word and begin praising Him openly and shamelessly. One of the reasons He came was so you could have life and have it more abundantly!

Don't wait for things around you to change. Nothing around you will change until you do. Bad things can't stay in the presence of bold praise. Ask me how I know. Praise and worship in spite of the pain is one of the major weapons of faith that brought me victory over the last three months.

Let's praise our way out of 2004 and into 2005—The Year of Overflow. We are going to overflow in '05. It's our choice whether that overflow is abundance of God's grace and all things good or more pain and debt. God has already made His choice. His choice for us was Jesus. Life abundant. Overflow of the fruits of righteousness. He has done everything except make the choice for us.

Read Deuteronomy 30:19:

19   I call heaven and earth to record this day against you, that I have set before you life and death, blessing and cursing: therefore choose life, that both thou and thy seed may live.

Speaking of why Jesus came, let's talk about that. Why did He come? Why was He born into this earth? The first and most dramatic clue is found in Luke 2:13-14:

13   And suddenly there was with the angel a multitude of the heavenly host praising God, and saying,

14   Glory to God in the highest, and on earth peace, good will toward men.

Notice that phrase "good will toward men." It's not "among men," the way most people read it. In the Garden of Eden there was a great separation between God and man. Satan started another war with heaven—sin against righteousness.

All things bad came into the earth in the form of a curse. But, thank God, the sacrifice for Adam's sin was born into this earth in Bethlehem. And God, who calls things which be not as though they were, shouted His faith and announced through angels: "The war between heaven and earth is over. Good will from Me toward all men!" Separation between God and man was never God's idea.

Let's go to Genesis 1:26-28 and see just exactly what the will of God was:

26   And God said, Let us make man in our image, after our likeness: and let them have dominion over the fish of the sea, and over the fowl of the air, and over the cattle, and over all the earth, and over every creeping thing that creepeth upon the earth.

27   So God created man in his own image, in the

image of God created he him; male and female
created he them.

28 And God blessed them, and God said unto
them, Be fruitful, and multiply, and replenish
the earth, and subdue it: and have dominion
over the fish of the sea, and over the fowl of
the air, and over every living thing that moveth
upon the earth.

Those are the words that created Adam. Words of authority.
Authority over everything God had created. <u>Everything.</u>

Psalm 8:5-6: "You have made him a little lower than *[Elohim—*
Yourself*]*, and You have crowned him with glory and honor. You have
made him to have dominion over the works [creation] of Your hands"
(New King James Version). In verse 3 it says the heavens, the moon and
the stars are included in that dominion. <u>Now that was and always has
been God's perfect will for man.</u> It was not His will for a debunked,
fallen angel to have authority over man or anything else that belonged
to heaven.

From Malachi 3:6, "For I am the Lord, I change not..." and Hebrews
13:8, "Jesus Christ the same yesterday, and today, and for ever," we know
that God never changes. Once His will is made known, then that's His
will forever. Jesus came into this earth not only to make that will known
by taking authority over sickness, disease and death, the wind and
the water, and all devils including satan himself, but also to get that
dominion back for men.

Let's look at Matthew 28:18:

18 And Jesus came and spake unto them, saying, All
power is given unto me in heaven and in earth.

<u>All</u> power, or authority, in <u>both</u> heaven <u>and</u> earth. Then the first
thing He did was the same thing His Father had done in the Garden of
Eden. He delegated to men His authority over earth: "Therefore you go
into all the earth."

The pattern of this authority—the chain of command—was made known to Jesus' disciples in Matthew 18:18-20:

> 18   Verily I say unto you, Whatsoever ye shall bind on earth shall be bound in heaven: and whatsoever ye shall loose on earth shall be loosed in heaven.
>
> 19   Again I say unto you, That if two of you shall agree on earth as touching any thing that they shall ask, it shall be done for them of my Father which is in heaven.
>
> 20   For where two or three are gathered together in my name, <u>there am I in the midst of them.</u>

"You bind, I'll back it. You loose (the devil's grip), I'll back it. Any two of you <u>on earth</u> agree, I'll back it. Not only with our heavenly Father but also <u>with My personal presence.</u>"

That's what He is anointed to do. He is the High Priest appointed by God to see to it that His words in our mouths come to pass. He came into this earth to pray the most powerful prayer ever uttered through human lips: "Thy will be done on earth as it is in heaven!" He came. He prayed it. He did it.

To ask Him to do something outside the framework and order of that chain of authority is to ask Him to do something out of the will of God. HE WON'T DO IT! To ask Him to bind the devil won't work. He has told *us* to bind him. Not only bind him, but also cast him out.

This may come as a shock, but He did not say, "I am going into all the world and I'm going to preach the gospel, come follow Me." He said, "You go into all the world and preach the gospel, and I'll go <u>with you</u> and confirm the Word <u>you</u> preach with signs following." He did not say, "I have on the armor. Stay behind Me." He said, "<u>You</u> put on the whole <u>armor of God,</u> His armor, and you stand against the devil. You bind, I'll back it. You loose, I'll back it. <u>I'll send you the same Holy Spirit of power that backed My authority when I was ministering in the earth, and He will dwell in you and back you in My Name. My authority.</u>"

No wonder that angel shouted, "I bring you <u>good</u> news!" Take it. Rise up right now with a renewed faith in the words of Jesus' authority in your mouth. Put the devil on the run. Cast the mountain of debt into the sea. Take authority over sickness and disease.

In your mind "see" Jesus standing right behind you with fire in His eyes and a smile on His face. You are standing right in the middle of His perfect will for you and your life. You are on your way. To where? <u>To victory!</u> Overwhelming victory. Victory in the Blood. Victory in the Word. Victory in the Name of Jesus.

Now begin to talk louder about it.

Don't whisper. Shout!

People talk about how loud-mouthed Americans are—especially Texans. That's because we're winners at heart. Well I am a loudmouth in Jesus, because He's the greatest winner of all time and it's my victory He won.

You'd better know I'm back in the saddle again, and with a louder mouth than ever. WE WIN!!

May you have the greatest <u>Christ</u>mas you've ever had and an overflowing year of victory in 2005.

Gloria and I love you more than ever, and we pray for you every day.

Love,

<u>Ken</u>

Kenneth reading letters from his Partners at the prayer cabin in Arkansas.

Perfect, Entire, Wanting Nothing!

Dear Partner

My, what a year 2004 was—both for this ministry and for Gloria and me personally! So many things we had believed for came to completion in '04.

I am shouting my thanksgiving from the housetops to the Lord Jesus for my complete healing. Not only is my back totally pain free, but some other things have been healed and cleared up as well. I'm out of rehab and back in training, going for the overflow. I am on my way to becoming stronger than I have ever been in my life! Not only physically but I have learned and grown spiritually by leaps and bounds.

That's the thing about staying with the Word and overcoming by faith—you remember the Lord and you did it. So not only can you do it again if you have to, but you can also teach and help someone else win the same fight of faith in their lives.

Let's talk about a key element to every faith victory in Christ Jesus: PATIENCE. James 1:4 tells us:

4   But let patience have her perfect work, that ye
         may be perfect and entire, wanting nothing.

Look at it again. <u>Perfect,</u> <u>entire,</u> <u>wanting nothing</u>! That's a word from heaven that you can hold onto. I did. It did. And I am!

The Greek word *patience* in James 1:3-4 can be translated endurance, constancy—or just simply the state of being constantly, consistently the same regardless of the circumstance. It does not mean to put up with. We don't put up with the devil and his attacks on our lives. No! Not ever! We attack him with greater force and <u>never</u> let up no matter what.

We are not just talking about patience. We are talking about patience <u>and</u> faith. We must never look at faith by itself. Nor should we ever look at patience by itself. They are dependent on one another. Faith does the work. Patience won't let faith quit. And there is nothing in this world order that faith will not overcome.

Pain is the enemy of patience. The greater the pain the greater the desire to just give up and die. That's the time when it is so important to stay on the Word—the promises of God. His Word never changes. He never changes. The blood of Jesus never changes. Get on it and stay on it. That's the key to victory.

Patience is not only dependent on faith. It is also dependent on decision. Quality decision. The strong decisions you have made are what will carry you through when the attacks come. And the attacks are coming. There's no getting around that. But when you have already made the decision to stay on the Word regardless of what gets thrown against your life, <u>victory is already yours.</u> Like they say: "<u>It's only a matter of time. I win!</u>"

Another thing faith and patience totally depend on is love and its commandment. Faith works by love. And patience must be accompanied by its twin brother, faith, or the whole thing just falls apart.

So now we're back to the place of decision. The best decision you ever made was to receive Jesus as your Lord and Savior. The next best decision you could possibly make is to do what He says always, every time, <u>regardless!</u> This is an absolute decision. No change. For no reason. No excuses.

This is the ultimate decision of quality and should be made over the Communion table with the body and blood of Jesus in hand. It's that important. It's life. It's abundance. Without that decision of quality, life is full of ups and downs—mostly downs. The reason is simple. Without Jesus being in full control there's no real stability. Without His ministry in our lives we're doomed to make the same disastrous mistakes over and over and never really know the abundance and joy that He went to the Cross to provide for us.

I can hear His words in my spirit right now as I'm writing this: "Why call ye me Lord, Lord, and do not the things which I say?" That's not the will of my heart, and I know it's not yours. My greatest heart's desire is to do <u>every</u> word He says. His words are our lives. His words are our health. His words are our victory over hell.

Without His words, we are doomed. But, thank God, we're not without Him or His words. <u>Victory is only a decision away.</u>

2005 is the year of <u>overflow.</u> Thanks to Jesus, *our* overflow is the abundance of everything good. The world is headed into a time of judgment—the overflow, or harvesting, of the seeds it has sown. That's what judgment is.

If there is any kind of sin or disobedience in your life, confess it and stop the thing from harvesting <u>immediately.</u> I mean right now. Before you <u>read any more of this letter, repent.</u> Dig up the seed. Don't let it go one more second.

This is the most important time of our lives. We are going to snatch millions of people out of judgment and into glory this year. We are going to preach more Word to more people than ever before in our 38-year history. It is a massive assignment but, thank God, we're ready. Together we can and will get it done.

I can <u>never</u> thank you enough for praying for me and for my family in 2004! Your prayers, letters and phone calls put us over the top. None of us, especially me, will ever be the same. We love you so very much.

As you sow your financial seed this month, name it *overflow.* Flood stage. Over the top. Magnum victory. Super abundance. Jesus magnified in everything I do in 2005! We set ourselves in agreement with that. It's done. Now shout for about an hour.

Again, Gloria and I love and appreciate you, and we pray for you every day.

Love,

Ken

Overflow Is Here BIG TIME!

Dear Partner

For more than a year now, we have talked about overflow and that it is coming. Well it's here. The Spirit of overflow has been released in the earth. It's time to either rejoice or repent.

Let's talk a bit about how it works. Picture God doing His part to see to it that a piece of land has just the right amount of rain at just the right time and blessing the soil to produce at its maximum potential. Think about Him controlling the weather and temperature all year long and giving instructions to His angels to protect this piece of land from any interference from the devil and his destroyers.

If God did all that, what would happen to that farm? That soil would grow <u>whatever</u> seed had been planted, producing a bumper crop—overflow proportions. <u>Whatever seed!</u> That's as clear a picture as I know how to present of the Spirit of overflow. That's what is here. There are massive harvests from seeds that have been planted for whole lifetimes that are ready to suddenly explode into manifestation. God will not plant seed into that land for you. You have already planted it, good or bad.

This is not such good news for the troublemakers and disobedient who have ignored the commandment of Jesus to love God and their neighbor as themselves. But this is really good news to those who have been sowing the seeds of love and compassion. This is a time of rejoicing for those who over the years just kept on walking by faith and tithing and giving offerings in obedience to heaven's commands, even when it looked like to everyone else it was a foolish thing to do. Payday is here! Healing time is here! Harvest time. The time to dance in the streets before the God of heaven.

This also means we have the biggest job of our lives in front of us. That's the redeeming of the lives who are suddenly overwhelmed with bumper crops of hell on earth into which their sin seeds have exploded into. After all, that's what our abundance is all about. That's what Jesus is all about. That's what Love does. Love reaches out to save not condemn. It's time to harvest the greatest crop of all—PEOPLE. Souls into the kingdom of God. More people are being saved right now all over the world than ever before. More people will get saved this year than in all the years of human history. This is the time our heavenly Father has dreamed of since before the foundation of the world. His house is about to be filled to <u>OVERFLOWING.</u> This is the time all the prophets saw would one day come to pass. Think about it. <u>This is it and you and I are right in the middle of it all.</u> We will "snatch" millions of hurting, overwhelmed people out of the heartache of judgment into the glory of God the Father.

But in order to take full advantage of this time of overflow there are some things that are extremely important.

First, judge yourself. Not others.

Take the time to have an accounting of your life. Just you and Jesus take a good look at everything you are doing. Ask yourself, *Is this something the Father directed me to do or did I direct me to do this?* Sometimes this can get painful but it's certainly worth it. Don't hold on to things for yourself. If it's something you need you walk away from, so be it. There's something far greater waiting at the door trying to come in.

Another thing that <u>must</u> happen is the absolute commitment to the Law of Jesus. Everything—I mean everything, including your very life—depends on it. This is no time to sow any seed of disobedience. <u>The Law of Jesus</u> is the key to the success of everything. Nothing in God's kingdom works without it.

This time imagine with me someone with a bunch of curtains trying to hang them over a window, and all the while having no curtain rod upon which for them to hang. He is running to and fro frantically trying to get these curtains to stay up and they are falling down just as fast as he hangs them up. In my mind it looks like some old-time movie comedy. This fool is tangled up in a pile of curtains. As he runs around hanging up one, another is falling on his head.

This is not so funny when you notice the names written on the curtains. There's the curtain of faith. The curtains of healing... deliverance...prosperity...righteousness. The whole thing becomes even less funny when you hear this poor fellow's cries of desperation: "Oh God, why is this happening to me? I'm serving You. It seems as though my faith doesn't work right. I'm sick though I believe in healing. I believe in abundance, yet I'm behind in my bills. The only abundance I have is debt and lack. What's wrong??!!"

Then, as you look even closer, you see little snakes crawling around in the pile of curtains nipping at his heels. This is a tough picture to swallow but let's face it. It's far too true in the lives of believers everywhere.

However, look over in the corner of the room. Standing there is a huge, <u>tremendously strong,</u> golden curtain rod. It's been standing there all the time just waiting to be hung. Written on it in huge red letters is Matthew 22:37-40:

THOU SHALT LOVE THE LORD THY GOD WITH ALL THY HEART AND WITH ALL THY SOUL AND WITH ALL THY MIND. THIS IS THE FIRST AND GREAT COMMANDMENT. THE SECOND IS LIKE IT. THOU SHALT LOVE THY NEIGHBOR AS THY SELF. ON THESE HANG ALL THE LAW AND THE PROPHETS.

Spiritual laws govern all life. There's the law of faith, but it <u>hangs</u> on the MASTER LAW—LOVE. Why? Simple. God is Love and He is life. That's just simply the bottom line. Without Him there is no life. Faith worketh by Love. Suddenly the voice of the Lord is heard, "Hang the rod. Not the curtains. The curtains are already attached to the rod!"

What now? I mean after the commitment is made to walk in the Law of Jesus? Let's look at 2 Peter 3:1-2:

1   This second epistle, beloved, I now write unto you; in both which I stir up your pure minds by way of remembrance:

2   That ye may be mindful of the words which were spoken before by the holy prophets, and

of the commandment of us the apostles of the
Lord and Saviour.

There is only one way to stir up your mind to remember something
or to have something on your mind all the time regardless of what else
is going on around you. It must be in your mouth and in your eyes.

The very first thing that must come out your mouth in the morning
when your eyes open is Matthew 22:37 "I love You, Father, with all my
heart, all my soul and all my mind and strength." And it must be the
very last thing you think and say before you close your eyes at night.

If you can't sleep, lie there and say it over and over until you fall
asleep. Don't lie there thinking and worrying about other stuff. You
can't do anything about all that anyway. Remember, stop trying to hang
the curtains. Hang the rod. The curtains are already attached to it.

Did you get that? Don't pray about other things until this is settled.
Don't talk about anything else to God except how much you love and
appreciate Him. Say all this out loud all day. You are going to be shocked
at how rapidly things start happening in your favor. When you begin
practicing the Love of God He responds. You are cultivating roots in
your inner man. You are being rooted and grounded in Love—in God.

I'll close this letter today with Ephesians 3:14-20. Read it very
carefully. This is YOU! It's happening to you and for you right now. As
you sow your tithes and offerings sow them in Love words to Jesus and
to the Father. The Spirit of overflow—Love Himself—is being poured
out. Jump into the river of His Love.

Gloria and I love you so very much and we pray for you every day.

Love,

Ken

"For this cause I bow my knees unto the Father of our Lord Jesus Christ,
of whom the whole family in heaven and earth is named, that he would

grant you, according to the riches of his glory, <u>to be strengthened with might by his Spirit in the inner man;</u> that Christ may dwell in your hearts by faith; <u>that ye, being <u>rooted and grounded in love,</u></u> may be able to comprehend with all saints what is the breadth, and length, and depth, and height; and to know the love of Christ, which passeth knowledge, <u>that ye might be filled with all the fulness of God.</u> Now unto him that is able to do exceeding abundantly above all that we ask or think, according to the power that worketh in us" (Ephesians 3:14-20).

This is what is happening every time you confess the great command.

Jump into the River of His Love!

Dear Partner

I tell you, I am so thrilled and excited about this time we're living in and all that's happening around us, I can hardly put it into words! If there ever were a time to walk with and serve the Lord Jesus, it is now. The miraculous is exploding into manifestation on every hand. I'm thinking right now of something the Lord said to me in the visitation I received in December '03:

This is the time you've been waiting for, hoping for and believing for.

Oh, my, how very true that is. It's time to jump into the flow—His flow—of the wonderful, marvelous works of the Spirit.

Let's go to the Word in 3 John 2:

> 2   Beloved, I wish above all things that thou mayest prosper and be in health, even as thy soul prospereth.

Notice where the *King James Version* says "I wish," the Greek text says "I pray." This, with the fact John identifies himself as "the elder" in verse 1, really settles something extremely important when you stop and meditate on it. This was written by a man who had many years earlier walked with Jesus as a personal disciple and aide. This is the man Jesus turned His own mother over to when He was on the cross. If anyone understood the divine importance of words, John did. And he said, "I pray <u>above</u> <u>all</u> <u>things</u> that you may prosper and be in health."

Why do you suppose John was so strong about that? I'll tell you why. Many years before, he had heard Jesus preach it and teach it over and again.

For example, in John 10:7 he recalls the time Jesus referred to

Himself as the door to the sheepfold. Now let's look at the 10th verse:

> 10   The thief cometh not, but for to steal, and to kill, and to destroy: I am come that they might have life, and that they might have it more abundantly.

The *Amplified* translation of John 10:10 gives us an even better insight into why John wrote 3 John 2.

> 10   ...I came that they may have and enjoy life, and have it in abundance (to the full, till it overflows).

Glory! Abundance to the full till it overflows! That's what is happening right now.

Now read that version again, only don't stop. Read the next line: "I have come that you might have full, overflowing abundance. I am the Good Shepherd." It is His calling from God the Father. It's His job to overflow His goodness, abundance, prosperity and health in our lives. Well, why hasn't He done it, then? He has! Our religious unbelief and hardness of heart has in so many cases for so many years stopped the flow. But no more! We are finally beginning to open our hearts and minds to overflow.

In teaching on this on the *Believer's Voice of Victory* TV broadcast, Brother Keith Moore said, "When you want what God wants for the same reason He wants it, you become...unstoppable." It is His divine will for you and me and this ministry to take this overflow to the whole Body of Christ all over the world.

It's time to prosper. It's time to be well. It's time to go, go, go. It's time for a tsunami of God's love to wash over the dark, dry places of the world bringing hope and joy where there has never before been any chance of abundant life. The time is now and the message has been placed in our hands. The anointing is here. The treasure house of heaven has been poured out.

In closing let's look at Amos 9:13, *The Amplified Bible:*

> 13 Behold, the days are coming, says the Lord, that the plowman shall overtake the reaper, and the treader of grapes him who sows the seed; and the mountains shall drop sweet wine and all the hills shall melt [that is, everything heretofore barren and unfruitful shall overflow with spiritual blessing].

Now that's overflow in your face! Harvest just as fast as you sow. That's also the reaping of seeds sown in the past. The time for all this is NOW!

Double up on your time in God's Word. Strengthen your confessions of His promises. Praise, praise and more praise. Repent for things that are not right and change them. First and foremost, put His commandment of love absolutely first place over everything else in your life. Let's go back to the elder, John's gospel chapter 14, verse 21. Remember now, it was only four chapters before where we were told by Jesus that He came that we might have abundant, overflowing life:

> 21 He that hath my commandments, and keepeth them, he it is that loveth me: and he that loveth me shall be loved of my Father, and I will love him, and will manifest myself to him.

The life of overflowing abundance is in the life of Love. <u>Wealth in the hands of Love is most magnificent.</u>

As you sow your seed this month, by faith release the Love of God on and through it. Lay your hands on it and tell your Lord God you love Him with all your heart, all your soul, and all your mind and strength and your neighbor as yourself.

The chains of lack cannot remain under the divine pressure of obedience to the Great Command.

Oh, how wonderful these times are. Put everything else behind you and jump into the river of His love.

Gloria and I love you and pray for you every day.

Love,

Ken

Becoming Love-Inside Minded

Dear Partner

I bring you greetings from your fellow KCM Partners in Singapore. I just returned to my hotel room after our Partner service here. I tell you, it was delightful!

It is always amazing to me how God's people are the same anywhere in the world. The language may be different (they do speak English here) and the clothes may come from different cultures, but born-again Jesus people react to the Word the same. They laugh, shout, dance and rejoice at the victory of the Lord Jesus over death and fear.

What a God we serve!

Let's look at some very familiar verses of Scripture in this letter, but give special attention to a part that is almost never discussed. Mark 10:17-21:

17 And when he was gone forth into the way, there came one running, and kneeled to him, and asked him, Good Master, what shall I do that I may inherit eternal life?

18 And Jesus said unto him, Why callest thou me good? there is none good but one, that is, God.

19 Thou knowest the commandments, Do not commit adultery, Do not kill, Do not steal, Do not bear false witness, Defraud not, Honour thy father and mother.

20 And he answered and said unto him, Master, all these have I observed from my youth.

21 Then Jesus beholding him loved him, and said unto him, One thing thou lackest: go thy way, sell whatsoever thou hast, and give to the poor, and thou shalt have treasure in heaven: and come, take up the cross, and follow me.

Many, many sermons and teachings have been derived from this incident in the life and ministry of Jesus. However, almost nothing has been said about the first phrase of verse 21: "Then Jesus beholding [or looking at] him loved him."

This is not something that occurred because of anything the young man did or did not do or say. Jesus ministered to him through the "look of Love." He ministered to the man by releasing the Love of God. He not only released the Love by and through what He said but also through His look. The Love and Anointing of God will and should flow through the eyes as well as the mouth and hands of a believer. For this to happen in our lives, there are several things we must do to become more "Love-of-God-in-me-now minded."

First, we must act on the Word and receive the Love by faith. Look at John 17:23:

> 23 I in them, and thou in me, that they may be made perfect in one; and that the world may know that thou hast sent me, and hast loved them, as thou hast loved me.

Jesus said that God loves you as much as He does Jesus. Receive that Love. Begin confessing it out loud continually.

Second, believe the Love. First John 4:16: "We have known and believed the love that God hath to us." Believe the Love!

Third, believe that Love NEVER fails (1 Corinthians 13:8). I don't care how impossible the situation may seem, nothing is too difficult for our God...who is Love! God is Love and Love is God!

Fourth, believe it is in you NOW! Romans 5:5:

> 5 And hope maketh not ashamed; because the love of God is shed abroad in our hearts by the Holy Ghost which is given unto us.

Now look at what Jesus prayed in John 17:26:

26   And I have declared unto them thy name, and will declare it: that the love wherewith thou hast loved me may be in them, and I in them.

The very same Love wherewith <u>God</u> the Father <u>loves</u> <u>Jesus</u> is in you. Now! Read that again. The same Love that Jesus released through His Word, His hands, His eyes—the Love of the Father—is living inside the spirit of every born-again believer.

Fifth, and most important, totally commit yourself to the laws of Jesus, His command to the Church. First John 3:21:

21   Beloved, if our heart condemn us not, then have we confidence toward God.

The way He gave commandment is Matthew 22:37-40:

37   Jesus said unto him, Thou shalt love the Lord thy God with all thy heart, and with all thy soul, and with all thy mind.

38   This is the first and great commandment.

39   And the second is like unto it, Thou shalt love thy neighbour as thyself.

40   On these two commandments hang all the law and the prophets.

As we begin to confess and act on that command in that order, Ephesians 3:16-17 immediately begins working. Love Himself begins to strengthen your inner man with His might. Powerful roots of Love and faith begin to grow deeper and stronger until there's no room left in your spirit, soul or body for fear. Fear is cast out—completely out. Faith, which works by Love, begins to flow, not just when you pray or believe for some need to be met but all the time. Every word becomes a word of faith. The Love of God begins to flow like a river from your innermost being. A river of living water. You're becoming more and more Love-inside minded. Your eyes will sparkle as the Love of Jesus flows through them releasing His compassion for hurting, sick people. This is the Body of Christ, the Anointed, in action.

The time has come for the Church to be who we really are. We are His very Body doing the works He did, and even greater works, because He went to the Father and the Father came—Love Himself came—and is dwelling in us now.

As you sow your financial seeds from now on, make it a practice of Love to lay your hands on your offering and release the Love of the Father on the gift and also toward whomever you are sending it. That Love is the source of all increase and overflow abundance.

Well, I must prepare for this evening's service. Gloria and I love you very much and we pray for you every day.

Love,

Ken

That Wicked One Touches Him Not!

Dear Partner

Can you imagine a place in the Lord Jesus and in His Anointing where the devil can't get to you?

I'm not talking about after you go to heaven. Of course he can't touch you there. He won't even be there. He got kicked out of there a long time ago and he's never going back. No, I'm talking about right here on this earth.

I think we've all sensed in our spirits that a place like this existed, but we have had no idea how to enter into it. Religion has always taught that it was totally impossible. But religion has also held up satan to be as strong as Jesus and death as strong as, or stronger than, life. That is not true. What God did in Jesus on the cross is far greater and far stronger than what satan did in Adam.

Let's begin by looking at 1 John 5:18:

18   We know that whosoever is born of God sinneth not; but he that is begotten of God keepeth himself, and that wicked one toucheth him not.

The key phrase in the book of 1 John is "God is Love." So he that is born of Love sinneth not. He keeps himself in Love (who is God), and the devil can't get to him.

Another thing to remember right here is there is no fear in love. Of course not. God is Love. What's there for Him to fear? The devil? You gotta be kidding! There is no fear in Love, and satan is the spirit of fear. That's the reason Love at work in a believer casts out fear. First John 4:18 declares that to be true:

18   There is no fear in love; but perfect love

casteth out fear: because fear hath torment.
He that feareth is not made perfect in love.

Let's go to the first chapter of 1 John and look at another verse. The fifth verse says:

> 5   This then is the message which we have heard
> of him, and declare unto you, that <u>God is light,</u>
> and in him is no darkness at all.

Here again satan is the spirit of darkness. Darkness can <u>never</u> enter into light. Darkness is always the result of the removal of light. It can never ever replace it by its own power. I don't care how dark it is, it is powerless to overcome light.

God, our wonderful Father, who is Light, has given us through Jesus, the Son of Light, the very Light of Himself. In the Gospel of John, He is the Light of men (1:1-5). James 1:17 says He is the Father of Lights. First Thessalonians 5:5 states:

> 5   Ye are all the children of light, and the children of
> the day: we are not of the night, nor of darkness.

Doesn't that put a thrill through your soul? Well, if that's a thrill, look at Ephesians 5:8:

> 8   For ye were sometimes darkness, but now are
> ye light in the Lord: walk as children of light.

<u>YOU</u> <u>ARE</u> <u>LIGHT.</u> You don't just have light. Light Himself is YOUR Father. You're born of Light. You don't just have Love. You are born of Love. You are joint heir with the Son of Love—THE LIGHT OF THE WORLD! Stand up and shout!

Romans 13:9-12 declares the results of keeping the commandment day in and day out—never breaking it without immediately repenting. The breaking of the command to love is an act of darkness. The results of that should be plain enough. Let's look at Romans 13:9-12:

9   For this, Thou shalt not commit adultery, Thou
    shalt not kill, Thou shalt not steal, Thou shalt
    not bear false witness, Thou shalt not covet;
    and if there be any other commandment, it is
    briefly comprehended in this saying, namely,
    <u>Thou shalt love thy neighbour as thyself.</u>

10 Love worketh no ill to his neighbour: therefore
    love is the fulfilling of the law.

11 And that, knowing the time, that now it is
    high time to awake out of sleep: for now is our
    salvation nearer than when we believed.

12 The night is far spent, the day is at hand: let us
    therefore cast off the works of darkness, and
    <u>let us put on the armour of light.</u>

Remember, now, this protective Light comes from the inside out. From inside your innermost being—your reborn spirit—and is manifest through your body as armor. Sometimes people may even see it. However, we know for certain the devil and demons not only see it and flee from it, the angels of God (or, of Light) love it. That's where they live and excel in strength.

Let's put some scripture together.

John 14:21:

21 He that hath my commandments, and keepeth
    them, he it is that loveth me: and he that loveth
    me shall be loved of my Father, and I will love
    him, and will manifest myself to him.

John 15:10:

10 If ye keep my commandments, ye shall abide
    in my love; even as I have kept my Father's
    commandments, and abide in his love.

First John 1:6-7:

6   If we say that we have fellowship with him, and walk in darkness, we lie, and do not the truth:

7   But if we walk in the light, as he is in the light, we have fellowship one with another, and the blood of Jesus Christ his Son cleanseth us from all sin.

First John 2:3-11:

3   And hereby we do know that we know him, if we keep his commandments.

4   He that saith, I know him, and keepeth not his commandments, is a liar, and the truth is not in him.

5   But whoso keepeth his word, in him verily is the love of God perfected: hereby know we that we are in him.

6   He that saith he abideth in him <u>ought himself also so to walk, even as he walked.</u>

7   Brethren, I write no new commandment unto you, but an old commandment which ye had from the beginning. The old commandment is the word which ye have heard from the beginning.

8   Again, a new commandment I write unto you, <u>which thing is true in him and in you:</u> because the darkness is past, and the true light now shineth.

9   He that saith he is in the light, and [loveth not] his brother, is in darkness even until now.

10   He that loveth his brother abideth in the light, and there is none occasion of stumbling in him.

11   But he that [loveth not] his brother is in darkness, and walketh in darkness, and knoweth not whither he goeth, because that darkness hath blinded his eyes.

Finally let's look at Jesus walking in this Light and that wicked one touching Him not.

John 8:59:

> 59   Then took they up stones to cast at him: but Jesus hid himself, and went out of the temple, going through the midst of them, and so passed by.

Luke 4:28-30:

> 28   And all they in the synagogue, when they heard these things, were filled with wrath,
> 29   And rose up, and thrust him out of the city, and led him unto the brow of the hill whereon their city was built, that they might cast him down headlong.
> 30   But he passing through the midst of them went his way.

Darkness could not touch Him when He "hid" Himself in the armor of light.

Confess the sin. Confess the commandment. Stay in the Light!

This is your and my assignment. This message must go throughout the entire Body of Christ. Now! Together we can do it. I know now what the Lord meant Friday, Oct. 18, 2001, when I heard Him say, "Launch a war against fear. Strip it out of the Body of Christ. I have delivered My people from fear. They have no business with it."

We'll pull down its strongholds and boldly declare, "Hands off, satan! You don't touch God's property. We're the children of Love, Light and power—God's power!"

In fact make that statement over your financial seed from now on. Make it bold because 1 John 4:17 says, "As He is so are we in this world."

Gloria and I are under the strongest anointing ever. We depend on your prayers. We love you and pray for you every day.

Love,

Ken

Many of the KCM products you know and love have been translated into other languages. Together we are reaching the world!

Believe <u>THE</u> Love!

Dear Partner

As I write this letter, Gloria and I have just finished our third Victory Campaign in the month of April. The first week we were in Brighton, England, and my, what a time we had! The following week we had six glorious services in Frankfurt, Germany. Then this week we were in Belfast, Northern Ireland. Next week we will complete this tour with services in Dnepropetrovsk, Ukraine.

In each city, the anointing steadily grew in intensity until it seemed to me as if it couldn't get any stronger. But then it did! This truly is overflow. The spiritual momentum is just awesome. All of this makes me wonder what's going to happen by this summer in the Prosperity Overflow Conventions!

Neither Gloria nor I named the conventions that. The word of the Lord came and instructed us to start calling them "Prosperity Overflow Conventions." I spoke with Brother Creflo two days ago, and he's about to explode with excitement over what the Lord has been saying about what's coming. I can hardly wait.

Let's look together at something that has been almost totally ignored in the lives of most believers. First John 4:16:

> 16 And we have known and believed the love that
> God hath to us. God is love; and he that dwelleth
> in love dwelleth in God, and God in him.

Notice the phrase "we have known and believed the love God hath to us." The Word *known* means we have experienced His Love. Certainly we have. No one can receive Jesus as Lord and Savior without experiencing the Love of God. That's what got us born again. That was John 3:16 in action.

The neglect has come on the second half of that phrase: "...and have <u>believed</u> the love." Everyone mentally agrees with the fact that

God loves us all, but very few have actively believed it. Far too many Christians have lingering doubts about God <u>really</u> loving them: "I just don't see how God could love someone like me."

So let's look first at what Jesus said in John 15:10:

> 10   If ye keep my commandments, ye shall abide in my love; <u>even as</u> I have kept my Father's commandments, and abide in his love.

He stayed in His Father's love by keeping His commandments. Remember what He said about the greatest commandments? Matthew 22:37-40:

> 37   Jesus said unto him, Thou shalt love the Lord thy God with all thy heart, and with all thy soul, and with all thy mind.
> 38   This is the first and great commandment.
> 39   And the second is like unto it, Thou shalt love thy neighbour as thyself.
> 40   On these two commandments hang all the law and the prophets.

Now think about it. <u>For Jesus not to love you would be a sin!</u> He would have to break that second commandment, and He's not about to do that over you or me or anyone else. His loving you has nothing whatsoever to do with you. <u>It has to do with obeying the Father's command.</u>

That also takes care of the idea that maybe He loves others more than He does ol' me. That can't be. He must love you and me as Himself. Also John 17:23 totally dispels that lie from hell:

> 23   I in them, and thou in me, that they may be made perfect in one; and that the world may know that thou hast sent me, and hast loved them, as thou hast loved me.

<u>The Father loves you just as much as He loves Jesus!</u> <u>Glory be to God!</u> Now that that's settled, let's believe <u>the</u> Love. Believe you receive

it just like you did when you received Jesus as Lord. Believe it in your heart and say it with your mouth: "God loves me just as much as He does Jesus. He loves me with all His heart, all His soul and all His might. Jesus loves me as Himself!"

So, believe the Love:

1. Believe it's in you. (Romans 5:5)

2. Believe it NEVER fails. (1 Corinthians 13:8)

3. Believe it is God. (1 John 4:15-16)

Now Hebrews 13:6 will become a living reality in your daily life:

> 6   So that we may boldly say, The Lord is my helper, and I will not fear what man shall do unto me.

Stop right now and boldly confess that verse at least five times.

This is the message that roots out fear wherever it finds it. The anointing on it is increasing and becoming more overwhelming by the day. We have a job to do, and this is the Word from heaven that will get it done. This is the core of the healing message. This is the very essence of the prosperity message. This is the heart and soul of the message of salvation. It is the heart of Love Himself. Together we will take it to the whole world.

As you sow your financial seed this month, release the Love of God over it and "see" it loving people from the top of the world to the bottom.

There's never been a time like this when the whole earth is so ready to hear that Jesus loves them. They are going to hear it from us.

Gloria and I love you and pray for you every day.

Love,

Ken

I have a Daddy!
I have a Father!
And He's Rich!

Dear Partner

As you know, Gloria and I were in four different cities in Europe for the entire month of April. It was a real eye-opener to what the Spirit of God is doing among believers everywhere. It was especially thrilling to hear testimonies about the TV broadcast.

Since there were people who came into the meetings from other countries—countries such as Russia, India, the Balkans and too many others to mention here—we heard from a lot of places. It's working! People are learning to live by faith, and they are using their authority as believers to change things.

Just think about what happens when we all come together as Partners. Not only do we have the finances to get things done, but more importantly we join our faith together.

Corporate faith is a very, very powerful thing. Things happen when we all believe together—things that would not happen with just one or two.

For instance, whole nations are being changed. Leaders of state are declaring Jesus as Lord over their countries. That has just happened in Ukraine. It has happened in Uganda. It is in the process of happening in cities and former strongholds of the devil everywhere. Thank God, you and I are a part of that! Stop right now and give the Lord praise.

But God is not only moving to change nations. Nations are made up of people. People make up households. Whole households are suddenly being swept into the kingdom of God. In many cases, yesterday it looked as if the whole bunch was headed to hell, and today they are praising God with their whole heart. And they are searching for everything they can find out about His Word. These are the days we believed for. We knew they would come "someday." Well, "someday" is here!

For the past few weeks I have been especially impressed with the phrase found in 1 John 4:9: "That we might live through Him." Let's look at verses 7-9:

7   Beloved, let us love one another: for love is of God; and every one that loveth is born of God, and knoweth God.

8   He that loveth not knoweth not God; for God is love.

9   In this was manifested the love of God toward us, because that God sent his only begotten Son into the world, <u>that we might live through him.</u>

If a very wealthy person were to adopt a very poor person, the poor person would live his life from that point on through his new father. That's what happened when we were born again in Jesus.

Let's illustrate this with the birth of an unwanted orphan child. Say this baby is immediately abandoned at birth. He has no hope. No future. No heritage. His only inheritance is death.

But that all changes if a wonderful, wealthy, loving, Christian family adopts this child. They give him their name. They withhold nothing from him. The moment those covenant adoption papers are signed, for all practical and legal purposes that baby has been "reborn."

This time he has a future. He has heritage. He has inheritance both in this natural world and in God if he listens to his new parents. Now he is living his life "through" them.

Now that's exactly what happens when someone receives Jesus as Lord, with one outstanding difference. In a natural adoption, the baby remains genetically linked to his natural birth parents. However with Jesus, adoption goes further than that. Any man who is in Christ Jesus is <u>a new creature.</u> Old things have passed away and <u>all</u> things have become new and <u>all</u> things are of God.

Suddenly he has a new Father. The richest Father there is. The most powerful Father that exists. Not only that, he is loved by his new Father beyond human knowledge. He has a new name. He is named after his blood brother, Jesus, and at that Name devils fear and tremble.

His new heritage is love, joy, righteousness and peace forever. His new inheritance is joint heir with Jesus—all authority both in heaven and earth, wealth beyond his wildest imagination, and all blessings in heavenly places. A new life plan has been put in place that is filled with healing, deliverance and success in this earth and a heavenly home in the future.

He has inherited all of that and more—much more. And with only one requirement—one command: "Believe on the name of his Son Jesus Christ..." (1 John 3:23). Well, that shouldn't be too hard to do. After all he just did that, and with the help of the family Director and Guide, the Holy Spirit, he should be able to learn to depend completely on that Name and the Word of His covenant that it guarantees. "...And love one another as he gave us commandment."

My, that's easy. After all, loving the One who just set him free from death, hell and fear, sin, sickness, and devils should be no problem at all.

Now loving his neighbor as himself as Jesus commanded (Matthew 22:39) may be a bit of a challenge. But if that's what pleases his Father, he can and will commit to being a good steward of that commandment. In fact, he will spend the rest of his new life with that commandment first priority in everything.

Can you see how thrilling the words of Jesus should be to you and me? "I have come that you might have life and have it more abundantly." This is worth living for, and worth dying for if need be.

This sick world must hear this. They are hearing it. They are listening. The news media doesn't know it yet, but they are. And you and I are right in the middle of it all.

If you haven't already, take hold of your new heritage with boldness. If you have already, renew your commitment to the commandment of Love and the lifestyle of Jesus. Together, as a team, as a family, we'll walk in the light as He is in the light, and His Blood cleanses us from all sin.

Remember what the Spirit said to Gloria and me a few years ago? He said we would be the biggest Holy Ghost "gang" on the earth. Well, we are! Together, we can get it done!

Lay your hands on your financial seed this month and shout, "I have a Daddy! I have a Father and He loves me just as much as He does Jesus!! John 17:23 says so!"

Gloria and I love you very much and we pray for you every day.

Love,

Ken

The Tide of the Glory Is Rising!

Dear Partner

My, how this year has flown by! We are over halfway through it and the Lord has certainly been true to His Word. We are in the midst of overflow on every hand.

What has been so amazing to me is the major shift in nations around the world. The same nations in which only a few years ago terrible people like Idi Amin in Uganda were heads of state, now have declared themselves Christian nations. This has just happened in Ukraine, and is in the process of taking place in a number of other places that we will hear from before the end of the year.

In fact, the last half of 2005 is going to be glorious. The tide of God's glory is rising.

Yesterday the word of the Lord came to me saying, "Do you remember what you preached almost all of 1983—that the glory was coming in great manifestation?" "Oh yes, I do," I said.

"Well," He said, "it's happening now and will continue to rise the rest of this year and all of next."

The statement He made to me in January 1983 came running back into my memory: "The glory has been manifested as the cloud. It has been manifested as the rain. It has been seen as lightning and also wind. But there's no place in the Word where it has come as all four at once. That would be a 'glory storm.'

"It's coming," He said. "It's coming. The glory's coming, the storm's coming."

He kept saying that to me and through me for over a year.

Well, it's here! Get in it!

Let's look again this month at 1 John 4:7-9:

7   Beloved, let us love one another: for love is of God; and every one that loveth is born of God, and knoweth God.

8   He that loveth not knoweth not God; for God is love.

9   In this was manifested the love of God toward us, because that God sent his only begotten Son into the world, that we might live through him.

Jesus came—the Father sent Him that we might live <u>through</u> Him. Now let's go to John 10:7-18:

7   Then said Jesus unto them again, Verily, verily, I say unto you, I am the door of the sheep.

8   All that ever came before me are thieves and robbers: but the sheep did not hear them.

9   I am the door: by me if any man enter in, he shall be saved, and shall go in and out, and find pasture.

10   The thief cometh not, but for to steal, and to kill, and to destroy: I am come that they might have life, and that they might have it more abundantly.

11   I am the good shepherd: the good shepherd giveth his life for the sheep.

12   But he that is an hireling, and not the shepherd, whose own the sheep are not, seeth the wolf coming, and leaveth the sheep, and fleeth: and the wolf catcheth them, and scattereth the sheep.

13   The hireling fleeth, because he is an hireling, and careth not for the sheep.

14   I am the good shepherd, and know my sheep, and am known of mine.

15   As the Father knoweth me, even so know I the Father: and I lay down my life for the sheep.

16   And other sheep I have, which are not of this

fold: them also I must bring, and they shall hear my voice; and there shall be one fold, and one shepherd.

17 Therefore doth my Father love me, because I lay down my life, that I might take it again.

18 No man taketh it from me, but I lay it down of myself. I have power to lay it down, and I have power to take it again. This commandment have I received of my Father.

Notice in the 18th verse the Father commanded Him to lay down His life. Now compare that with what we just read in 1 John 4:9. All of this—His coming, His being the good shepherd and His giving and laying down His life—was a manifestation of the Father's love toward us.

Take it personally. Toward you. That you might live through Him.

Now compare 1 John 4:9 with John 10:10: "I am come that they might have life [live through Me] more abundantly."

Would a good shepherd take food or water away from his sheep? No! Would a good shepherd open the door for sickness or disease to come among his sheep? Absolutely not. That would have to be the work of the thief whose only purpose is to steal, kill and destroy what belongs to the shepherd. Those are the works and lies that man-made religions and traditions have told us. And that's just what they are—lies of the thief.

How do we live through Him? We've already talked about the covenant side of being born again. It is like a child who was born to parents who cared nothing for him and who had no future. Then he was adopted by a loving, wealthy, Christian family. The moment those covenant papers were signed, he had a new father and mother. He had a new name, a future and an inheritance. He was reborn. From that moment, he began living his life THROUGH his new parents. That's what Jesus has provided for us. New life. Abundant life.

How do we take advantage of what He has made available to us? Through command and promise. The basic ground rules are simple.

They are laid out in 1 John 3:22-24:

22   And whatsoever we ask, <u>we receive of him,</u> because we keep his commandments, and do those things that are pleasing in his sight.

23   And this is his commandment, That we should believe on the name of his Son Jesus Christ, and love one another, as he gave us commandment.

24   And he that keepeth his commandments dwelleth in him, and he in him. And hereby we know that he abideth in us, by the Spirit which he hath given us.

And Matthew 22:37-40:

37   Jesus said unto him, Thou shalt love the Lord thy God with all thy heart, and with all thy soul, and with all thy mind.

38   This is the first and great commandment.

39   And the second is like unto it, Thou shalt love thy neighbour as thyself.

40   On these two commandments hang all the law and the prophets.

There is command and promise. Read it again. See how plain that is? Love came. Love gave Himself. Love died. Love rose again. Love took our sins and punishment so we could live abundantly through Him—LOVE! You can't live <u>through</u> Love and not love. You can't hear love without Love. You can't see love without Love. <u>Strife never connects to Love.</u> It connects with confusion and every evil work. Unforgiveness doesn't connect with Love. It connects with darkness.

Fear connects to the spirit of fear.

Faith connects to the Spirit of faith.

Hate connects to the spirit of hate.

Love connects to the Spirit of Love.

Sin connects to the spirit of sin, which is death.

Repentance connects to the Spirit of forgiveness, which is eternal life.

Command and promise.

When we stand on His Word, our first commitment is to His commandment. Being a good steward of the commandment of Love is job number one in the family of God. Everything else—I mean everything—depends on it. Life itself depends on it. Well, certainly it does. God is Love and He is Life.

Make the commitment. Do it right now. Do it out loud. Let Love be priority number one. Put His Word first place—final authority in your life. Love has sent the Spirit of Love Himself to stick closer than a brother to you, empowering you to live through Him in His glory and abundance.

As you sow your seed financially this month, lay your hands on it and sow it in <u>Love.</u> In <u>Him.</u> See it going <u>through</u> Him. It's no longer just your offering to Him. It has gone through Him. It has taken on His nature, His power, His glory, His ability to save, heal and deliver. <u>Blessed!</u> It has become precious seed, and it <u>will</u> produce a like harvest. It cannot help it. That's just the way Love is—<u>abundant.</u>

Pray for Gloria and me as we go into the rest of this year. "For I know that this shall turn to my salvation through your prayer, and the supply of the Spirit of Jesus [the Anointed One]" (Philippians 1:19).

We love you so very much and we pray for you every day.

Love,

Ken

Repentance—The Key to Overflow

Dear Partner

Do you remember when the Lord first talked to me about 2005 being the year of overflow? It was December 2003. He said 2004 would be the year of fullness and 2005 would be the year of overflow. *How much overflow,* He said, *depends on how much seed you sow toward it in 2004.* Later on in 2004 He explained that overflow is when all the seed comes up to harvest. Good seed overflows to great joy. Bad seed overflows to judgment.

It is God who, through His laws of seedtime and harvest, causes the increase to come—good or bad, joy or judgment—according to Galatians 6:7-8:

> 7   Be not deceived; God is not mocked: for whatsoever a man soweth, that shall he also reap.
>
> 8   For he that soweth to his flesh shall of the flesh reap corruption; but he that soweth to the Spirit shall of the Spirit reap life everlasting.

All of any person's bad seed can be brought to naught through the wonderful gift the Father has given us through Jesus and His precious blood. That gift is repentance. He is faithful and just, or righteous, to not only forgive us our sins but also to cleanse our spirit being, the real us, from all unrighteousness. CLEAN! Not just forgiven, but clean.

Repentance should come quickly, immediately, when one breaks the Law of Jesus or the commandment of Love. First John 1:7 tells us why and how:

> 7   But if we walk in the light, as he is in the light, we have fellowship one with another, and the blood of Jesus Christ his Son cleanseth us from all sin.

Now let's take a closer and deeper look at how the spiritual system of the reborn human spirit works. First of all, it is vitally important to <u>know</u> that you were born again of <u>incorruptible seed,</u> the Word of God. <u>There are no spiritual birth defects.</u> No, not one. No one was born in Christ Jesus short of faith, righteousness or any other attribute of our heavenly Father. Galatians 5:22-26 spells it out clearly:

22   But the fruit of the Spirit is love, joy, peace, longsuffering, gentleness, goodness, faith,

23   Meekness, temperance: against such there is no law.

24   And they that are Christ's have crucified the flesh with the affections and lusts.

25   If we live in the Spirit, let us also walk in the Spirit.

26   Let us not be desirous of vain glory, provoking one another, envying one another.

Notice that when all these forces of the spirit are working together, the flesh is brought under control. It doesn't work the other way around. Look at verse 16:

16   This I say then, Walk in the Spirit, and ye shall not fulfil the lust of the flesh.

It does not say stop the lusts of the flesh and then you'll be able to walk in the spirit. Walking in the spirit is walking in Love by faith, standing on the rock of the Word. When the flesh rises up, REPENT. NOW, not LATER.

When this system is working at its best—when you are clean of unforgiveness, strife and the world's way of life—the anointing is allowed to grow and do its powerful work of removing burdens and destroying yokes. First, in your life. Then, in the lives of those around you.

That's why being a good and faithful steward of the Law of Jesus is so very important. The more faithful you are with His Love Commandment, the more you can be trusted with His power. This is laid out plainly in John's Gospel, chapter 14. Let's read verses 12-15:

12   Verily, verily, I say unto you, He that believeth on me, the works that I do shall he do also; and greater works than these shall he do; because I go unto my Father.

13   And whatsoever ye shall ask in my name, that will I do, that the Father may be glorified in the Son.

14   If ye shall ask any thing in my name, I will do it.

15   If ye love me, keep my commandments.

Now verses 21 and 23:

21   He that hath my commandments, and keepeth them, he it is that loveth me: and he that loveth me shall be loved of my Father, and I will love him, and will manifest myself to him.

23   Jesus answered and said unto him, If a man love me, he will keep my words: and my Father will love him, and we will come unto him, and make our abode with him.

What happens when this system is violated? Let's look at Acts 24:16:

16   And herein do I exercise myself, to have always a conscience void of offence toward God, and toward men.

"A conscience void of offence." What does that mean? Has your "conscience" ever hurt or bothered you? Certainly it has. In simple terms, that's your spirit's voice witnessing to you, *Repent now!* Or, *Get this dirt out of our system. This is bad for the anointing. Repent!*

Let's look at some other scriptures.

Romans 9:1:

1   I say the truth in Christ, I lie not, <u>my conscience</u>

also bearing me witness in the Holy Ghost.

First Timothy 1:5:

> 5 Now the end of the commandment is charity out of a pure heart, and of <u>a good conscience,</u> and of faith unfeigned.

Now verse 19:

> 19 Holding faith, and a <u>good conscience;</u> which some having put away concerning faith have made shipwreck.

And 3:9:

> 9 Holding the mystery of the faith in a <u>pure conscience.</u>

Verse 2 of Chapter 4 is an eye-opener:

> 2 Speaking lies in hypocrisy; having <u>their con-science seared</u> with a hot iron.

The <u>voice of the conscience</u> can be silenced. That's what has happened with so many Christians who ignore the command of Love. The results have been disastrous!

How important was the <u>voice of conscience</u> to the Apostle Paul? Look at 2 Timothy 1:3:

> 3 I thank God, whom I serve from my forefathers with <u>pure conscience.</u>....

The Apostle of Love explains its workings in more detail in 1 John 3:21-22:

> 21 Beloved, if our heart condemn us not, then have we confidence toward God.

22   And whatsoever we ask, we receive of him,
        because we keep his commandments, and do
        those things that are pleasing in his sight.

Let's look at these two verses in the *New Living Translation:*

21   Dear friends, if our <u>conscience is clear,</u> we can
        come to God with bold confidence.
22   And we will receive whatever we request
        because we obey him and do the things that
        please him.

That's about as clear as you can get. When violation of the law of Love occurs (sin), your spirit stops everything else and centers up on itself to get you to repent and receive your cleansing. Now there is conflict between your reborn spirit and your flesh. Your believing for other things has momentarily shut down. You are vulnerable to the enemy. Your defenses are down. The pressure is on.

Let's go back to Galatians 5. This time, to verse 17. Before we read this, however, let me point out one very important fact. There are no capital letters in the original text. Certain words were capitalized at the privilege of the translators. The capital "s" on the word "spirit" in these verses in Galatians 5 is not correct. Verse 17 is not talking about the Holy Spirit. It is referring to your reborn spirit. In this case, <u>your conscience.</u> Now let's read it:

17   For the flesh lusteth against the spirit, and the
        spirit against the flesh: and these are contrary
        the one to the other: so that ye cannot do the
        things that ye would.

Do you see what that said? Read it again. You <u>cannot</u> do the things that you would. Your spirit is having to put pressure against your flesh. Love, joy, peace, longsuffering, gentleness, goodness, faith, meekness and temperance have all been compromised. The anointing is in danger. Bad seed has been planted.

STOP! REPENT!

That's why Jesus went to the cross! He loves you more than Himself. He's not down on you for missing it. Confess that sin, whatever it is. Boldly call it by its ugly name. When you confess it before Him is not when He finds out about it. That's when you get rid of it. The beautiful part of it all is that your heavenly Father will never treat you as though you have sinned. Thank God for the blood of Jesus!

Take the time right this minute and deal with whatever your conscience is witnessing to you about. Then apply Mark 11:24:

> 24 Therefore I say unto you, What things soever ye desire, when ye pray, believe that ye receive them, and ye shall have them.

Don't listen to your flesh. Instead, ignore all symptoms of guilt once confession has been made. It may take a while for those symptoms to go away. Repentance is an act of obedience, not feelings. It is an act of faith in the lordship and faithfulness of Jesus. Your flesh will have to come in line. And it will.

Center up on His Love, not judgment. He is Love. He keeps His own Commandment. He loves you with all His heart, all His soul and all His might. He would have to break His own Commandment not to. He is not about to do that. Give the Lord praise!

The rest of this year is going to be glorious. Pull out all the stops and go all out for God's best of everything. Gloria and I love you very much, and we continue to pray for you every day.

Love,

Ken

Jesus Is the Sweetest Name I Know

Dear Partner

Everything is about the Cross!

We <u>must</u> <u>never,</u> <u>ever</u> forget that.

What happened to Jesus on that tree and why does it affect us more than 2,000 years later?

To begin answering those questions, let's go to Deuteronomy 28:15:

> 15   But it shall come to pass, if thou wilt not hearken unto the voice of the Lord thy God, to observe to do all his commandments and his statutes which I command thee this day; that all these curses shall come upon thee, and overtake thee.

The curse that was released on Adam, his wife and all the earth was the result of disobedience to the Creator and the laws He used when He created us. That curse came upon every living thing. The ground was cursed. Consequently, everything the ground produced was cursed. *Everything*—spirit, soul and body—fell under the power of death. It was separated from Life, who is God. That is the true definition of poverty—CURSE.

The basic definition of *curse* in Deuteronomy 28:15 is "to make bitter." Everything God created was good or "sweet." The Creation chapters in the book of Genesis state over and over again: "God created... and saw that it was good." It was sweet. Eden was a sweet place. There was no bitterness at all. There was no bitterness between the animals and man. There was no bitterness in the food. It did not exist. Adam knew nothing of it. There was no concept of death, grief, sickness, lack or any other bitter thing.

When Adam sinned, his disobedience brought bitterness into every cell of his body. The root of bitterness lodged in his spirit, and there was no way he could remove it. Bitterness came into his thinking. It was in everything, on everything and through everything on earth. Nothing escaped. Bitterness—death—was everywhere.

Then the worst part of the curse became apparent. The seed of everything was cursed. No one could prevent the passing of this curse from one generation to the next. Oh! Woe is ours forever! Only the Godhead knew the plan of redemption. No one else even knew there was a plan. It was a mystery hidden in Christ Jesus.

The answer was another Adam. But where would he come from? The first Adam's body was made from the earth, but that had been cursed. Had the Creator used the same material, the second Adam's body would have also been cursed.

But wait. What did the Father use to create the earth in the beginning? <u>His WORD!</u> Thank God, His Word cannot be cursed. Let's remind ourselves of John 1:1-3:

> 1   In the beginning was the Word, and the Word
>   was with God, and the Word was God.
> 2   The same was in the beginning with God.
> 3   All things were made by him; and without him
>   was not any thing made that was made.

Think about that. His written Word is just as much a manifestation of God as His Son Jesus and His Holy Spirit! Take time to walk around your prayer room holding your Bible in your arms knowing that by giving you the authority to walk in His Word and release it through faith, God has allowed you to handle His very being—Himself.

His Word became the seed in Mary's womb that gave birth to the second Adam, YESHUA MASHIACH—Jesus the Anointed—Son of the living God! Finally! A man in the earth in whom there is no bitterness—not in one cell of His being. He is a free man. He—not death—is in control.

But now what? He did the unthinkable.

Philippians 2:8:

> 8   And being found in fashion as a man, he
>   humbled himself, and became obedient unto
>   death, even the death of the cross.

He was free. He didn't have to do that. No, but He chose to in order to face death and defeat it. He took away the authority of the bitterness and released the blessing—heaven's sweetness—back into the earth. Look at the startling statement the Holy Spirit made through the Apostle Paul in 2 Timothy 1:10:

> 10   But is now made manifest by the appearing of
>   our Saviour Jesus Christ, who hath abolished
>   death, and hath brought life and immortality
>   to light through the gospel.

Look at that! To this point, we have scarcely believed that, but now we are beginning to believe it and act on it like no other generation of believers.

Now let's look at Galatians 3:13-14:

> 13   Christ hath redeemed us from the curse of the
>   law, being made a curse for us: for it is written,
>   Cursed is every one that hangeth on a tree:
> 14   That the blessing of Abraham might come
>   on the Gentiles through Jesus Christ; that
>   we might receive the promise of the Spirit
>   through faith.

That's what happened to Jesus on that cross and then in hell. He not only paid the awful price for what Adam did, but He also broke the power of the curse and then broke the authority of satan to use it on any believer who would walk in his or her redemption.

Now let's look at Deuteronomy 28:1-2:

> 1   And it shall come to pass, if thou shalt hearken
>   diligently unto the voice of the Lord thy God,

> to observe and to do all his commandments
> which I command thee this day, that the Lord
> thy God will set thee on high above all nations
> of the earth:
>
> 2 And all these blessings shall come on thee,
> and overtake thee, if thou shalt hearken unto
> the voice of the Lord thy God.

We're back to obedience to God. We're back to where Adam was before he sinned. Commandment!

Jesus is the key issue to everything. His commandment, then, is priority No. 1. Sweetness or bitterness? Life or death? Blessing or cursing? The choice is ours. God made *His* choice. He chose to lay that entire curse on Jesus. Jesus chose to bear it. Now it's our choice to walk in it by obeying the commandment of Love. That commandment renders the curse helpless to function in the life of the obedient believer.

Remember the words "...will come on you and overtake you"? That's what happens when the commandment becomes the No. 1 priority in our everyday lives. Everything heaven has done depends on it. Disobedience is no different now than it was then. Break the command and fear connects to that bitter life and draws it in. Repent and it stops. Claim your forgiveness and your cleansing, and Jesus is faithful and just to get it done. What is happening? Jesus is backing His Word of Love with heaven's power of Love.

That commandment is everything. All of the law and the prophets hang on it. IT IS LIFE!!

First John 3:22-23:

> 22 And whatsoever we ask, we receive of him,
> because we keep his commandments, and do
> those things that are pleasing in his sight.
>
> 23 And this is his commandment, That we should
> believe on the name of his Son Jesus Christ, and
> love one another, as he gave us commandment.

Matthew 22:37-40:

37   Jesus said unto him, Thou shalt love the Lord
         thy God with all thy heart, and with all thy
         soul, and with all thy mind.
38   This is the first and great commandment.
39   And the second is like unto it, Thou shalt love
         thy neighbour as thyself.
40   On these two commandments hang all the
         law and the prophets.

This is the message you and I are taking to the Body of Christ all over the world, and through the Body to this curse-filled world. It is the answer to all the bitterness death has brought. Jesus has come that we might have life and have it more abundantly.

Say it out loud right now: "I am redeemed from the curse. Jesus was made a curse for me. The blessing of Abraham has come on me and on my life. I am committed to being a good steward of the commandment of Love. It is my life." Say that over and over. Write it down. Keep it before your eyes until it gets down into your deepest inner being. Keep it there. Confess it over everything you have—I mean *everything*.

Let's close with John 14:21:

21   He that hath my commandments, and keep-
         eth them, he it is that loveth me: and he that
         loveth me shall be loved of my Father, and I
         will love him, and will manifest myself to him.

Isn't that the heart's desire of every believer? Well, obedience makes it a done deal. This is the good news. We won't stop shouting it until it has filled the earth.

Make your seed-faith offerings seeds of Love. Claim your money for the kingdom of Love. Bind it to the blessing and to God's use forever, even after it leaves your hands. This earth is ours NOW!

Marvelous things are happening in this ministry all over the world.

OVERFLOW! It's happening. Give the Lord a shout and jump into the flow with all your might.

Gloria and I love you and pray for you every day.

Love,

Ken

It's Time for the Glory!

Dear Partner

It's time for the Glory!

I heard that word on my way to preach in New York City, September 18, 2005, at 41,000 feet. Oh, my, how good that was to the ears of my spirit. So much disaster. So much heartache and pain in the world.

It's like the world is convulsing. <u>It is.</u> From what? <u>Sin!</u> No, God's not punishing the world. The world has been harvesting its own darkness. <u>It's called judgment.</u>

The Lord told us what was coming in 2005. Overflow. That's when all the seeds sown, good or bad, come to full harvest. Sin and darkness can become so heavy, the earth and its atmosphere can't contain it any longer. When that happens, something breaks. Jeremiah 12:11 says:

> 11   They have made it desolate, and being deso-
>   late it mourneth unto me....

Then Romans 8:22:

> 22   For we know that the whole creation groaneth
>   and travaileth in pain together until now.

That's the reason it is so vitally important that every believer keep the bad seed out and continue to sow the seeds of Love and faith. Keeping the Law of Jesus and being a good steward of that commandment is the <u>most</u> important thing in life. Especially when judgment and so much death and destruction are all around us.

We don't have to wait for the Glory. We walk in it. We walk in <u>the</u> Light. We walk in the secret place of the Most High God. That's what walking in Love is. <u>Love</u> is <u>God.</u>

There has never been a time in history when it has been as important to be on guard over every thought, every deed, and every word that comes out of our mouths. First John 5, verses 1-5, 14 and 15, and then especially verse 18 make clear how vitally important this is, especially in our day:

1 Whosoever believeth that Jesus is the Christ is born of God: and every one that loveth him that begat loveth him also that is begotten of him.

2 By this we know that we love the children of God, when we love God, and keep his commandments.

3 For this is the love of God, that we keep his commandments: and his commandments are not grievous.

4 For whatsoever is born of God overcometh the world: and this is the victory that overcometh the world, even our faith.

5 Who is he that overcometh the world, but he that believeth that Jesus is the Son of God?

14 And this is the confidence that we have in him, that, if we ask any thing according to his will, he heareth us:

15 And if we know that he hear us, whatsoever we ask, we know that we have the petitions that we desired of him.

18 We know that whosoever is born of God sinneth not; but he that is begotten of God keepeth himself, and that wicked one toucheth him not.

Untouchable right in the middle of all this. Psalm 91:7:

7 A thousand shall fall at thy side, and ten thousand at thy right hand; but it shall not come nigh thee.

The Glory of the Lord has been growing in intensity all this time. The stronger we, the Body of Christ, become in faith, hope and Love, the brighter the Glory is manifest. Remember, His Glory is already in the earth. He's here! It's time for 2 Corinthians 4:1-7 to explode on the scene of all this darkness:

1   Therefore seeing we have this ministry, as we have received mercy, we faint not;

2   But have renounced the hidden things of dishonesty, not walking in craftiness, nor handling the word of God deceitfully; but by manifestation of the truth commending ourselves to every man's conscience in the sight of God.

3   But if our gospel be hid, it is hid to them that are lost:

4   In whom the god of this world hath blinded the minds of them which believe not, lest the light of the glorious gospel of Christ, who is the image of God, should shine unto them.

5   For we preach not ourselves, but Christ Jesus the Lord; and ourselves your servants for Jesus' sake.

6   For God, who commanded the light to shine out of darkness, hath shined in our hearts, to give the light of the knowledge of the glory of God in the face of Jesus Christ.

7   But we have this treasure in earthen vessels, that the excellency of the power may be of God, and not of us.

We're there! It's happening now! Don't get caught up in the media's hash and rehashing of the disasters. Get caught up in the Glory. Begin to praise like never before. We are in a "tsunami" of Love. We are in the middle of a Holy Ghost "storm" of His lightning and His winds of salvation and healing. The flood of His power is flowing.

Go where it's happening and get in it. Not only at church and in meetings, but go get into the flow of ministry. It's everywhere like never before. Take the joy of the Lord to someone. Go feed somebody and love them into knowing Jesus. Pray and be led of the Holy Spirit. <u>Obey.</u> Do something by faith. It is our job to snatch people out of judgment and into the Glory.

We don't have much time. The time is all gone. We must do our job of preaching this uncompromised word of Love and faith like never before. Jesus is coming sooner than we all think.

2006 is the year of total fulfillment. I heard Bishop Keith Butler say that by the Spirit a few months ago, and it literally exploded in my heart. It has been ringing in my spiritual ears ever since. Put it in your mouth. Say it, shout it, sing it, tell everybody that 2006 is the year of total fulfillment. I believe it. I receive it.

As you sow your financial seed this month, sow toward that. Lay your hands on your seed and name it: "This is the seed of total fulfillment."

God has been so good to us. Gloria and I love you and we pray for you every day.

Love,

Ken

The Glory of the Lord Shall Be Revealed and
All Flesh Shall See It TOGETHER! Isa. 40:5

Dear Partner

Well, thank God we are finally here—2006! The year of the Glory, the year of total fulfillment, is just around the corner.

I have been looking forward to 2006 more than any other year. It has seemed to me that ever since the year 2000, everything has been leading up to right now. 2006 will be remembered as the year we saw the Glory manifest. The Glory of God has been here all the time and has manifested in many ways but very seldom has it been seen by everyone—sinner and saint alike—at one time. That time has come.

The way the storms came in '05, the Glory will come in '06!

The Glory is Almighty God making His presence known above and beyond what ordinary men have seen. He will reveal Himself in ways unheard of—ways no one has ever thought or asked. I have enclosed the study outline on "Glory" from the KCM Reference Edition Bible. Look up all the scriptures. They tell their own story. Study them for yourself. Claim every one of those promises. They belong to every believer. After all, we are the glorious Church. We preach the glorious gospel of the glorified Savior, Jesus the Son of Glory.

In this letter today, I want to talk to you some more about the precious gift of repentance. Every believer knows that repentance is important. But most don't understand the power of faith that is involved and what makes it so important.

Faith is what pleases the Father—not how sorry and guilty you feel for sin in your life. The reason for that is His interest in cleansing you from all unrighteousness and restoring your spirit to complete spiritual health. His purpose is seeing to it that your joy may be full (1 John 1:4) and that you might have and live life in abundance (to the full, till it overflows).

Faith always takes the written Word and acts on it. Faith is action.

Believing is an action word. Faith is <u>never, ever</u> based on anything in the natural, seeing, feeling world. It is always Word-based and Love-dependent.

Faith <u>cometh</u> by hearing and hearing by the Word of God, and faith worketh by Love. And that is a perfect example of what I'm talking about. <u>Faith comes!</u> <u>Faith works!</u> Get the Word part right, and faith always comes. Get the Love part right, and faith always works. Now add to that 1 John 5:4—faith always overcomes <u>the world:</u>

> 4   For whatsoever is born of God overcometh the world: and this is the victory that overcometh the world, even our faith.

There is nothing—no-*thing*—in this world order that faith will not overcome.

That includes what we read about in 1 John 1:9:

> 9   If we confess our sins, he is faithful and just to forgive us our sins, and to cleanse us from all unrighteousness.

That is a bold statement, and it comes straight from the Father. Chapter 2, verse 1 directs us to whom we make that confession—Jesus. He is the One in charge. He is the One appointed as High Priest over our confessions of faith—not just of sin but of faith.

Now you can see where faith comes in. Faith <u>believes</u> that Jesus is faithful and just (or righteous) to forgive us our sin and cleanse us of all unrighteousness. When? <u>NOW!</u> The moment we confess them. Or really, the moment we believe and take Him at His Word—not when we stop feeling guilty about it.

Faith is always now. Feelings follow. Faith changes feelings. Faith overcomes, remember?

Now look at chapter 1, verse 7:

> 7   But if we walk in the light, as he is in the light,

we have fellowship one with another, and the blood of Jesus Christ his Son cleanseth us from all sin.

Walking in the light is walking by faith and not by sight. Without faith there is no light.

The next step in this process is what makes repentance so precious. Not only to us, but even more importantly to the Father. Remember <u>He is Love.</u> Let's look at Isaiah 43:25-26:

25   I, even I, am he that blotteth out thy transgressions for mine own sake, and will not remember thy sins.

26   Put me in remembrance: let us plead together: declare thou, that thou mayest be justified.

Here again is the Word straight from our Father. Take it. Act on it. Declare it: "Thank God my sins are blotted out right now! It's done!"

Does He have the power to remember and know the future forever? Yes, He does. Everyone believes that.

However, very few have considered the same power in the opposite direction. He has the supernatural power to not just forget, but also to blot out. Think about a page with your sins written on it. He does not simply stamp "Forgiven" over the writing. No! He totally blots it out or eradicates it. It becomes a clean, blank page. We're not just looking at a book. We are looking at His memory.

What now? Does it just stay blank until we sin again? No. Look at the rest of what He says in verse 26:

26   Put me in remembrance: let us plead together: declare thou, that thou mayest be justified.

Remember in verse 25 where He said He blots out <u>for His own sake?</u> He is a wonderful, loving Father. He has absolutely no desire whatsoever to remember something bad and unlovely about you, or me, or anyone else. That is the reason Jesus shed His precious blood. That's the joy that was set before Him in Hebrews 12:2.

In verse 26, He is offering us the <u>precious</u> gift of <u>filling His blank memory!</u> Think about that: "Put me in remembrance."

What are you going to <u>remind</u> Him? Look at that word: re-mind. It's a gift. It's the information upon which He will build your future. What are you going to do? "Oh, God, I'm so unworthy. I've been so worthless. I'm so broke. I'm so sick. No one loves me. Etc., etc."? Is that what you want Him to remember? Certainly not. Did Jesus die so you could say that? A million times no! He died so you could confess who you have become in Him:

"Father, I receive my forgiveness right now. I receive my cleansing from all unrighteousness according to Your Word. Thank God, I'm saved. I'm the righteousness of God. I know Jesus, and He has made me free. I am healed, well, strong in the Lord and in the power of His might. I thank You, Father, that I'm free from sin. I walk in the Light as Jesus is in the Light, and His blood cleanses me from <u>all</u> sin. I'm clean. I'm a believer. I'm supposed to be free. I'm supposed to be healed. I'm supposed to be prosperous and very wealthy. I can do all things through Christ, the Anointed One, which strengthens me."

Can you see it? Fill His mind and remembrance with <u>His</u> Word, <u>His</u> redemption. As you do that not only does your remembrance of that sin go away, but also guilt just melts, along with all the flesh desires and problems that caused all the trouble in the first place. You are blotting out and reprogramming your own memory—renewing your own mind. With that comes the fullness of joy. The joy of the Lord which is our strength.

Now you can see why repentance done in faith is such a precious thing.

Sow your financial seeds under the influence of this revelation. The results will be a joy in giving that is beyond anything you've ever known. It's time for the Glory and this is the way you release it in your life.

What a way to go into Christmas! Celebrate the Anointing. Celebrate the Gift. Celebrate the Life of the One who made it all possible.

JESUS. LORD. SAVIOR. And giver of Abundant Life in Him.

Merry Christmas and a glorious 2006.

Gloria and I love you and pray for you every day.

Love,

Ken

Glory

A Study Outline from the *KCM Reference Edition Bible*
Foundation scriptures: Second Corinthians 3-4

If Moses had looked on the glory of God he would have died. Had the people looked at Moses' face they would have died. Without the new birth being available that would have been the end. Second Corinthians 3:17-18 says that is what happened to us; except after death we were brought to life—eternal life. Chapter 4 goes on to say that a physical manifestation of God's glory is a manifestation of the power that is already resident in the gospel. Second Corinthians 4:7 says that we possess this precious treasure, the LIGHT OF THE GOSPEL, in our bodies (the Spirit in our spirits, in our bodies). We are born of this power.

The Glory Is in God's Presence

I.   The whole earth shall be filled with My glory
  A.   The word *glory* in Hebrew means "heavy with everything good—splendor"
    1.   Ephesians 1:17—The Father of Glory
    2.   Acts 7:2—The God of Glory
    3.   Psalm 29:3
  B.   Glory and honor are in God's presence (1 Chronicles 16:27)
    1.   Man was crowned with glory and honor, i.e., God's presence

      a. When God's presence departed, Adam became naked

      b. Romans 3:21-23—Man fell short of the glory

      c. 1 Corinthians 2:6-8—The plan or mystery is God's plan to return man to glory (God's presence)

        (1) Satan did not know this or he would not have killed Jesus

        (2) Colossians 1:26—God wants the mystery known now

        (3) 2 Corinthians 4—Christ in us, our hope of glory

      d. The knowledge of His glory is the knowledge of His presence—the way it shines in Jesus' face (Matthew 17:2)

      e. Mark 9:2—They saw Jesus in God's presence

  2. Jesus said to Lazarus' family, "You shall see the glory," or the presence

  3. When God said, "Light be," He said, "Me be," or "Let there again be a manifestation of My presence in the earth"

      a. This glorious gospel is full of His presence

      b. 2 Corinthians 3:18—We look into the Scriptures as a mirror for the glory—the revealed presence of the Father Almighty

      c. It produces "Me be" in us. It will take us from glory to glory—one level of His presence to another level of His presence

II. Goodness overcomes evil

  A. His goodness has come upon us a line at a time or it would overcome us (Isaiah 28:9-10)

  B. Eventually we will be glorified—gone!

  C. Jesus has God's presence flowing through His veins, giving life to His body

  D. Ephesians 5:25-27—Jesus washed the Church with the Word—making it a glorious Church

    1. Filled with the Father's presence

    2. Overwhelmingly filled with life and goodness

    3. Exodus 33:18-19 proves that glory is goodness

  E. Exodus 40:34—God's presence overwhelmed the tabernacle

  F. His goodness overwhelmed armies

  G. His goodness endures forever

God Will Send Bright Clouds

Foundation scripture: Zechariah 10:1

I. What is the glory? What is the cloud?

  A. Exodus 16:10—The glory appeared

  B. Exodus 24:16-18—The glory abode six days. The sight was like devouring fire

  C. Exodus 33:9-23—God was in the cloudy pillar

D. 2 Chronicles 5:12-13—The cloud filled the temple (6:1)
E. The glory is the presence of God
II. Where is it now?
   A. Luke 2:9—Accompanied the birth of Jesus
   B. Matthew 17:1-5—In Jesus
   C. John 11:25, 40—Resurrection
   D. 2 Peter 1:17—Power
   E. Colossians 3:4—We shall appear with Him in glory
   F. John 17:21-24—Jesus has given it to us
   G. Romans 6:4—Jesus was raised by the glory
   H. Acts 9:3-4, 22:6-8, 26:13-15—Jesus' voice came out of the glory
   I. Hebrews 2:9-10—Jesus and brethren crowned with glory and honor
   J. Acts 2:1-3—The fire appeared and sat on them
   K. Romans 8:18—The glory shall be revealed in us
III. What will it do in us?
   A. 2 Corinthians 4:1-7—The creative power is in us
   B. Colossians 1:27; Ephesians 1:18, 3:20—His riches are in the glory in us
   C. Philippians 4:19—Our needs are met according to His riches in glory
   D. Matthew 6:33—Seek the kingdom
IV. The Word is full of glory
   A. 2 Corinthians 4:4
   B. Romans 13:11-12—The Word is part of the armor of light
   C. The glorious gospel is our shoes
   D. Malachi 4:2-3—The sun-like splendor shall burn Satan to ashes under our feet

Fire, Light and Glory—A Scriptural Study

1. Hebrews 1—Ministers a flame
2. Psalm 104:2
3. Matthew 3:11—With the Holy Ghost and with fire
4. Habakkuk 3:4-5—Sun-like splendor
5. 1 John 1:5—God is light
6. Philippians 2:13-16—Lights in the world
7. 2 Corinthians 4:4-7—Knowledge of the light of glory
8. Proverbs 4:9—Crown of glory
9. Malachi 4:2—Sun of righteousness
10. 1 Corinthians 13:3—Body to be burned
11. Acts 2:3—Tongues of fire
12. Ezekiel 1:27-28—Fire from loins upward. This scripture ties the fire and the glory together. Also Ezekiel 8:2.

13. John 8:12—The light of life
14. John 1:4-5
15. Psalm 119:130
16. Zechariah 10:1—Lightnings
17. Acts 9:1-4—The light had a voice
18. Psalm 31:16
19. Proverbs 6:23—The law is light
20. Colossians 3:4—When Jesus appears we shall appear with Him in glory
21. Romans 13:11-12—Put on the armor of light
22. Luke 3:16—He will baptize you in wind (Greek) and fire

Works Revealed by Fire
Foundation scriptures: 1 Corinthians 3:12-15
I. Revealed by fire
   A. Not by men (John 12:48)
   B. Fire of the Holy Spirit through the Word (Acts 2:1-3; Jeremiah 5:14; Malachi 3:1-3, 4:1-3; John 15:3; 2 Timothy 3:12-17, 4:1-8)
II. The Lord—the Righteous Judge
   A. A very small thing to be judged by you (1 Corinthians 4:3-5)
   B. Romans 14:4—"Who art thou that judgest another man's servant?"
      1. To his own master he stands or falls
      2. He shall be held up by God
      3. God is able to make him stand
III. It is required in stewards to be found faithful
   A. Judging ministry (1 Corinthians 4:3)
   B. Judging sin (1 Corinthians 11:31)
   C. When we judge ourselves, we should not be judged. The *Lord* does the chastising—*NOT CONDEMNING*. How?? With His Word—*RECEIVE!!*
IV. Act on 1 John 1:9—Be restored, anointing, etc.
   A. 1 John 1:9—Jesus is faithful not only to forgive but to cleanse
   B. Believe you receive. Act as though Jesus is faithful
V. You that are *spiritual,* restore
   A. 1 John 2:10—Scandal comes from within
   B. Believe you receive your brother restored (1 John 5:16)
   C. When you see a brother sin—
      1. Mourn—intercede (1 Corinthians 5)
      2. Ask for life for him (1 John 5:16)
      3. Don't see scandal (1 John 2:10)
      4. Go restore (Galatians 5:14-26, 6:1-10)
VI. When you stand praying, forgive

Prayer for Salvation and Baptism in the Holy Spirit

Heavenly Father, I come to You in the Name of Jesus. Your Word says, "Whosoever shall call on the name of the Lord shall be saved" (Acts 2:21). I am calling on You. I pray and ask Jesus to come into my heart and be Lord over my life according to Romans 10:9-10: "If thou shalt confess with thy mouth the Lord Jesus, and shalt believe in thine heart that God hath raised him from the dead, thou shalt be saved. For with the heart man believeth unto righteousness; and with the mouth confession is made unto salvation." I do that now. I confess that Jesus is Lord, and I believe in my heart that God raised Him from the dead.

I am now reborn! I am a Christian—a child of Almighty God! I am saved! You also said in Your Word, "If ye then, being evil, know how to give good gifts unto your children: HOW MUCH MORE shall your heavenly Father give the Holy Spirit to them that ask him?" (Luke 11:13). I'm also asking You to fill me with the Holy Spirit. Holy Spirit, rise up within me as I praise God. I fully expect to speak with other tongues as You give me the utterance (Acts 2:4). In Jesus' Name. Amen!

Begin to praise God for filling you with the Holy Spirit. Speak those words and syllables you receive—not in your own language, but the language given to you by the Holy Spirit. You have to use your own voice. God will not force you to speak. Don't be concerned with how it sounds. It is a heavenly language!

Continue with the blessing God has given you and pray in the spirit every day.

You are a born-again, Spirit-filled believer. You'll never be the same!

Find a good church that boldly preaches God's Word and obeys it. Become part of a church family who will love and care for you as you love and care for them.

We need to be connected to each other. It increases our strength in God. It's God's plan for us.

Make it a habit to watch the *Believer's Voice of Victory* television broadcast and become a doer of the Word, who is blessed in his doing (James 1:22-25).

About the Author

Kenneth Copeland is co-founder and president of Kenneth Copeland Ministries in Fort Worth, Texas, and best-selling author of books that include *How to Discipline Your Flesh* and *Honor—Walking in Honesty, Truth and Integrity.*

Now in his 43rd year as a minister of the gospel of Christ and teacher of God's Word, Kenneth is the recording artist of such award-winning albums as his Grammy-nominated *Only the Redeemed, In His Presence, He Is Jehovah, Just a Closer Walk* and his most recently released *Big Band Gospel* album. He also co-stars as the character Wichita Slim in the children's adventure videos *The Gunslinger, Covenant Rider* and the movie *The Treasure of Eagle Mountain,* and as Daniel Lyon in the *Commander Kellie and the Superkids*_{TM} videos *Armor of Light* and *Judgment: The Trial of Commander Kellie.*

With the help of offices and staff in the United States, Canada, England, Australia, South Africa and Ukraine, Kenneth is fulfilling his vision to boldly preach the uncompromised Word of God from the top of this world, to the bottom, and all the way around. His ministry reaches millions of people worldwide through daily and Sunday TV broadcasts, magazines, teaching audios and videos, conventions and campaigns, and the World Wide Web.

World Offices
Kenneth Copeland Ministries

For more information about KCM and our products,
please write to the office nearest you:

Kenneth Copeland Ministries
Fort Worth, TX 76192-0001

Kenneth Copeland
Locked Bag 2600
Mansfield Delivery Centre
QUEENSLAND 4122
AUSTRALIA

Kenneth Copeland
Post Office Box 15
BATH
BA1 3XN
U.K.

Kenneth Copeland
Private Bag X 909
FONTAINEBLEAU
2032
REPUBLIC OF
SOUTH AFRICA

Kenneth Copeland
PO Box 3111 STN LCD 1
Langley BC V3A 4R3
CANADA

Kenneth Copeland Ministries
Post Office Box 84
L'VIV 79000
UKRAINE

We're Here for You!

Join Kenneth and Gloria Copeland and the *Believer's Voice of Victory* broadcasts Monday through Friday and on Sunday each week, and learn how faith in God's Word can take your life from ordinary to extraordinary.

You can catch the *Believer's Voice of Victory* broadcast on your local, cable or satellite channels.* And it's also available 24 hours a day by webcast at BVOV.TV.

Enjoy inspired teaching and encouragement from Kenneth and Gloria Copeland and guest ministers each month in the *Believer's Voice of Victory* magazine. Also included are real-life testimonies of God's miraculous power and divine intervention in the lives of people just like you!

To receive a FREE subscription to
Believer's Voice of Victory, write to:
Kenneth Copeland Ministries
Fort Worth, TX 76192-0001
Or call: 800-600-7395
Or visit: **www.kcm.org**

If you are writing from outside the U.S., please contact the KCM office nearest you. Addresses for all Kenneth Copeland Ministries offices are listed on the previous page.

* Check your local listings for times and stations in your area.